I08106O3

IMAGES
of America

PRESQUE ISLE COUNTY

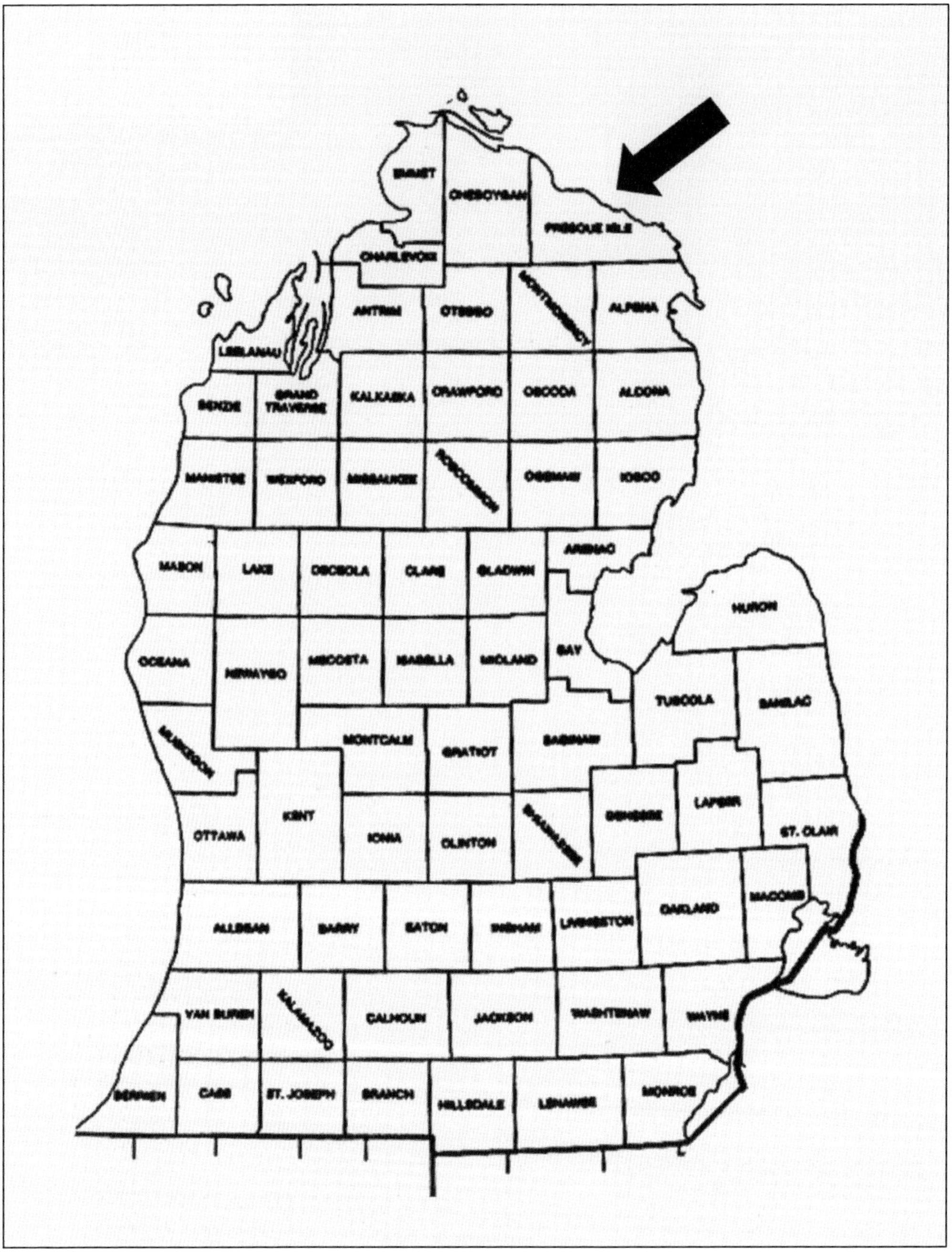

As seen on this map of Michigan's counties, Presque Isle County is located along the Lake Huron shore in the northeastern area of the Lower Peninsula. (Courtesy of the Presque Isle County Historical Museum.)

On the Cover: A large crowd was on hand on the grounds of the Presque Isle County Courthouse in Rogers City to celebrate the Fourth of July in 1902. (Courtesy of the Presque Isle County Historical Museum.)

IMAGES
of America

PRESQUE ISLE COUNTY

Mark Thompson

ARCADIA
PUBLISHING

ISBN 978-0-7385-9977-9

Published by Arcadia Publishing
Charleston, South Carolina

Printed in the United States of America

Library of Congress Control Number: 2012954652

For all general information, please contact Arcadia Publishing:
Telephone 843-853-2070
Fax 843-853-0044
E-mail sales@arcadiapublishing.com
For customer service and orders:
Toll-Free 1-888-313-2665

Visit us on the Internet at www.arcadiapublishing.com

To Madison and Jack Alspach, who I hope will appreciate and preserve the rich heritages of the Thompson and Alspach families

CONTENTS

ACKNOWLEDGMENTS

This book would not have been possible without the extensive photograph collections and other historical records maintained by the Presque Isle County Historical Museum. It also would not have been possible without the assistance of the more than 80 volunteers who are involved in every aspect of the museum's operations. Chief among them are the members of the museum's board of trustees, who have provided the resources and the progressive leadership to make a museum in a community with a population of just over 3,000 one of the finest local museums in the state.

Most significant, however, have been the contributions of the hundreds of past and present residents of the county who valued their heritage so much that they have supported the museum with their visits, their financial donations, and their donations of artifacts and other historical materials over the past 40 years. The rich history of our community has largely been preserved in the memories of those who have so willingly shared their knowledge with our museum and our community.

Unless otherwise noted, all images appear courtesy of the Presque Isle County Historical Museum.

INTRODUCTION

In the 1970s and 1980s, the *Little House on the Prairie* television show was just as popular with the people of Presque Isle County as it was with people across the United States. Life for the Ingalls family on the prairie of Minnesota was an interesting and often exciting mix of an idyllic frontier setting, colorful characters, and the pioneering life intertwined with frequent danger. It is unlikely that many residents of Presque Isle County, particularly the young people, realized that the history of their county could easily have provided the story lines for many seasons of *Little House* shows.

Native Americans arrived in the county at least 8,000 years ago, and many of their descendants still live here today. About 400 years ago, French explorers and missionaries began traveling through the area, trading with the Indians for valuable pelts that were in high demand in Europe. As far as what is known, however, no European immigrants actually settled in Presque Isle County until the middle of the 1800s. It was the rugged northern frontier of America at that time, and life was every bit as difficult and dangerous for those settlers as it was for the fictional Ingalls family.

For the earliest residents of Rogers City, for example, the winter of 1870–1871 came to be known as the "Famine Winter." The ship contracted to bring in a load of supplies to get the little colony through the winter months never arrived due to early ice on Lake Huron. The only supplies left in the village's single store were flour, salt pork, dried peas, syrup, and potatoes that had been damaged by frost. Those meager supplies were augmented by fish caught through the ice and game hunted in the surrounding forests. The first ship to call at Rogers City in the spring was greeted by hungry, but enthusiastic, villagers.

Rogers City was essentially a company town at that time, controlled by Albert Molitor, a German immigrant who ran the local sawmill and store. Molitor charged his workers exorbitant prices in his store, was abusive to women in the community, and, as a township official, rigged elections and stole tax money levied to build roads. In 1875, a large group of irate German farmers took the law into their own hands and assassinated Molitor. The local sheriff, one of Molitor's henchmen, investigated, but, undoubtedly fearing for his own life, he could not find the murderers.

Fires were also a constant threat in those early years. The communities of Providence and Metz were totally destroyed by forest fires, while half of Millersburg burned. The Metz fire of 1908 was particularly devastating. It burned more than half the county, destroying 150 homes, 75 barns, and six schools. The third-worst forest fire in the history of Michigan, it left 37 people dead and 1,851 totally or partially burned out. As was often the case, the exact cause of the fire was never determined. Many homes, barns, and businesses also burned as a result of other causes. With firefighting equipment commonly limited to nothing more than a bucket brigade, structure fires often spread to adjacent buildings. One such fire in Millersburg ended up destroying half of the village's business district. In 1926, an overheated piece of machinery set fire to a mill at the sprawling manufacturing complex of the Lobdell-Emery Company and its American Wood Rim subsidiary in Onaway. Before the day was over, the fire had destroyed all but two buildings and, in doing so, eliminated more than half of the jobs in what was then the largest community in the county. When the company's owners decided to rebuild elsewhere, people left Onaway in droves. The town survived, but it never really recovered from the fire.

Despite the many hardships, most newcomers persevered. The majority were tough German and Polish farmers who were accustomed to hard work. With their axes, hammers, and plows, they carved homesteads out of the towering forests, built homes, churches, schools, and roads, and founded communities, many of which still dot the landscape today. The early settlers seem to have willingly endured the many hardships as a fair toll for two things that had often been missing in their European homelands: freedom and land.

Those pioneering settlers and their descendants have always been tied to the land. The county's expansive forests of pine and hardwoods brought the first settlers to the area, and the lumber camps and sawmills and all sorts of related businesses provided most of the jobs for the first 50 years. As the forests gave way to the lumberjacks' double-bladed axes and crosscut saws, farmers laid claim to the land and gradually replaced acres of stumps with well-maintained fields of potatoes, corn, wheat, and even tobacco. While most farms in Germany and Poland were 40 acres or less, the immigrants who settled here often acquired a 160-acre homestead for as little as five dollars—and a lot of hard work. By European standards, the settlers in Presque Isle County were virtual land barons.

As the forests disappeared and the economic future of the county was uncertain, again the land provided sustenance. Under the layer of glacial till that covered the land was a rich deposit of limestone, the fossilized remains of marine creatures that occupied the warm water sea that covered the region millions of years ago. Limestone was a mineral needed to fuel many of the country's burgeoning industries, from steel to cement and glass to pharmaceuticals. For the past century, limestone mines have been the largest employers in the county.

While the timber and limestone industries are still vital to the economy of the county today, it may be the natural landscape that will have the most significant impact on the future of the area. With 99 inland lakes, 72 miles of Lake Huron shoreline, verdant forests covering about 70 percent of the land area, a population of less than 15,000, relatively low real estate prices and property taxes, and a laid-back lifestyle, Presque Isle County is becoming an increasingly popular destination for people who have tired of the hectic pace and high prices in many of Michigan's northern tourist areas. A growing number of people seem willing to forego the trendy shops, condo complexes, upscale restaurants, and big box stores in exchange for northeastern Michigan's slower paced and decidedly simpler lifestyle.

Presque Isle County's past is an epic, often heroic, saga. Portions of that saga are captured in the photographs and text in the following pages.

One

Our Unknown Past

From at least 6000 BC until the 1870s, most of the residents of Presque Isle County were Native Americans, mainly members of the Odawa or Ojibwe tribes. While both tribes have been here for thousands of years, neither is actually "native" to the region, as both seem to have originated in the Northeast, possibly as far north as Hudson Bay. In addition to the Odawa and Ojibwe, members of the Huron and Wyandot tribes often traveled into the region from their traditional homelands in the Detroit-Western Lake Erie area. Constantly harassed by the Iroquois to the east of their homelands, the Hurons reportedly traveled north seeking the protection of the French missionaries at St. Ignace.

Anthropologists and archaeologists have not found evidence to indicate that there were any large, permanent Native American settlements in the area. The Indians were largely hunter-gatherers and reportedly set up temporary settlements in the county during times of the year when foodstuffs were plentiful, such as when fish were spawning in the rivers or when wild berries were in season. They often went back to the same locations year after year. One of the most popular locations in Presque Isle County was at the mouth of the Ocqueoc River, an area frequented by Native Americans to both fish and harvest berries.

The Indian settlements at the Ocqueoc were observed by many European immigrants between 1870 and 1910. There are reports of as many as 150 Indians being encamped along the Lake Huron shore at the mouth of the Ocqueoc at one time, often drying sturgeon, which were plentiful in the river.

Because both the Odawa and Ojibwe were at least seminomadic, they carried all their possessions with them when traveling. They lived in domed or pointed wigwams made from birch bark attached to a simple framework of flexible saplings. The birch bark could be rolled up and transported easily in their canoes. Furniture inside their wigwams consisted largely of reed mats that could also be rolled up and carried along with them.

Indians were certainly very familiar with the shoreline areas of the county. Their preferred means of travel was by birch bark canoe, so they frequently coasted along the Lake Huron shore during their travels north and south. If traveling by foot, they would undoubtedly also have followed the well-worn foot trail that paralleled the shore from Saginaw Bay to the Straits of Mackinac.

The Indians did more than just pass along the forested coastline though. Many explored inland, probably following rivers and streams, and discovered many of the county's inland lakes, most of which were well stocked with fish. After finding a bountiful source of easily accessible protein, it is likely that Indians frequently lingered in the area for a season or possibly for years. Early

European settlers often found the remnants of Indian wigwams on the shores of the inland lakes that dot the county.

A second seasonal Native American settlement was at the south end of Black Lake, in the area now occupied by Onaway State Park. The Indians would have reached that area by traveling up the Cheboygan River and across Black Lake, a distance of about 30 miles. There is evidence that the Indians had established and maintained an orchard there, but it is unknown whether that was before or after the first European immigrants arrived in the area. Numerous Native American burial mounds were found at both the Black Lake and Ocqueoc River locations, suggesting the sites had been used over an extended period of time. There are reports that bands of Indians visited the Ocqueoc River location annually to honor their dead who were buried there.

To Native Americans, all things found in nature have spiritual significance, and greater spiritual significance is attached to unusual natural features. In Presque Isle County, there are reports that Indians considered both Sacred Rock and the falls of the Ocqueoc River to be particularly significant features. Sacred Rock, located on the Lake Huron shore about five miles north of Rogers City, is a massive rock of Engodine dolomite that was undoubtedly deposited along the shore by a glacier during the Ice Age. There are numerous reports that Indians traveling along the shore by canoe would stop at the unique rock and make offerings, including occasionally sacrificing a dog.

Indian legend has it that the boulder marked the boundary between the hunting grounds of two different tribes. Members of the tribes frequently trespassed on the other tribes' lands while hunting, and that led to quarreling and fighting between the two groups. All the fighting and quarreling was not pleasing to the "Great Spirit" Manitou, who resided in the Lake Superior region. On one occasion, when the chiefs of the two tribes were fighting, Manitou picked up the huge boulder and in anger threw it at the chiefs, burying both of them beneath the rock as a reminder to the two tribes that such quarreling and fighting had to stop.

The Indians' first contact with non-Indians was with early French explorers and fur traders. French Jesuits established their first mission to the Native Americans at the Straits of Mackinac in 1670. The Ojibwe and Odawa in the region would definitely have had knowledge of the Jesuits, who were headquartered first at Mackinac Island and then at St. Ignace. If as many as 150 Indians had gathered at the mouth of the Ocqueoc for any period of time, it is likely that Fr. Jacques Marquette or his assistants would have visited there. Fur traders would also have frequented the region, trading with the Indians for their valuable furs.

French military installations were established at Detroit in 1701 and at the present site of Mackinaw City in 1715. After that, there was regular military and commercial traffic between Detroit and Mackinaw under French, British, and American rule of the region, and they would have encountered local Indians as they traveled along the Lake Huron shore.

When the first European settlers arrived, there were Indians scattered throughout the county and frequent contingents paddling along the shore. Some Indians were living in the county, but there is little information about them. We know that an Indian named Thomas Shawviner was living in the Grand Lake area in the period after the Civil War. Shawviner knew how to use herbs, plants, and minerals to cure various injuries and illnesses, and settlers from nearby Presque Isle frequently called on him for medical assistance. By around 1900, an Indian woman named Susan Gilbert owned a farm near Millersburg, where she lived with her family. In addition to farming, Gilbert also made and sold Indian baskets. Farmers in the Onaway area occasionally hired Indians to assist with planting or harvesting during the early 1900s. Little is known beyond those few reports.

Most of our knowledge of the region's Indian cultures has come via early settlers, articles in the local newspaper, or from the reports of a few archaeologists. Our knowledge is embarrassingly limited; in fact, we know more about what happened last week in remote places around the world, even with a rover on Mars, than we know about the Native Americans who inhabited this area for 8,000 years and whose descendants contribute to our modern-day culture.

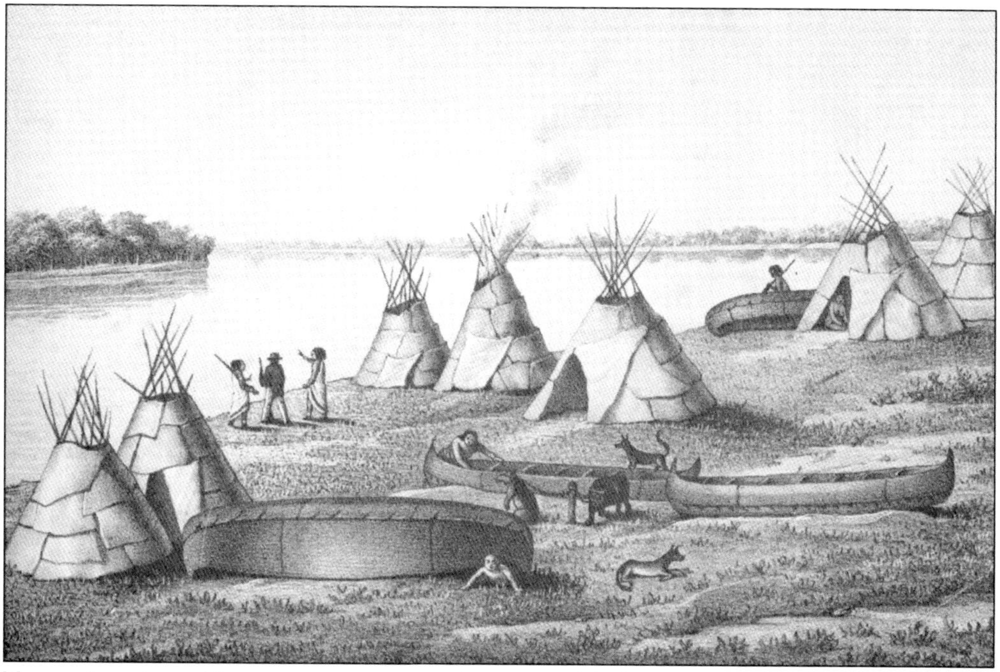

Native American villages or encampments in Presque Isle County would probably have looked very similar to the Odawa village seen in this 1842 drawing of Mackinac Island by Francis de Castlenau. The wigwams of the Odawa and Ojibwa tribes were covered with birch bark strips that could easily be rolled up and transported to a different location. (Courtesy of the Library of Congress.)

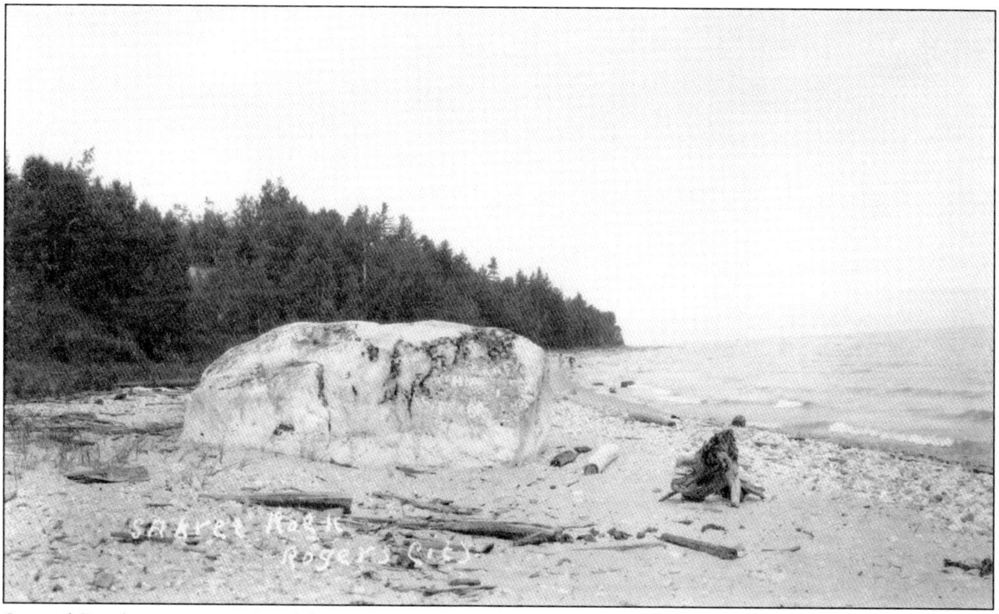

Sacred Rock, a massive boulder of dolomite, was undoubtedly deposited along the Lake Huron shore north of Rogers City by a receding glacier at the end of the last Ice Age. Native Americans reportedly attached a spiritual significance to the rock, leaving offerings whenever they passed by. The unique rock, seen here in the 1920s, is 20 feet long, eight feet wide, and six feet tall.

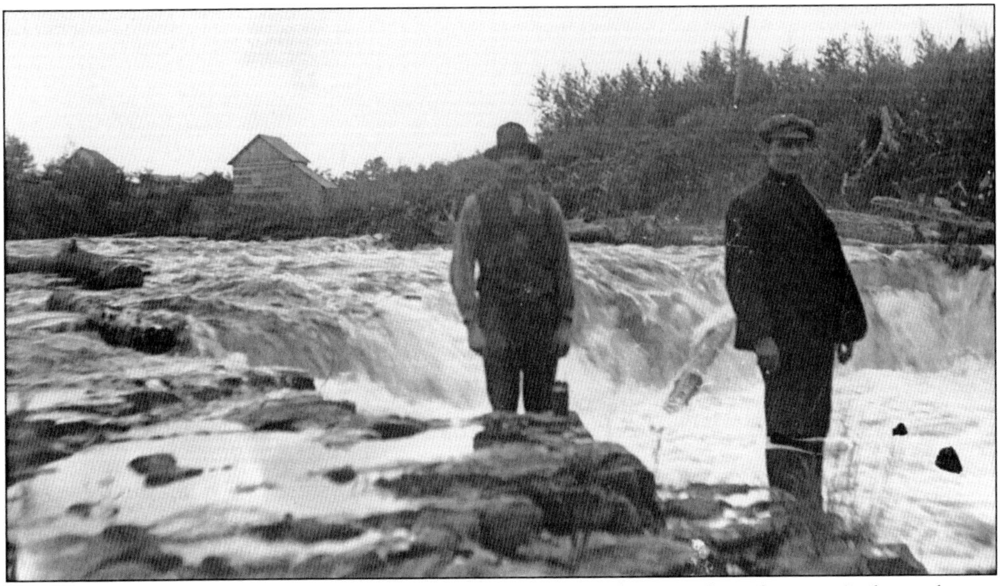

The Ocqueoc River, north of Rogers City, was a major gathering place for area Indians during portions of the year, particularly when fish were spawning or wild berries were in season. Major burial grounds are located near the mouth of the river at Lake Huron, and Indians explored as far up the river as Ocqueoc Falls, seen here. One of only two waterfalls in Michigan's Lower Peninsula, Native Americans regarded the unique natural feature with great reverence.

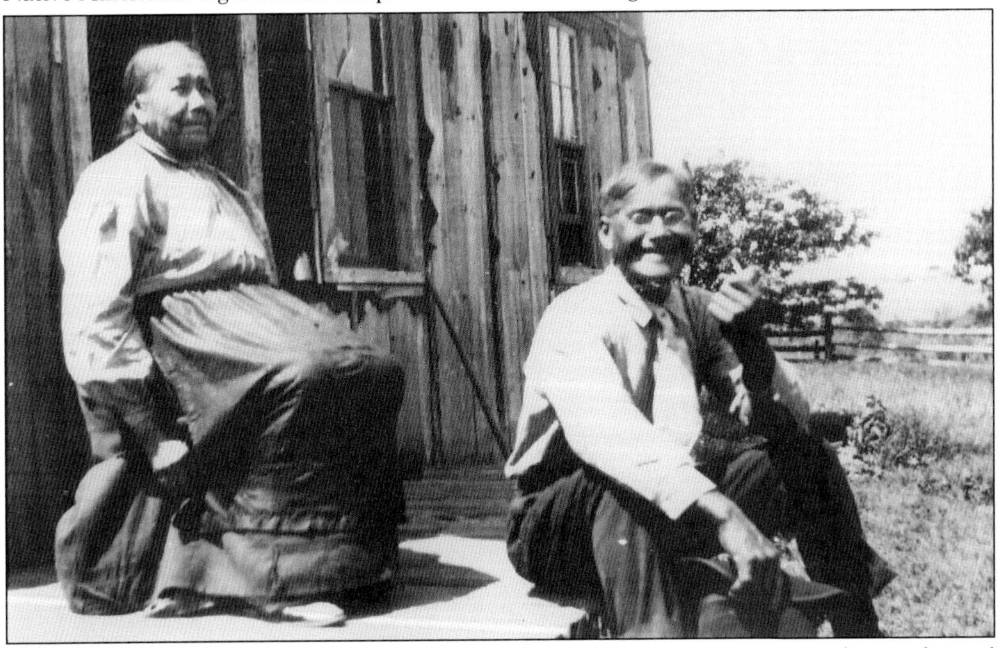

By the early 1900s, most Native Americans in the Great Lakes region had given up their traditional nomadic lifestyles. Many worked as farm laborers and some, like Susan Gilbert and her family, purchased land and operated their own farms while also practicing many traditional skills, such as basket weaving. Susan Gilbert, seen here with her son George, owned a farm in the Millersburg area, near the Ocqueoc River, and is reported to have lived to the age of 115. Many Indians eventually hid or denied their racial heritages in an effort to assimilate into white culture.

Two

They Came by Boat

Boats brought the first Europeans to Presque Isle County, and the forests kept them here. The first residents of European descent were Lemuel Crawford and his family. When the first government survey party arrived at Presque Isle aboard the passenger and freight steamer *Madison* in 1840, Crawford was operating a wooding station to supply wood to fuel the boilers of passing steamboats. At that time, Presque Isle was the only inhabited area between Mackinaw and Bay City. According to historian David Oliver, a member of that first survey party, Crawford's operation included a dock, a store, a frame house, a log barn, and a few shanties.

According to Oliver, Presque Isle was also the first fishing station on Lake Huron north of Saginaw Bay. Fishing was a seasonal business, however, so anglers tended to live in fairly rustic lodgings and return to their homes on the lower lake when winter set in.

In 1840, the federal government had a small lighthouse and keeper's cottage built at Presque Isle, marking the channel into Presque Isle Bay. In 1871, a taller lighthouse and keeper's residence was built at the tip of Presque Isle Point to provide navigational assistance to ships traveling up and down the lake. At 109 feet in height, New Presque Isle Light, as it is called, is almost three times as tall as the original light.

The second settlement in Presque Isle County was about 14 miles up the shore from Presque Isle. It, too, was settled by Lemuel Crawford and his family, who moved there from Presque Isle. The property, at what became known as Crawford's Quarry, was actually purchased by Crawford's wife, Cynthia, in 1861.

Crawford operated a very successful wooding station and shipping dock at the quarry. A large outcropping of limestone rock dominated the parcel of land owned by the Crawfords, and they thought it could be mined for use in construction. The rock proved to be too soft and too fractured for building purposes, but a small amount of it was quarried for other uses.

In 1869, the federal government ordered a coastal survey of the shoreline north of Crawford's Quarry. The survey party was headed by Lt. William Rogers, an 1867 graduate of the Military Academy at West Point. His survey crew included Albert Molitor, a German immigrant who had served in the Union army during the Civil War; Frederic Denny Larke, a highly educated English immigrant who had worked for the Hudson Bay Company; and John Raymond, a young French Canadian.

The area they surveyed was still covered with old-growth forest, and Rogers and Molitor decided to go into the timber business. They first tried to buy land at Crawford's Quarry but were turned down, so they purchased a section of land about two miles to the north. Larke was employed to recruit lumberjacks and other workers, and in the spring of 1869 he brought a large group of German and Polish immigrants north to work for the Rogers-Molitor Company. Robert Horn, one of the first settlers, later wrote that the village was a "forest primeval," with a clearing large enough for a tent or log house here and there, but no streets."

The beginning of the lumber boom in Presque Isle County can be traced to the start of the Rogers-Molitor operation. Soon, anyone with any extra cash was buying timberland around Crawford's Quarry and the Rogers-Molitor settlement, and the population grew rapidly. Albert Molitor's brother Edward, a government engineer in Detroit, drew up a plat for the village of Rogers in 1871. By the census of 1874, there were 896 people in Rogers Township and another 719 in Presque Isle Township. Most of the men in the county were employed in some facet of the timber industry.

Farmers followed on the heels of the lumberjacks. In fact, many of the early farmers had been brought north as lumberjacks. Very few were professional lumberjacks, however. For the most part, they were German or Polish farmers, but like all farmers they knew how to cut down a tree. As the land was cut over, much of it was purchased by the lumberjack-farmers, who removed the stumps, built homes—usually log cabins—planted crops, and began acquiring livestock. It was common practice in those days for men to work in the woods or sawmills in the winter months and then farm during the balance of the year. In those early years, lumbering was limited to the cold winter months, when the ground was frozen and large sled loads of logs could be moved easily on iced roads.

As both the lumber camps and farms spread out from Presque Isle, Crawford's Quarry, and Rogers, the population of the county grew rapidly. From 1,615 residents in 1874, the population doubled to 3,113 by 1880 and reached 8,821 by 1900. From 1869 to 1900, Michigan was the nation's leading lumber producer. The sprawling old-growth forests were cut over to provide the lumber needed to build the great cities of the Northeast and Midwest. By 1900, however, the prime forests had been cut, and the big timber operators moved on to Wisconsin, Minnesota, and eventually the West Coast. The future prospects for communities like Rogers, Crawford's Quarry, and Presque Isle did not look good.

That less-than-optimistic view of the future changed in the fall of 1910 with the announcement that William F. White's Michigan Limestone & Chemical Company was going to open a quarry and processing plant on 5,000 acres purchased around Crawford's Quarry. The plant went into operation in June 1912. The Calcite Plant produced an extremely high grade of limestone, and it could be shipped economically via freighter on the Great Lakes. The plant was an immediate success, with orders far exceeding even the most optimistic expectations.

Most of the stone from the plant went to steel mills around the Great Lakes, the largest of which was United States Steel. In 1920, the steelmaker purchased William F. White's controlling interest in the company. By that time, the Calcite Plant was the world's largest producer of limestone, shipping more than six million tons a year, much of it on large self-unloading freighters in the company's Bradley transportation fleet. At its peak in 1953, the sprawling quarry produced more than 16 million tons of stone.

The Calcite Plant, owned now by Carmeuse Lime & Stone, is still in business, but increased competition and market changes have resulted in significant declines in tonnage. In 2011, total shipments fell just below six million tons, about the same amount the quarry was producing 90 years ago.

While limestone, lumbering, and farming are all important elements in the economy of the county's shoreline communities, none of those sectors are as significant as they were in the past. More and more, residents are looking to tourism as offering the greatest potential for economic growth.

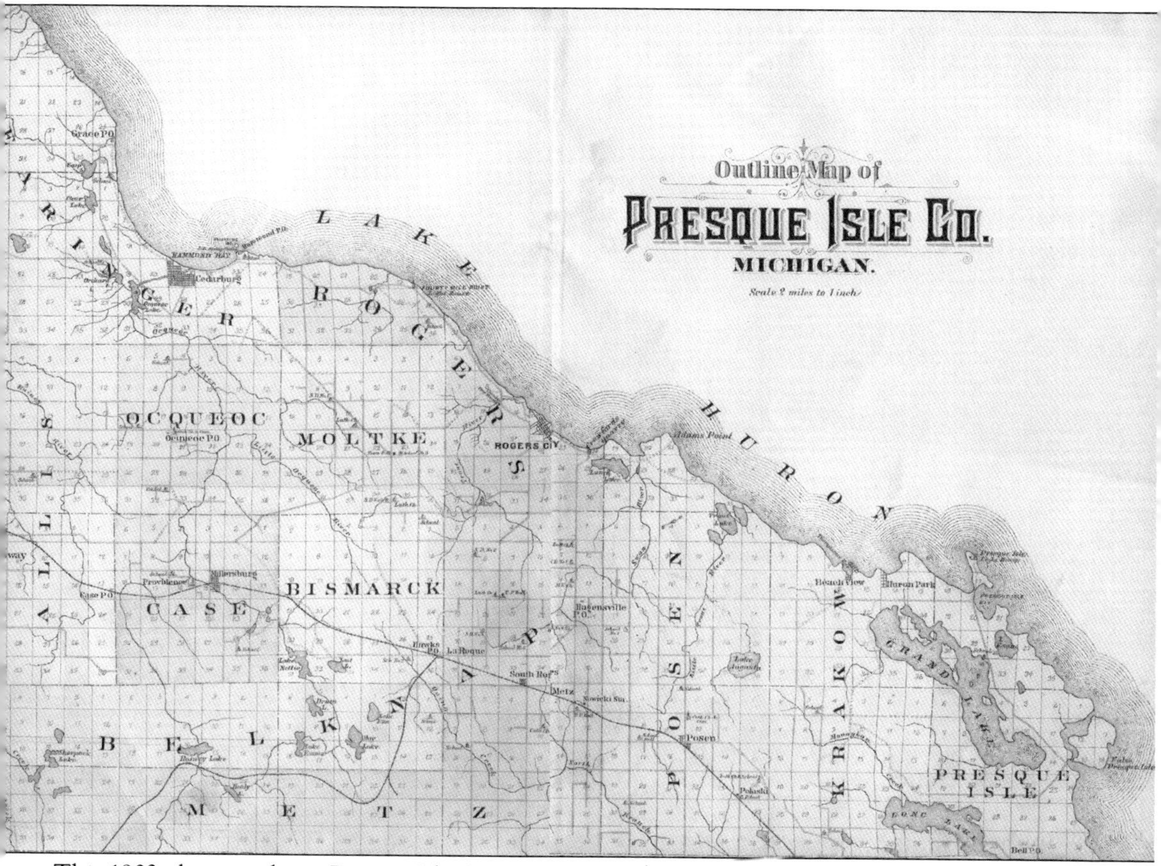

This 1903 plat map shows Presque Isle County, its townships, its communities at that time, and its long shoreline on Lake Huron. Originally French territory, it was ruled by the British after 1760 and was ceded to the United States in 1836. First surveyed in 1840, the county was legally established in 1875. Prior to that, it had been governed at various times by Mackinac, Cheboygan, and Alpena Counties. The original survey party described the area as "worthless."

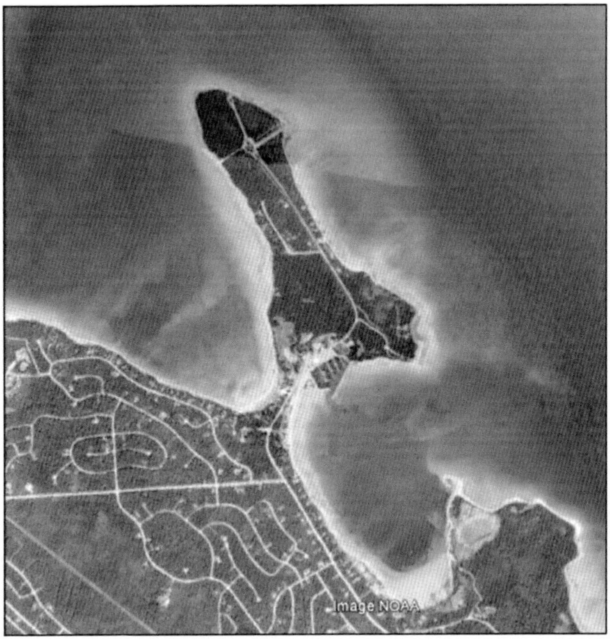

This is a satellite view of Presque Isle Point, in the southeastern part of the county. Identified by early French explorers and fur traders as Presque Isle, meaning "almost an island," or what would be called a peninsula, the description attached to the spit of land morphed into its formal name. The first area of the county settled by immigrants of European ancestry, the French name was given to the county when it was formed in 1875. It is pronounced locally as "presk eel" instead of the more common "presk ile." Indians traveling along the shore in canoes would portage across the base of Presque Isle Point, saving a trip of about seven additional miles to go out around the point.

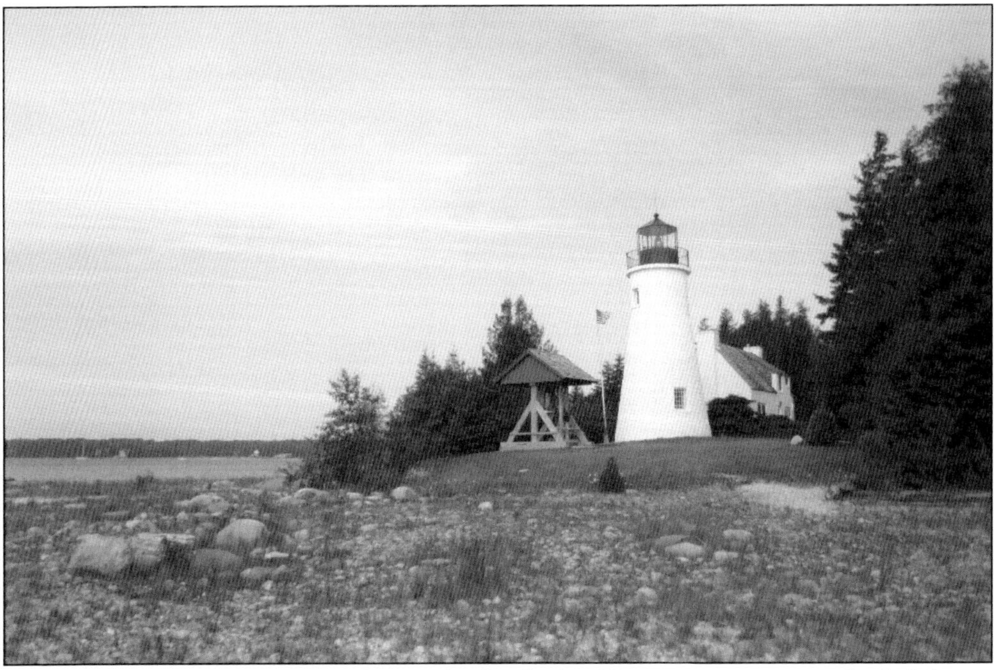

The county's oldest surviving residence of individuals of European ancestry is the lighthouse built on Presque Isle Bay in 1840. The lighthouse and adjacent keeper's cottage are a popular tourist attraction today. The area around the bay that is known today as Burnham's Landing was originally occupied by Lemuel Crawford, who operated a wooding station there prior to 1840, selling firewood to passing steamboats. Crawford and his family were essentially squatters on government-owned land.

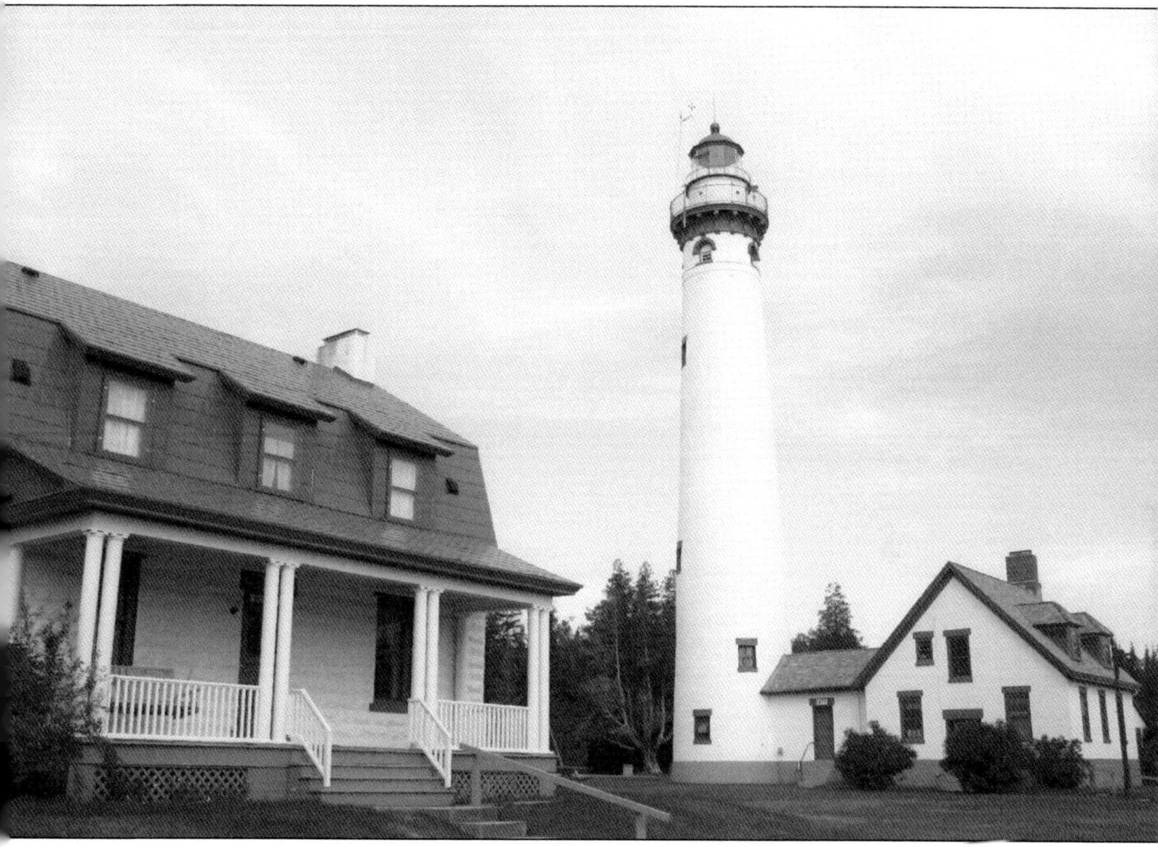

The 1840 Presque Isle Lighthouse, which marked the entrance to the bay, was replaced by a much taller lighthouse in 1871. It marked the end of Presque Isle Point and was an important navigational aid for ships passing up and down the coast.

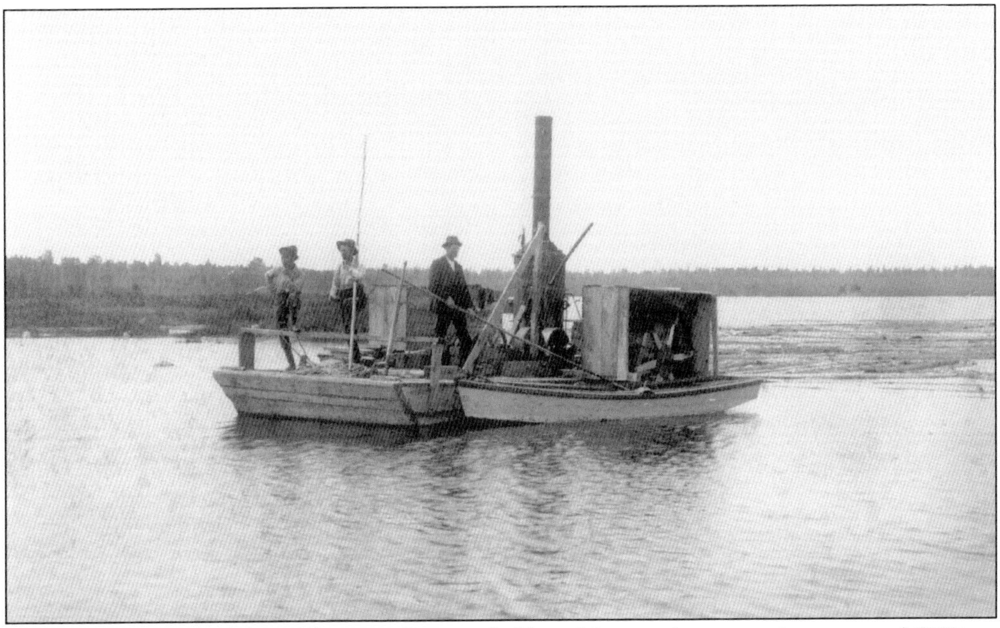

Francis Crawford (right) and his sons Francis (left) and Leonard are seen here around 1870 on their steam-powered barge towing a raft of logs along the shore near Crawford's Quarry. Whenever possible, logs were moved by water by floating them down rivers or towing them on lakes with barges, tugs, or steamboats. The Crawfords' crude barge was propelled by side wheels.

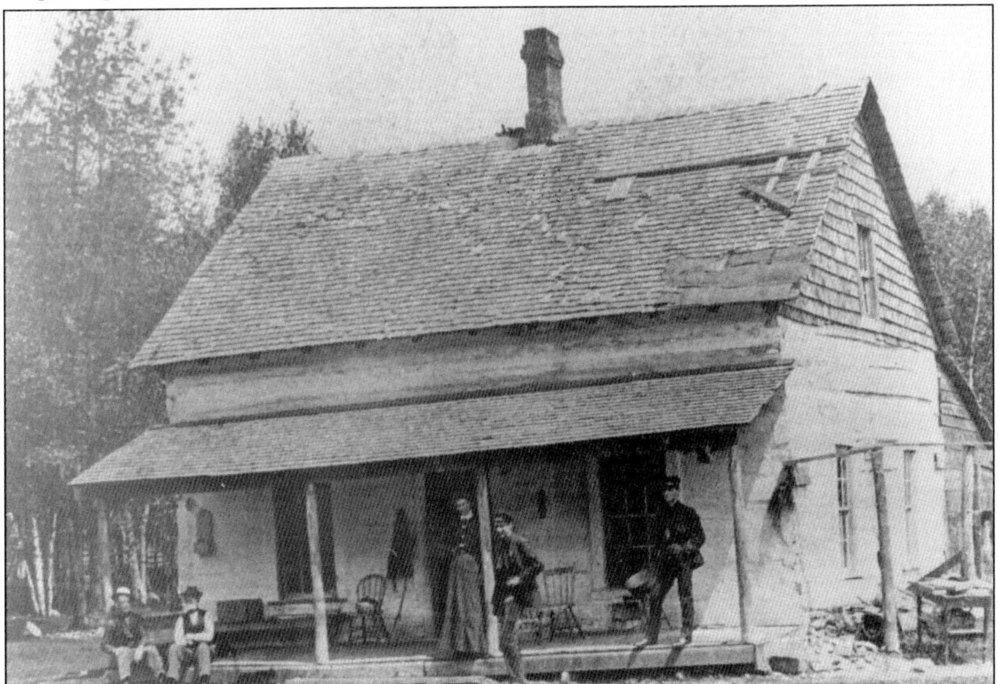

John Kauffman swam ashore at Presque Isle in 1862 when the boat he was traveling on sank. He remained in the area for the balance of his life. His log cabin, built in 1862 and seen here in the 1870s, still stands today at the Birch Hill settlement between Presque Isle Harbor and Grand Lake.

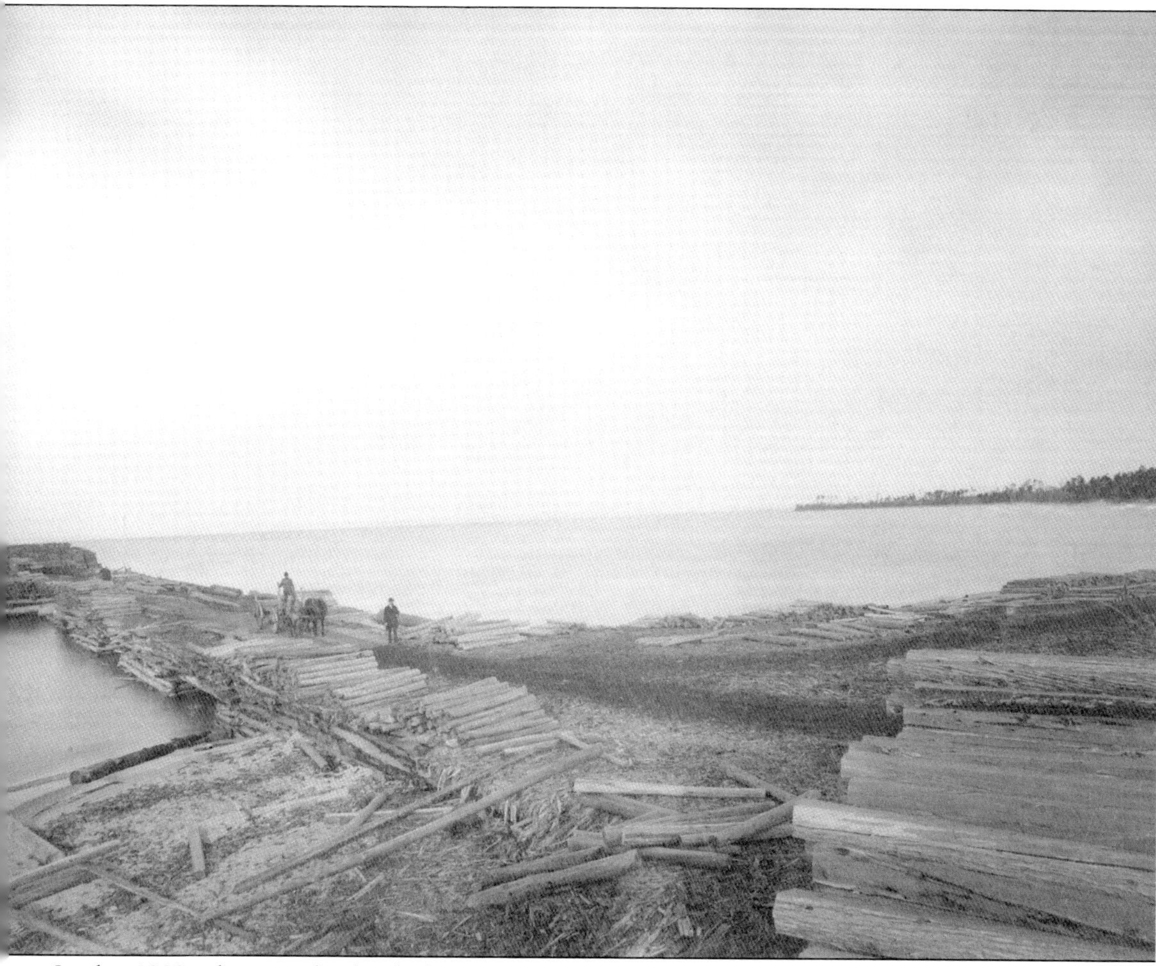

In this 1880s photograph, the dock at Crawford's Quarry is stacked with 140,000 cedar ties waiting to be shipped by boat to cities around the Great Lakes. Presque Isle County was one of the country's largest producers of cedar, which was used extensively for railroad ties and wooden sidewalks in cities.

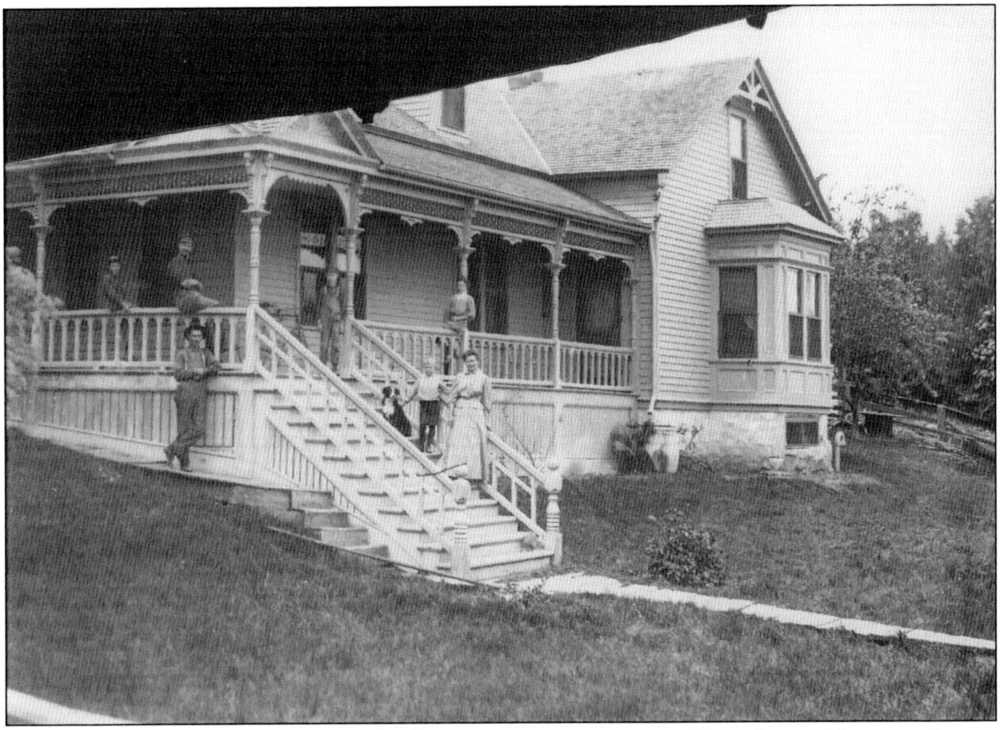

Crawford's Quarry was a prosperous little community at one time. This elegant Victorian home, seen around 1910, was owned by the Bittner family, which operated the local brewery and several other businesses. All of the property in Crawford's Quarry was eventually purchased by Michigan Limestone, and there are now few signs that the village ever existed.

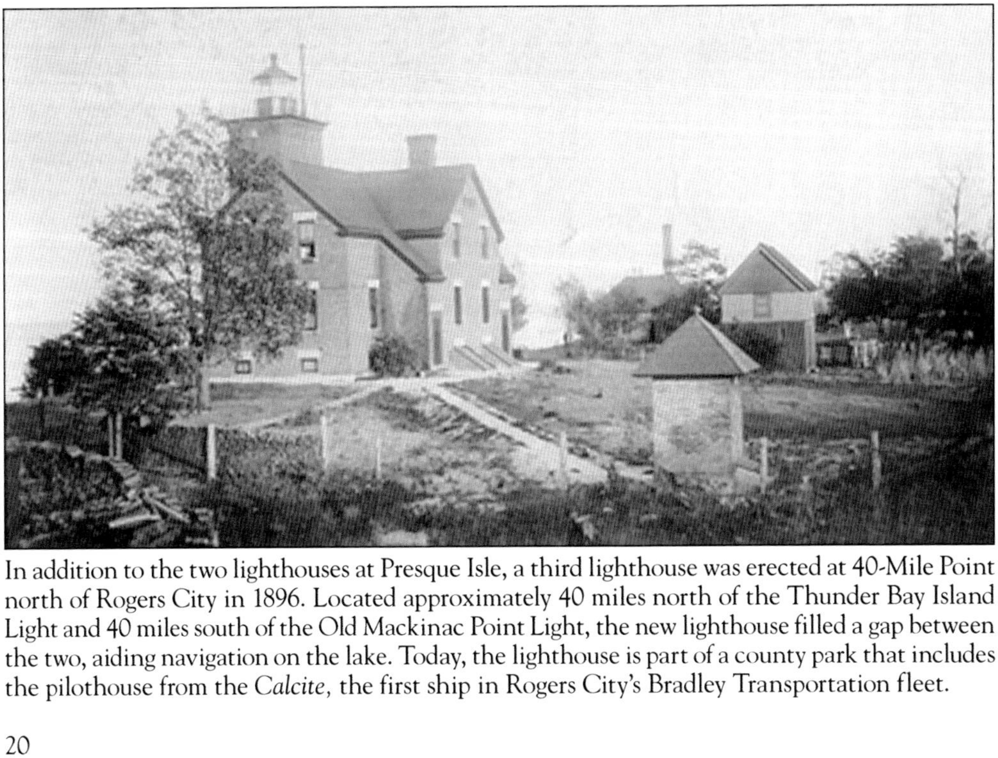

In addition to the two lighthouses at Presque Isle, a third lighthouse was erected at 40-Mile Point north of Rogers City in 1896. Located approximately 40 miles north of the Thunder Bay Island Light and 40 miles south of the Old Mackinac Point Light, the new lighthouse filled a gap between the two, aiding navigation on the lake. Today, the lighthouse is part of a county park that includes the pilothouse from the *Calcite,* the first ship in Rogers City's Bradley Transportation fleet.

William E. Rogers, the namesake of the village of Rogers, now Rogers City, is seen here in his cadet uniform from the Military Academy at West Point, which he graduated from in 1867. Rogers, who financed the Rogers-Molitor Sawmill, purchased the section of land that is now the heart of Rogers City, and donated the parcel of land where the courthouse stands today, never spent more than a few days in the community named in his honor.

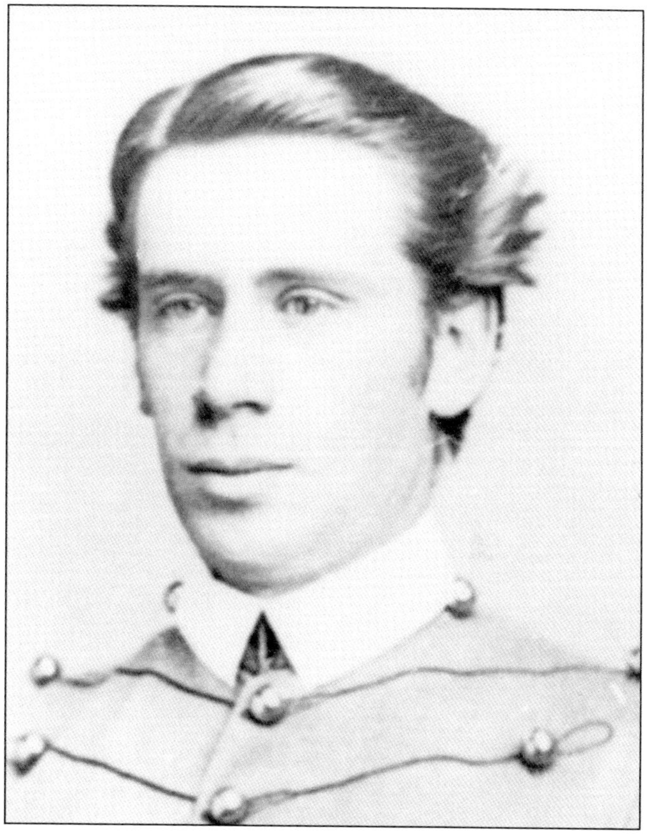

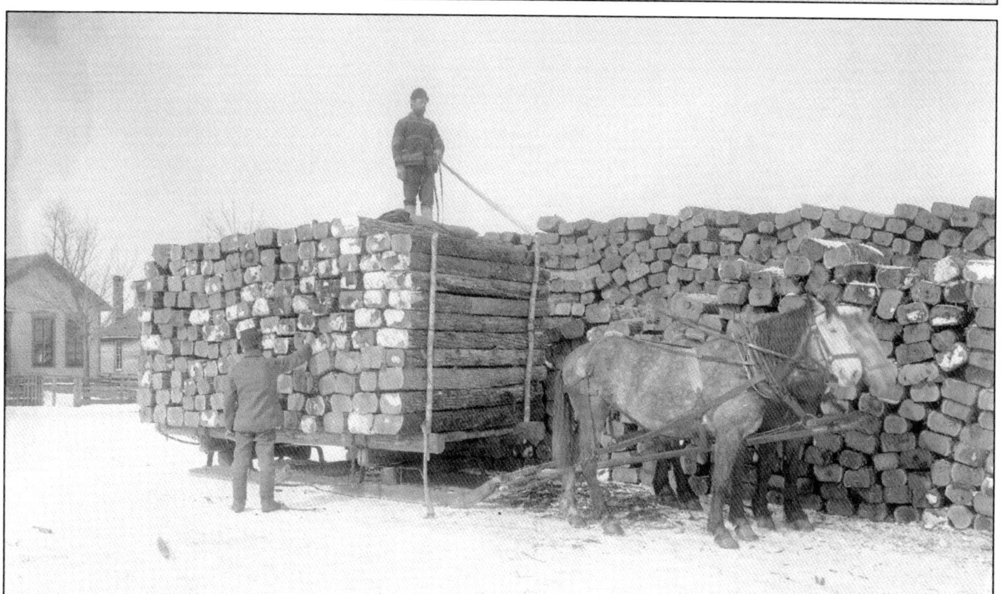

Rogers built up around the Rogers-Molitor Sawmill and the company store. Lumbering was the backbone of the community's economy until Michigan Limestone's Calcite Plant went into operation in 1912. Here, a sleigh loaded with cedar railroad ties waits to be unloaded at a dock in Rogers.

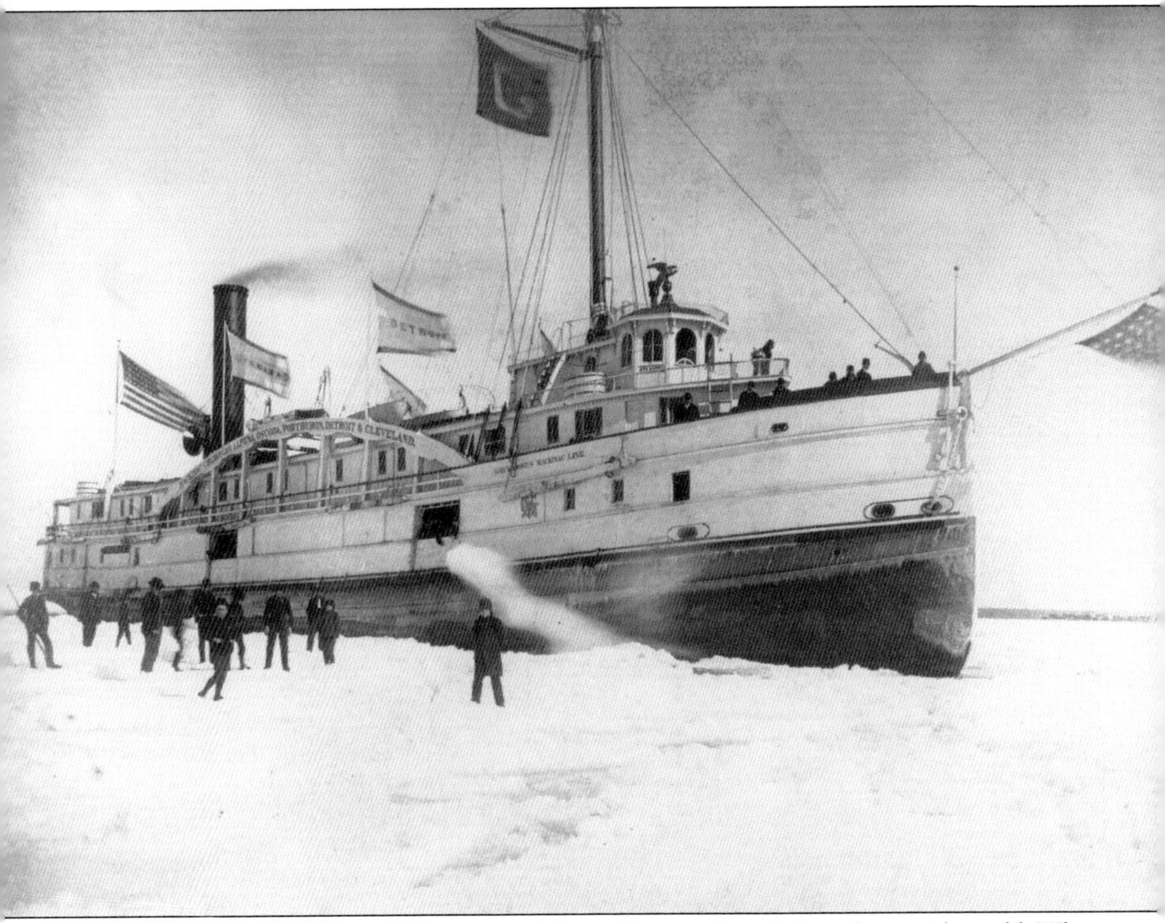

For residents of little Rogers, the steamer *Marine City* was their link to the outside world. When early ice prevented the ship from calling at Rogers with a large load of needed supplies in the late fall of 1869, residents suffered through what came to be known as the Famine Winter.

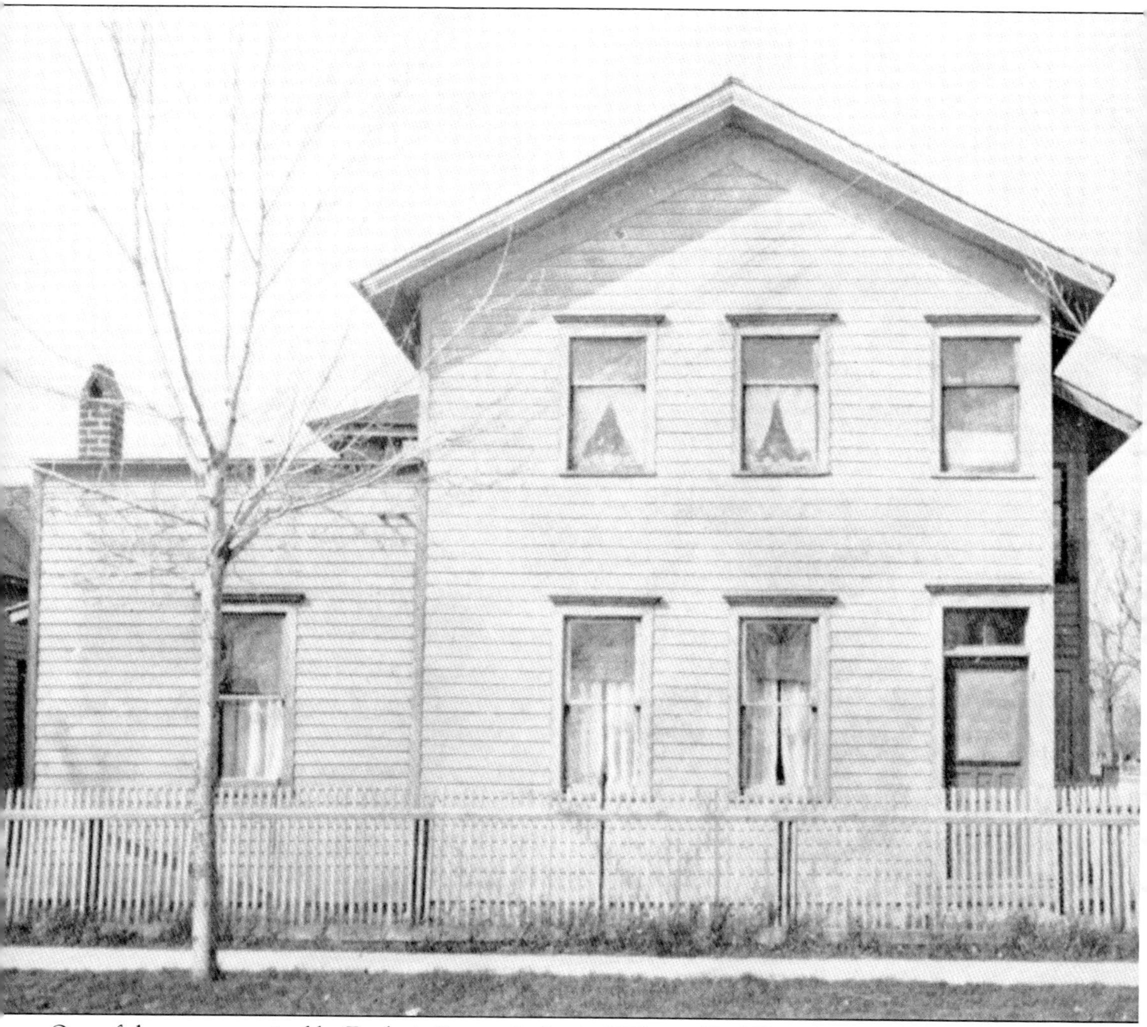

One of the men recruited by Frederic Denny Larke in 1869 was Karl Horn, a carpenter by trade. Horn built most of the early houses in Rogers, including his own (seen here). It was located at the southwest corner of First Street and Michigan Avenue.

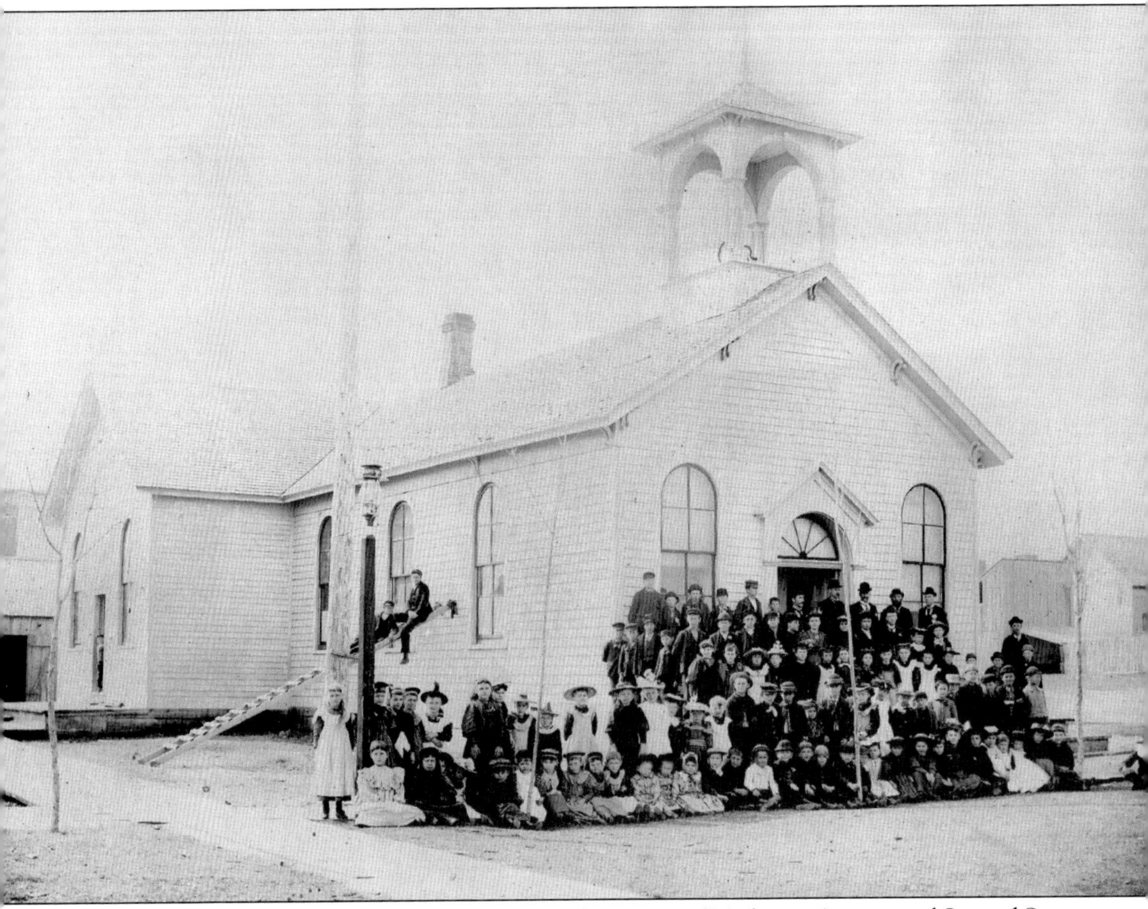

The first school in Rogers was built in 1872 at the corner of Michigan Avenue and Second Street, where the city hall is located today. It served the community until what was known as the yellow school was built in 1903.

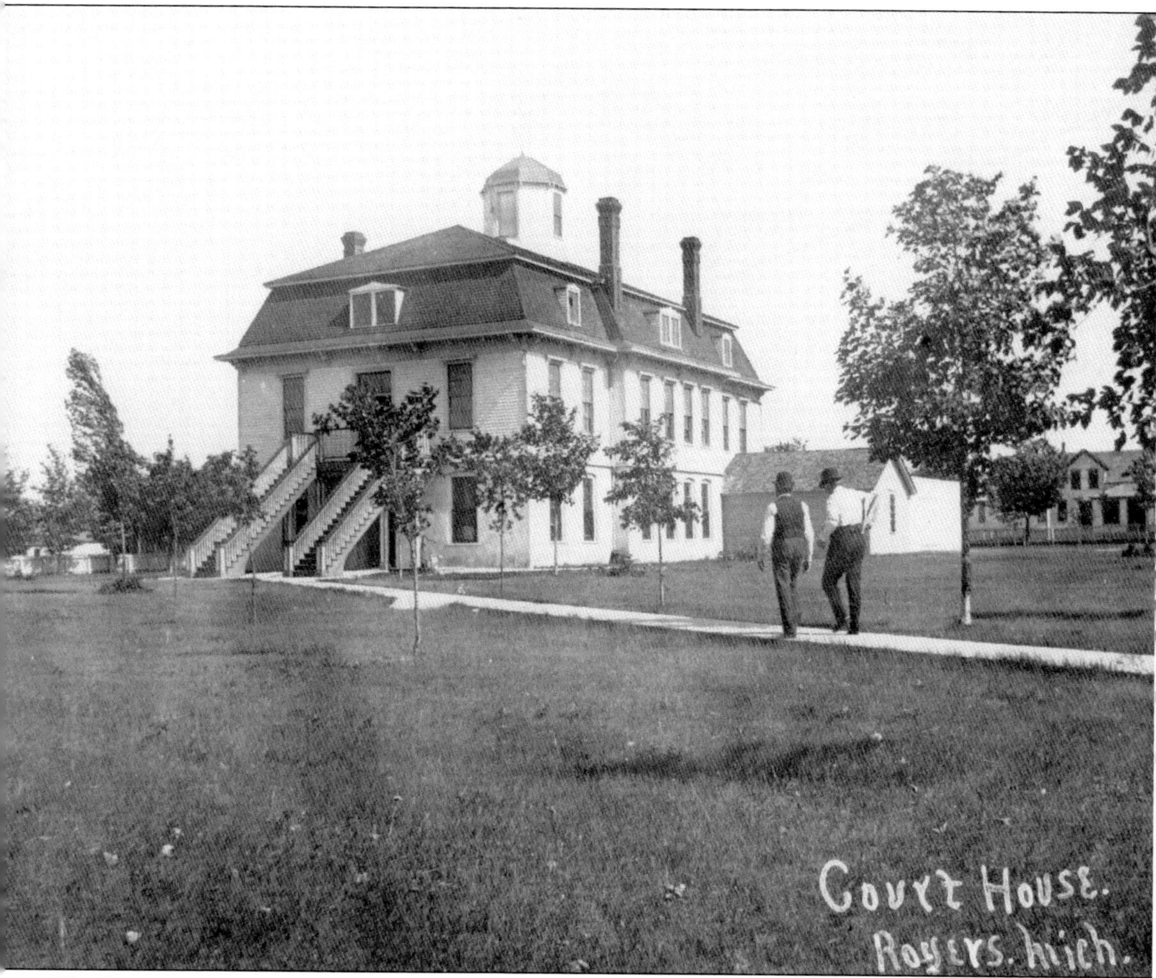

The first courthouse was built in 1872 on a parcel of land donated to the community by William Rogers. It burned in 1881, and this building was erected on the same spot in 1883. It is still in use today, although it has been surrounded with a number of additions.

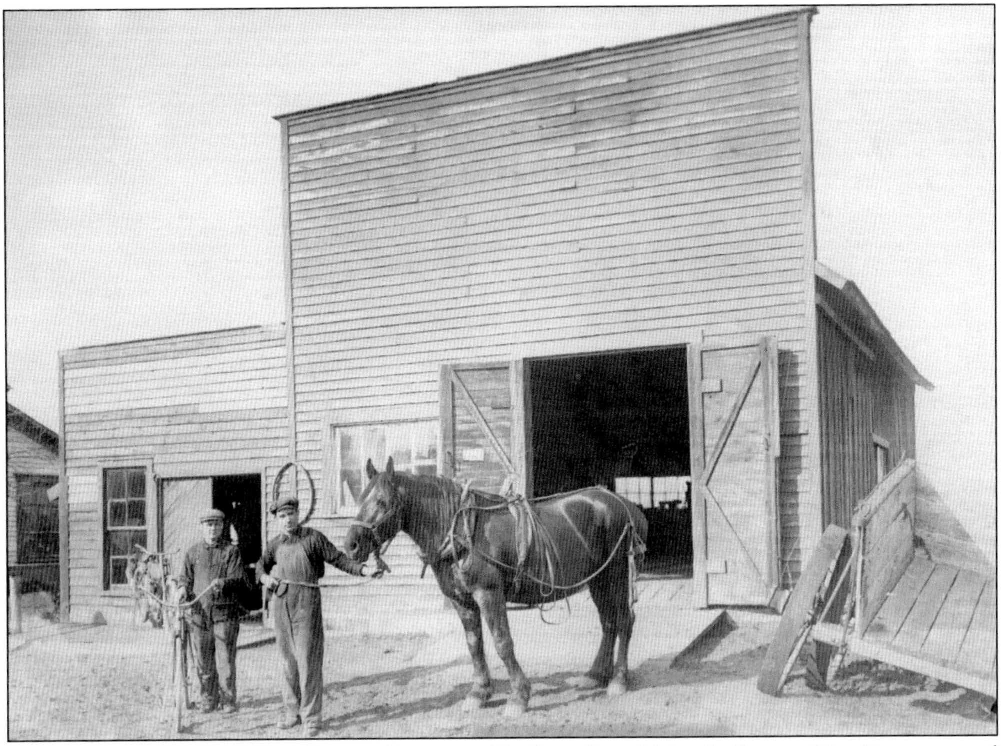

One of the early businesses in Rogers City was a blacksmith and bicycle shop on First Street owned by the Kelly family. Seen here in front of the building are Paul Clemens (left) and Walter Kelly.

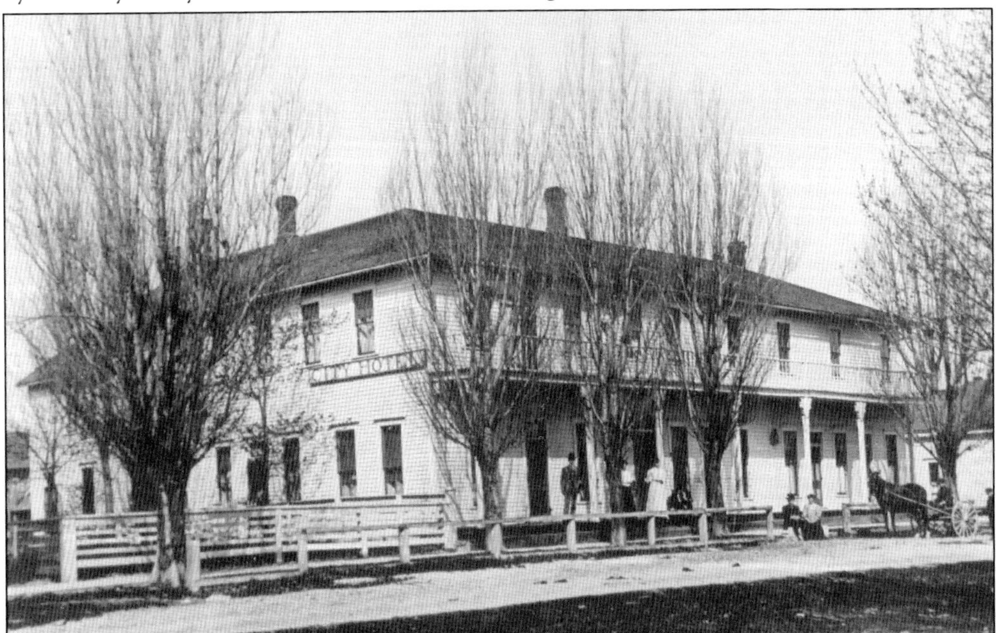

By the end of the 1870s, Rogers City had two hotels, the International and the City Hotel. The latter burned in 1884, and its replacement is seen here. The hotel operated until the early 1970s under a variety of owners.

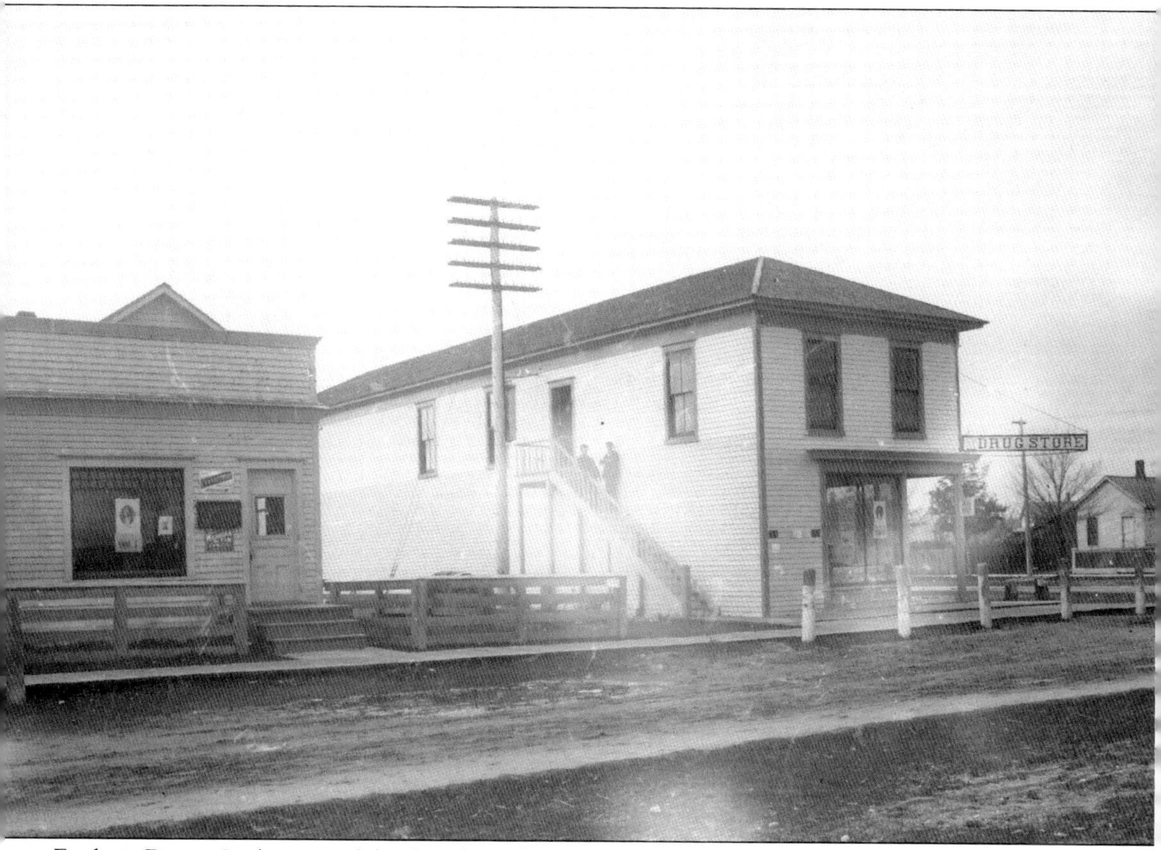

Frederic Denny Larke, one of the founders of Rogers City, and his wife, Augusta, built the two-story structure on the right as a general store around 1878. Located at the corner of Huron Avenue and Third Street, it was later converted into a drugstore operated by the Larkes' son Roland. The village's first telephone company was on the second floor of the building, which also housed the post office and the offices of the *Presque Isle County Advance*. Today, Grulke Hardware occupies the building. The structure on the left housed the Presque Isle County Savings Bank from the 1890s until 1911. It is also still in use today.

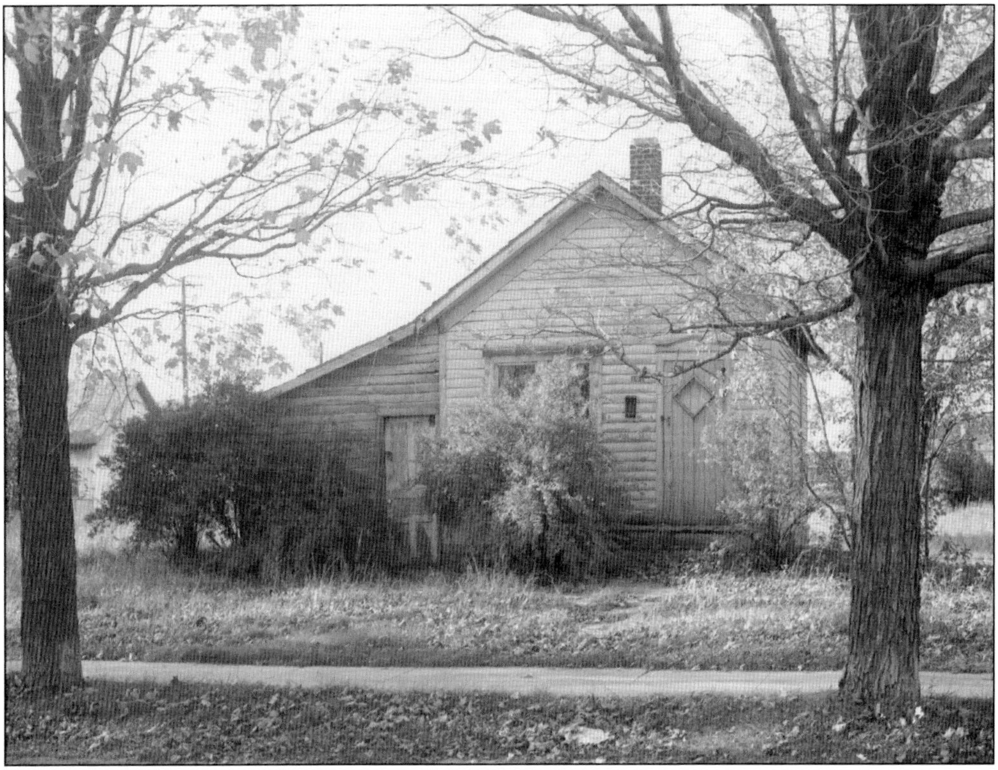

The first bank in Rogers City was in this small, rather inauspicious building on the north side of Huron Avenue, directly behind Frederic Denny Larke's Third Street home.

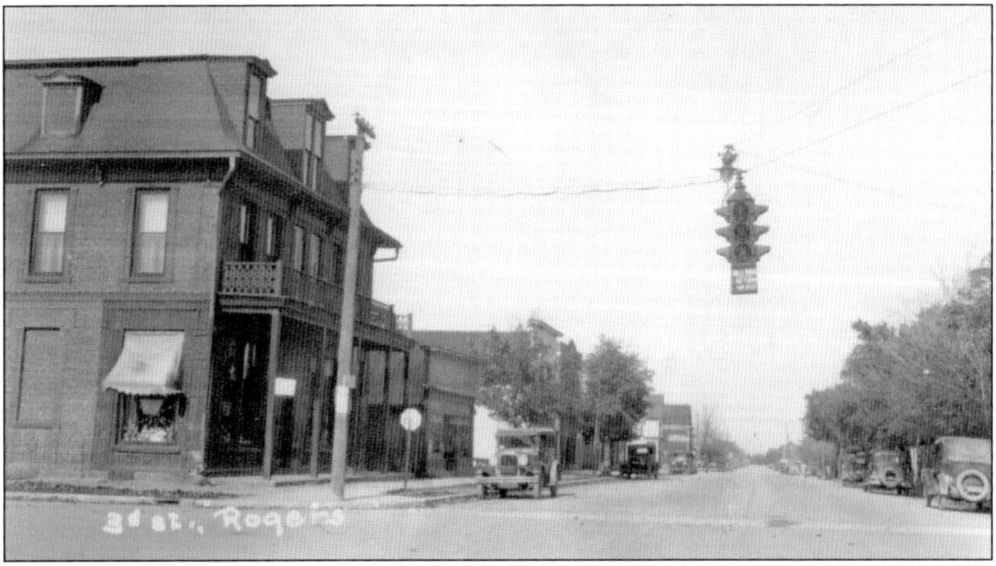

On the left in this c. 1920 photograph of Third Street is the three-story, redbrick Bertram Building, completed in 1887 on the outskirts of the village. When it was first built, it was reached by a path through the woods. The Bertram family operated a general store in the imposing structure until 1912, living upstairs. The building was demolished in the early 1970s as part of Rogers City's Urban Renewal Program.

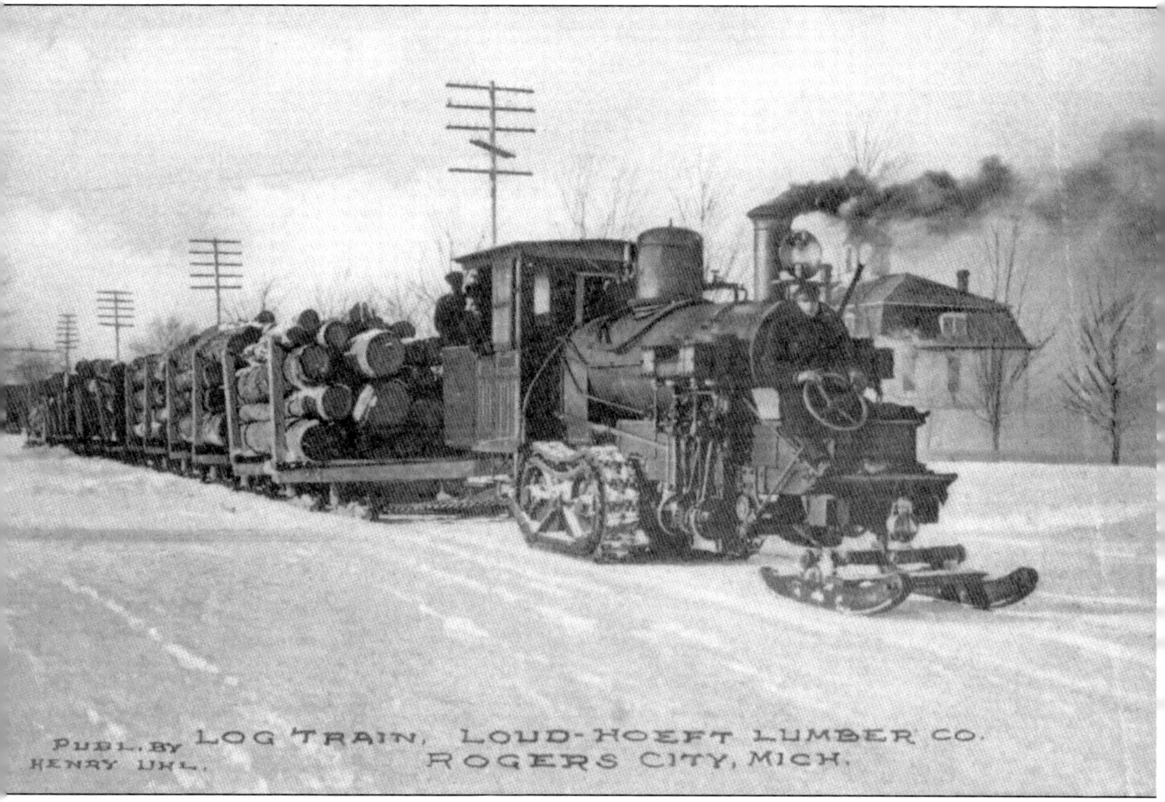

This c. 1910 postcard shows the Loud-Hoeft Lumber Company's log train, or steam hauler, towing heavily loaded sleighs of logs past the courthouse on Third Street. The engine of the log train was a small steam locomotive equipped with tracks that was steered by a worker perched over the skis at the front of the engine. The logs were hauled from a landing on the outskirts of the village to the company's mill on the lakefront at the foot of Erie Street.

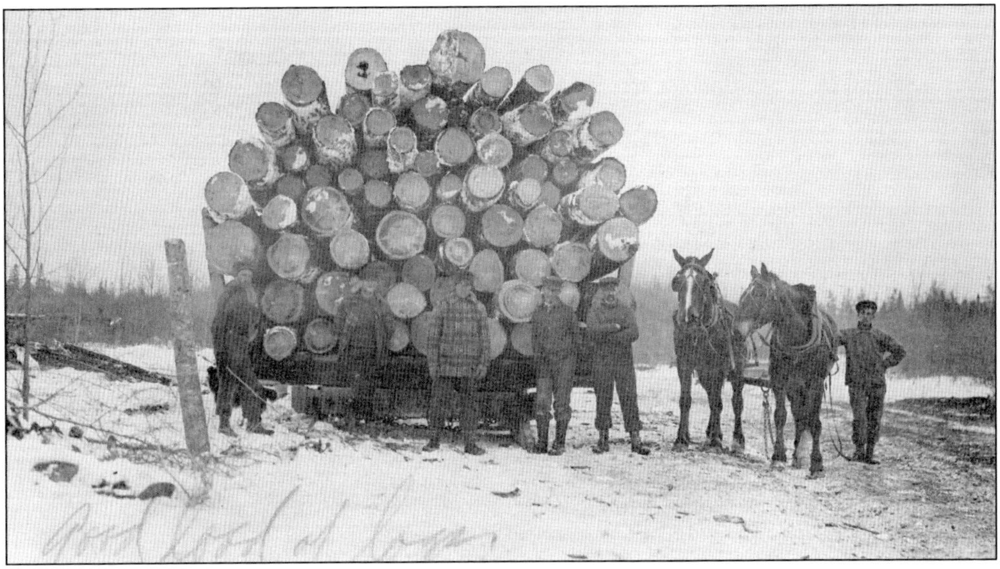

In this 1920s photograph, a sled loaded with pine logs is ready to be towed down to the Loud-Hoeft mill by the log train.

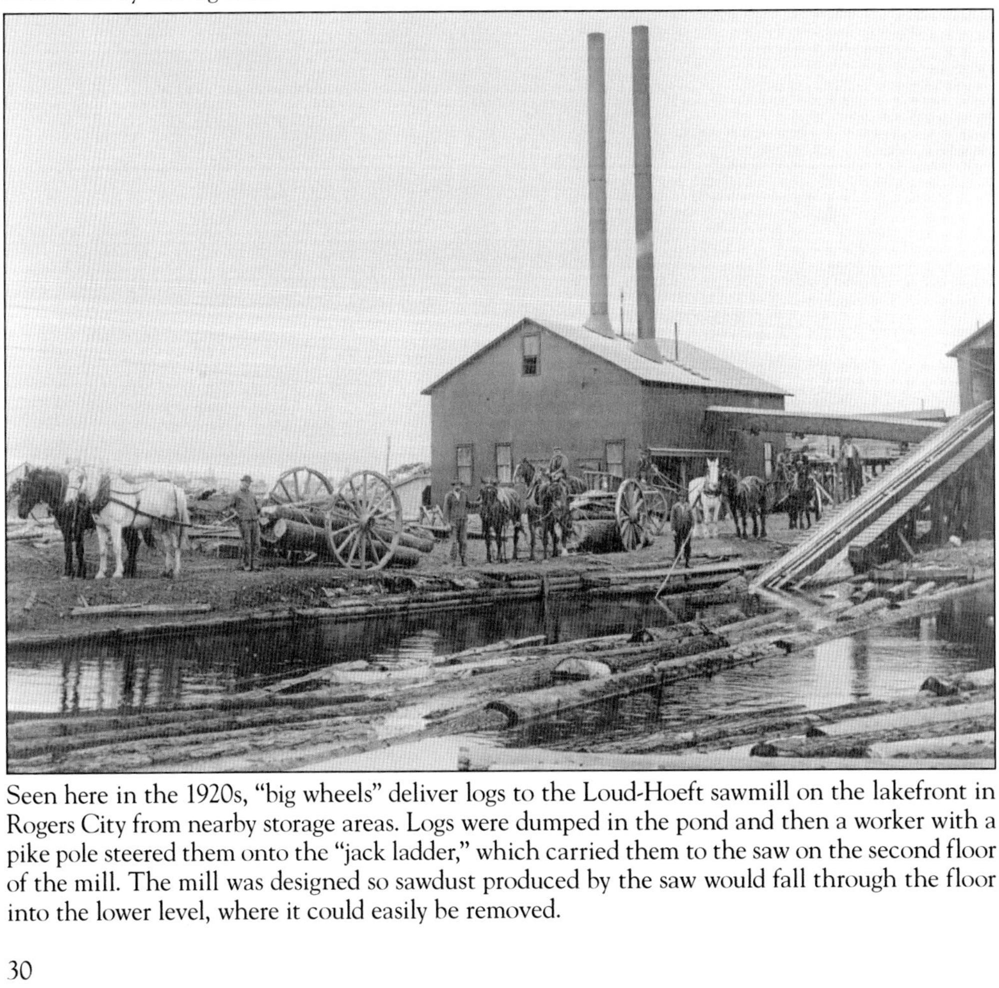

Seen here in the 1920s, "big wheels" deliver logs to the Loud-Hoeft sawmill on the lakefront in Rogers City from nearby storage areas. Logs were dumped in the pond and then a worker with a pike pole steered them onto the "jack ladder," which carried them to the saw on the second floor of the mill. The mill was designed so sawdust produced by the saw would fall through the floor into the lower level, where it could easily be removed.

Capt. William Crosby poses for a photographer while "dockwallopers" load Hoeft's *C.H. Starke* at the company dock at the foot of Erie Street in Rogers. Crosby, a popular captain, had a reputation for carrying the largest possible deck loads of timber on this ship. He captained the *Starke* for 23 years. (Courtesy of Harry Whiteley.)

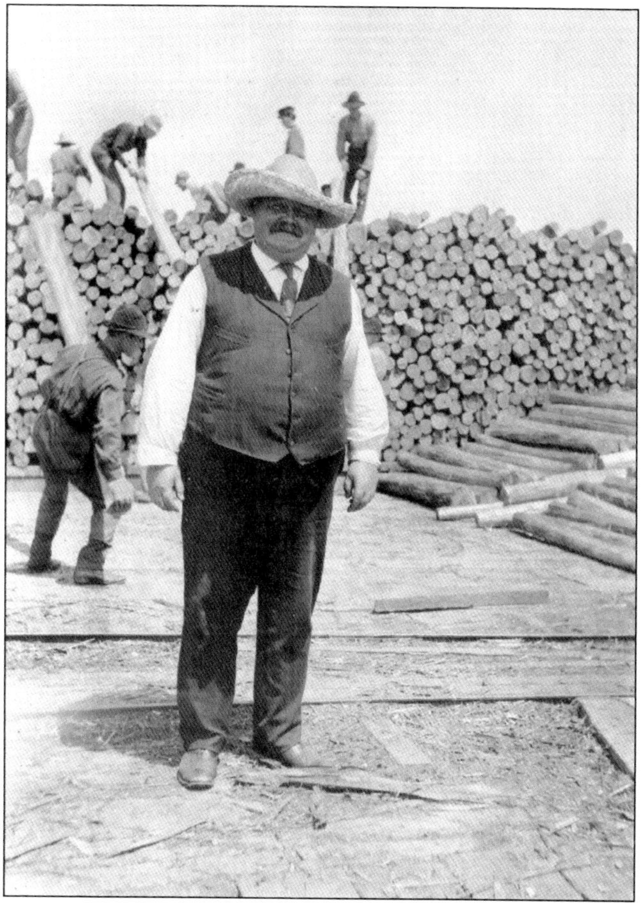

In addition to operating a sawmill that turned out dimensional lumber, the Loud-Hoeft operation also included a head and stave mill that produced staves and the circular ends, or heads, for barrels. Barrels were in high demand for use as shipping containers for a wide variety of products. This photograph shows all the stages in the process of making staves and heads. (Courtesy of Harry Whiteley.)

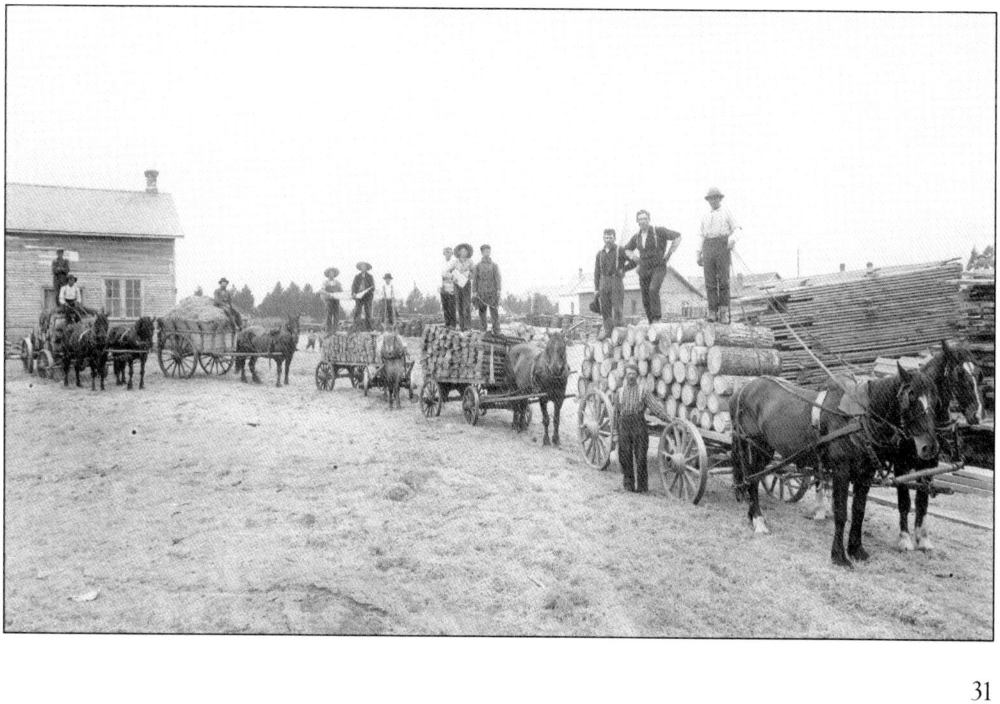

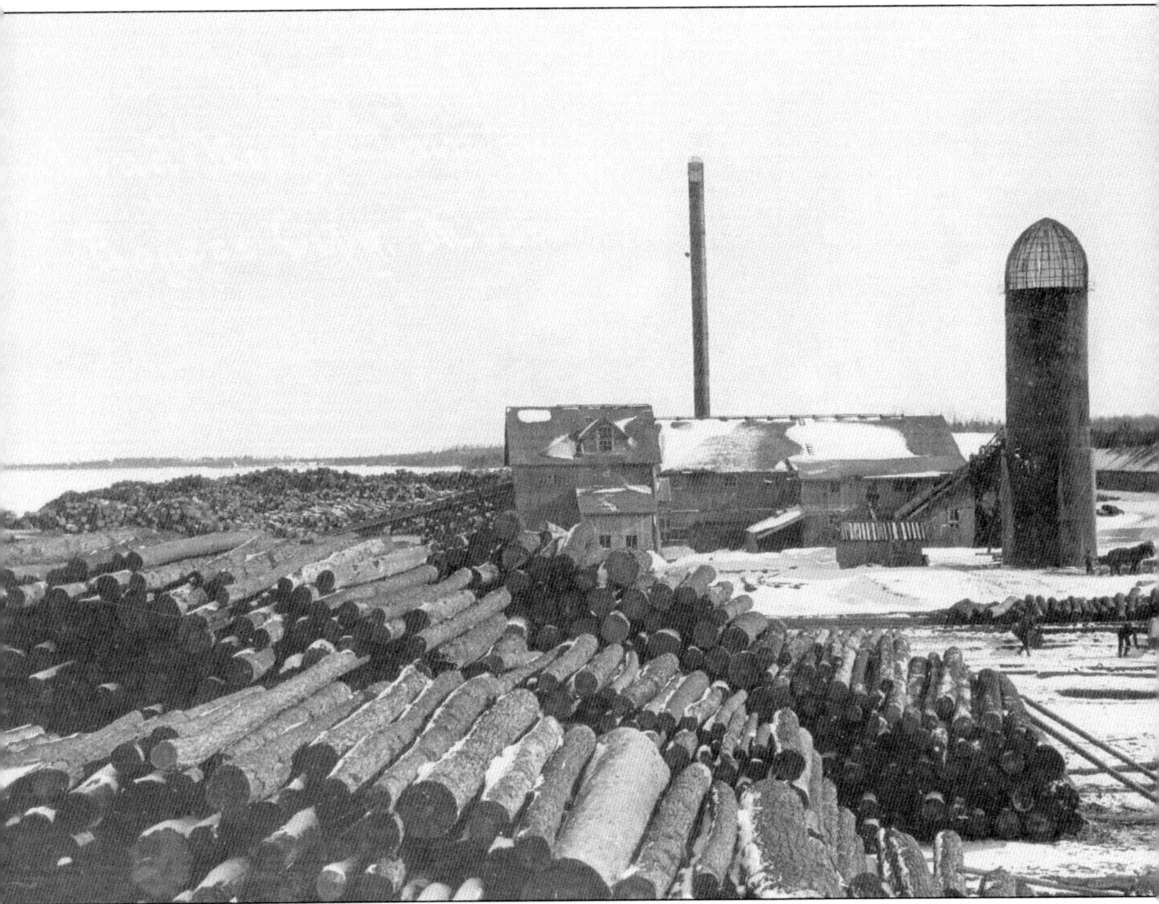

This is another view of the Loud-Hoeft mill, taken around 1910, showing the area used for log storage. Sawdust from the mill was burned in the tall silo on the right.

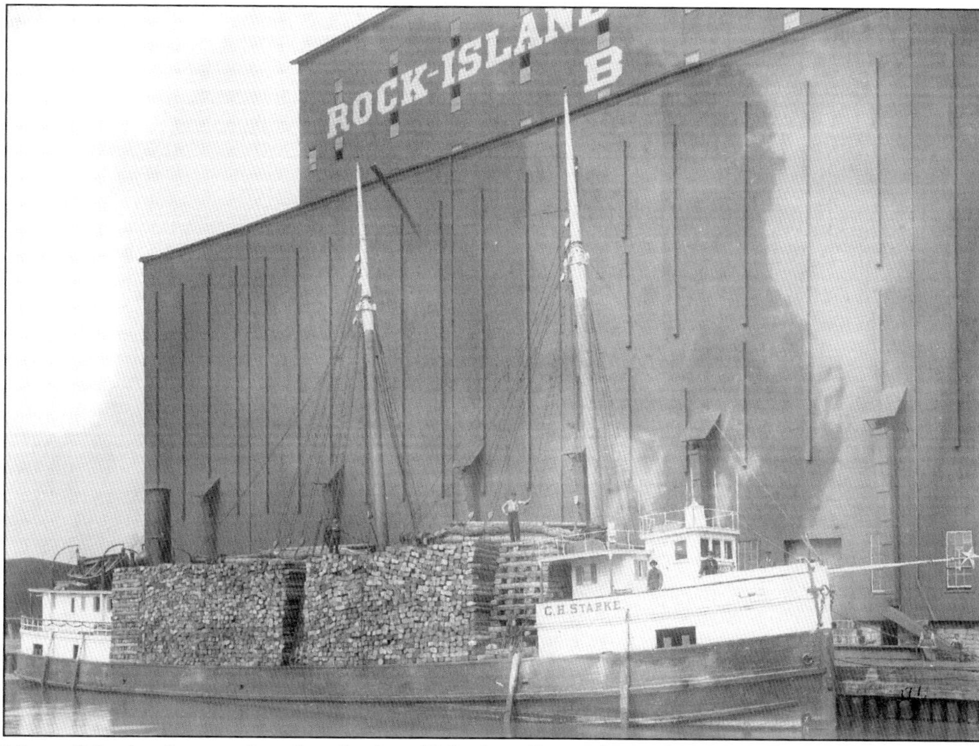

Most of the lumber produced at the Loud-Hoeft mill was shipped out on the company's steamer *C.H. Starke*. It is seen here in the 1930s delivering a load of cedar railroad ties to the Rock Island Railroad dock in Chicago.

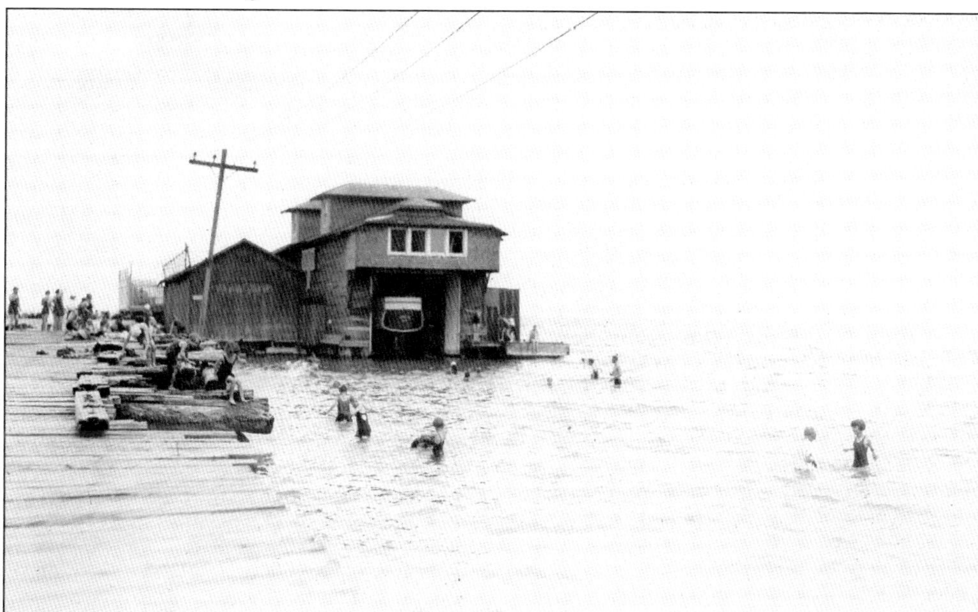
Hoeft's massive lumber dock had a large boathouse at the outer end where P.H. Hoeft kept his boats, the *Leila* and the *Topaz VI*. After the Loud-Hoeft mill closed down, the dock was a favorite venue for local swimmers, seen here in the 1930s.

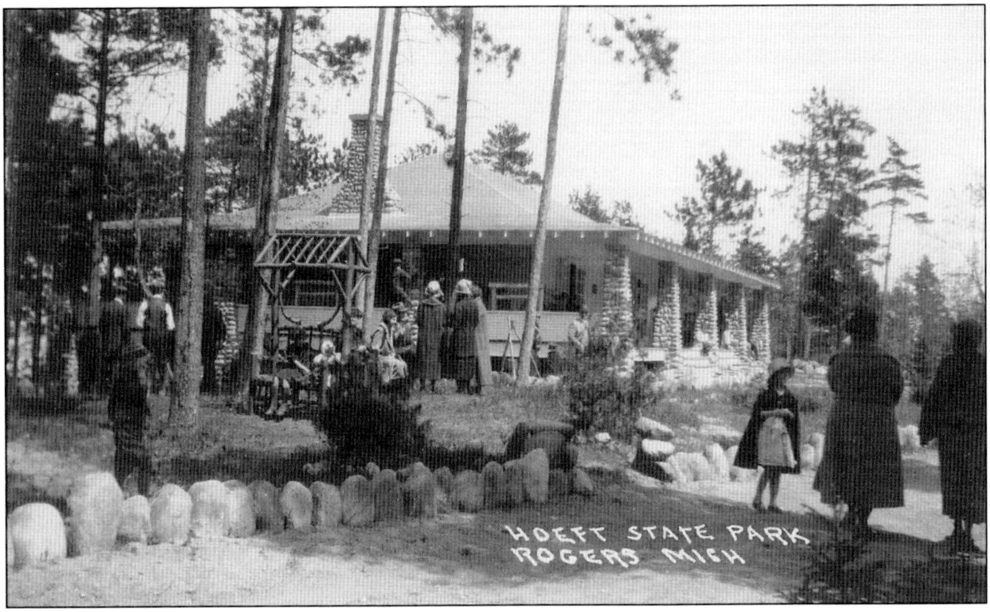

In 1921, businessman and lumber baron Paul H. Hoeft offered to donate 320 acres of land on a one-mile stretch of the Lake Huron shore north of Rogers City to the State of Michigan for use as a state park. His offer was accepted in 1922, and the park was one of the earliest developed in Michigan; it was named in Hoeft's honor. This c. 1930 postcard shows a weekend crowd around the park's pavilion.

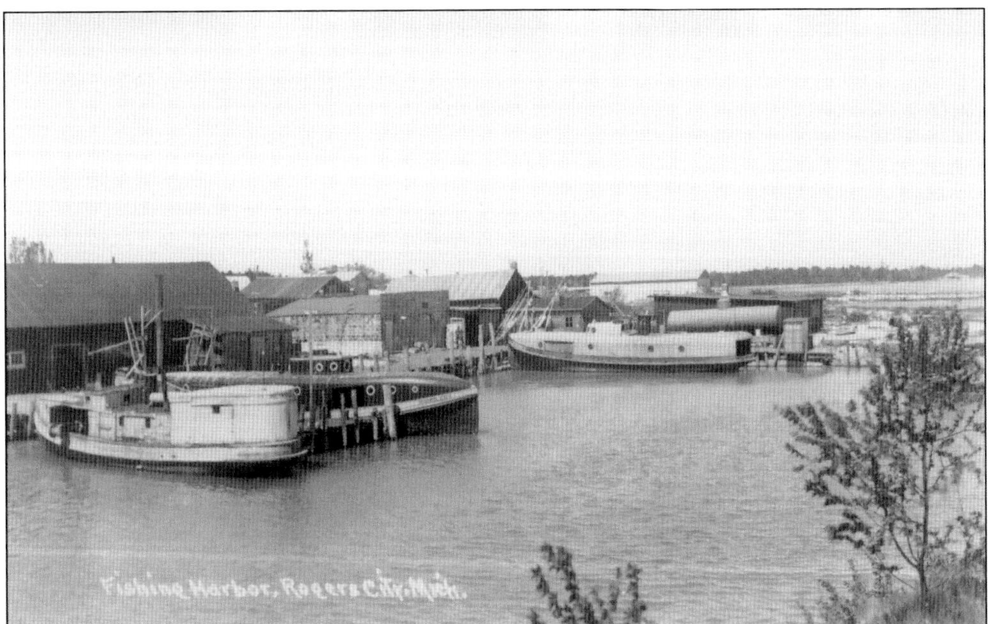

Commercial fishing was also an important local industry from the earliest days of Crawford's Quarry and Rogers City. The fish docks in Rogers, seen here in the 1940s, operated until the fish population in the area was depleted in the 1950s. The harbor used by fishermen was just north of the present Rogers City marina.

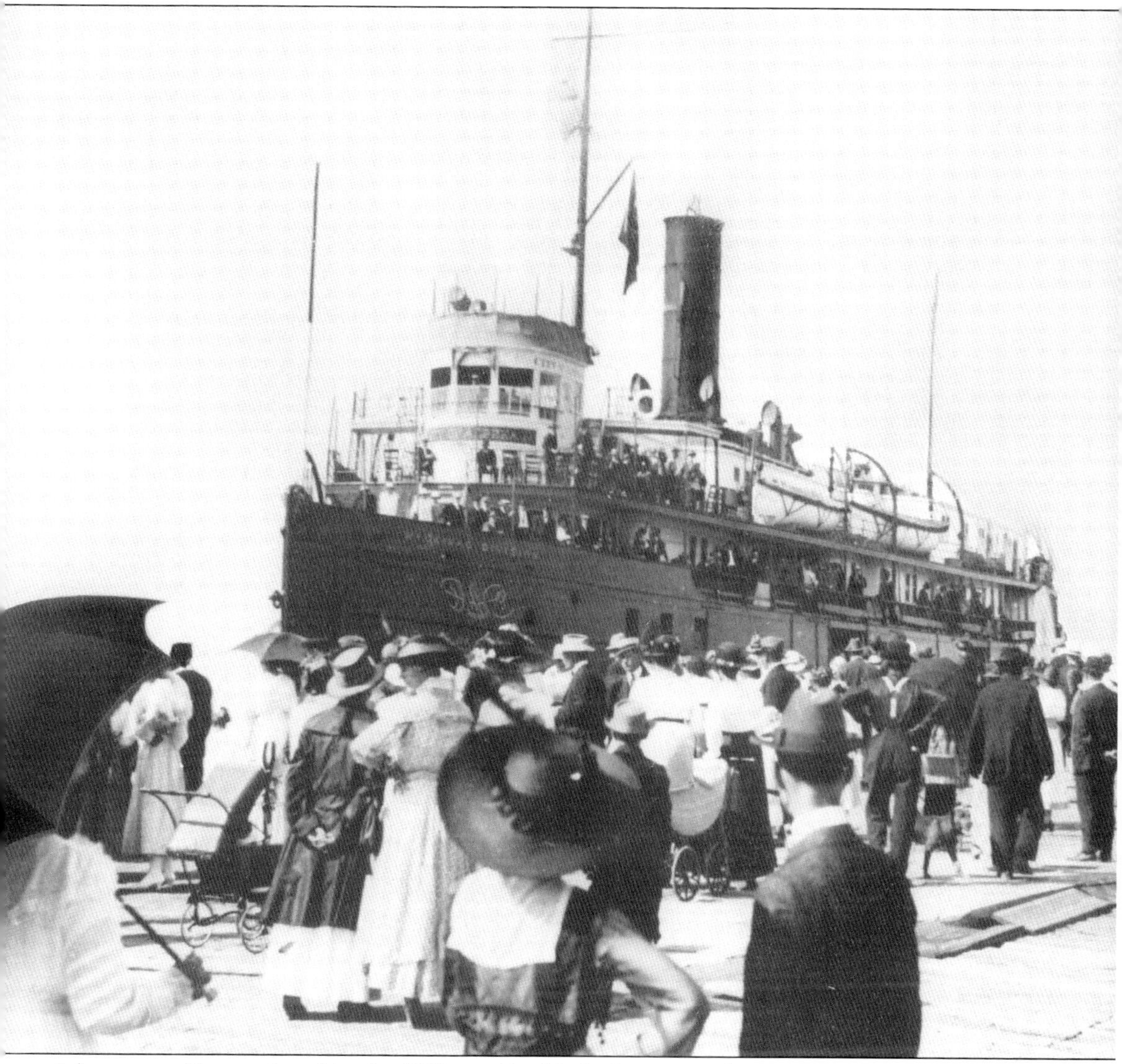

A large crowd has gathered in the 1920s on Hoeft's dock to greet the passenger steamer *City of Alpena* on one of its twice-weekly visits to Rogers City. Until the 1930s, most people traveling to or from Rogers traveled by boat.

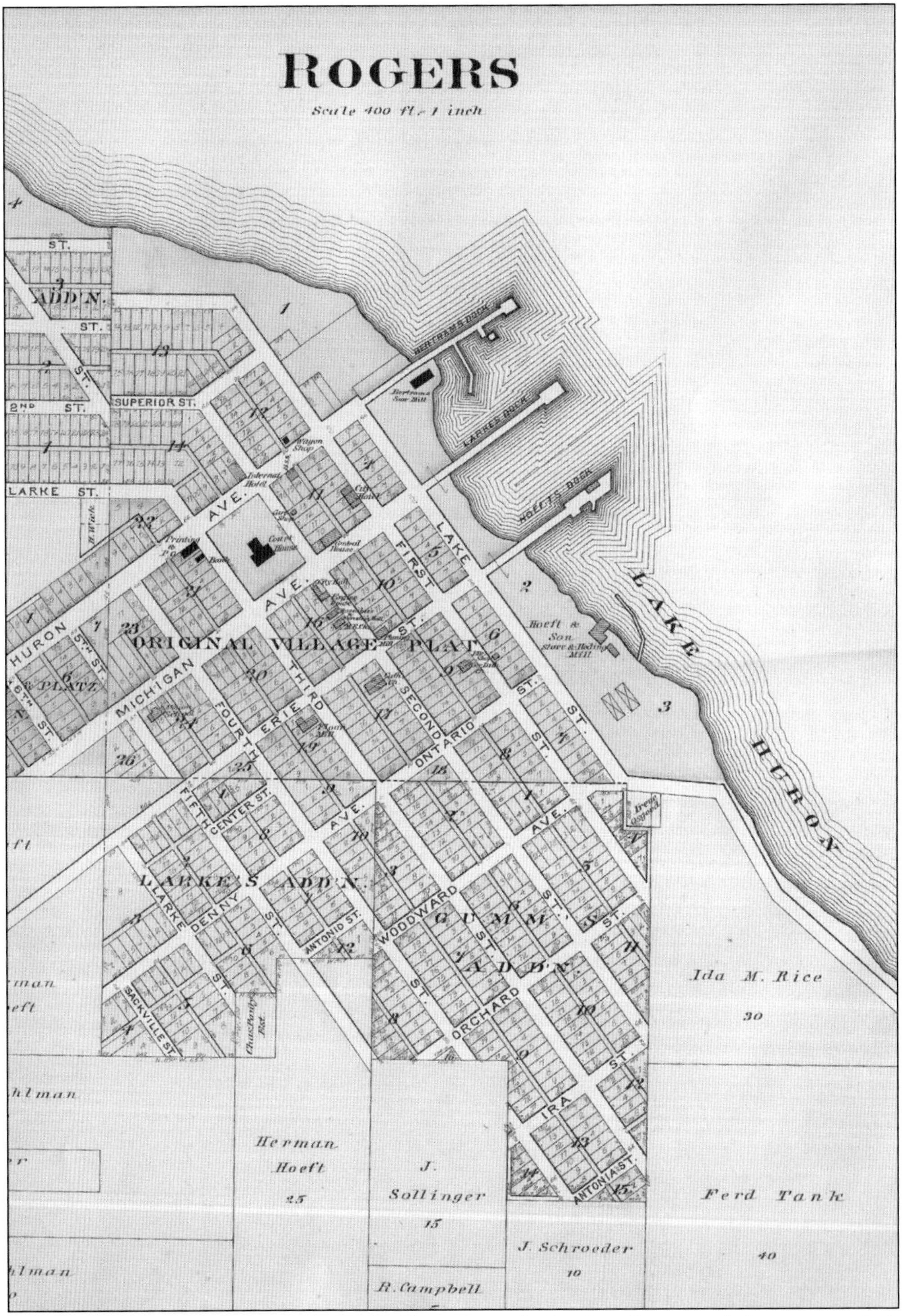

This 1903 plat of Rogers City shows the three large docks that dominated the community's waterfront. From top to bottom, they are the Bertram, Larke, and Hoeft docks. All were operated by lumber companies, and all were eventually removed after the lumber boom ended in the 1910s.

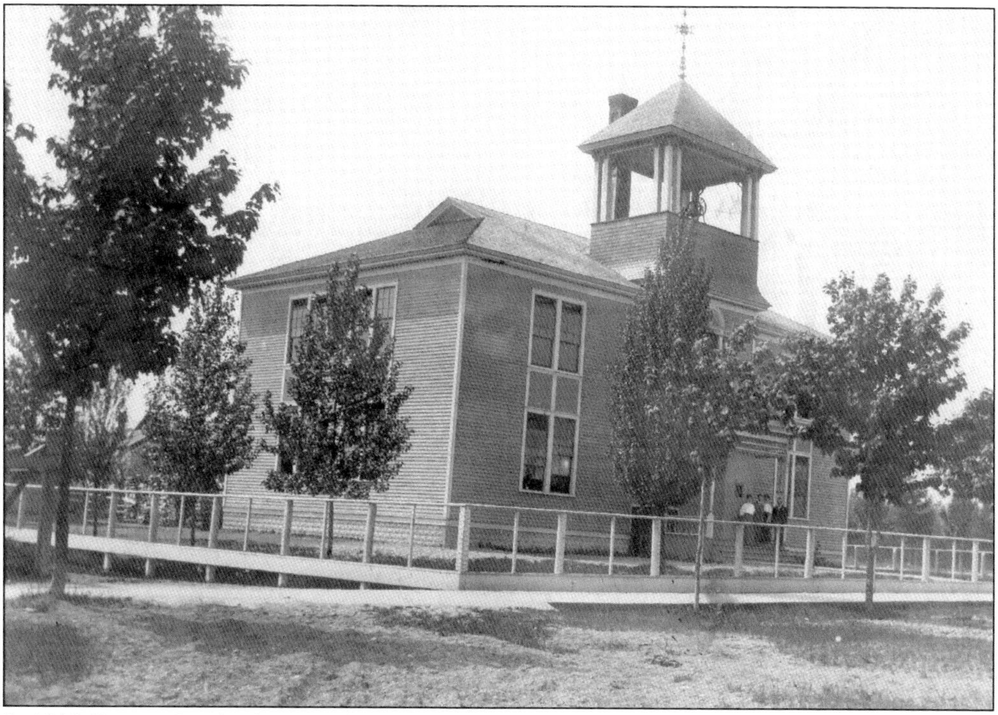

In 1903, Rogers City built a new four-room elementary school at the corner of Michigan Avenue and Fifth Street. Several years later, it was expanded to eight rooms to accommodate the growing student population. At that time, the school system only offered education through the eighth grade. The building was used by the schools until it was demolished in 1964. It is pictured here sometime between 1903 and 1907.

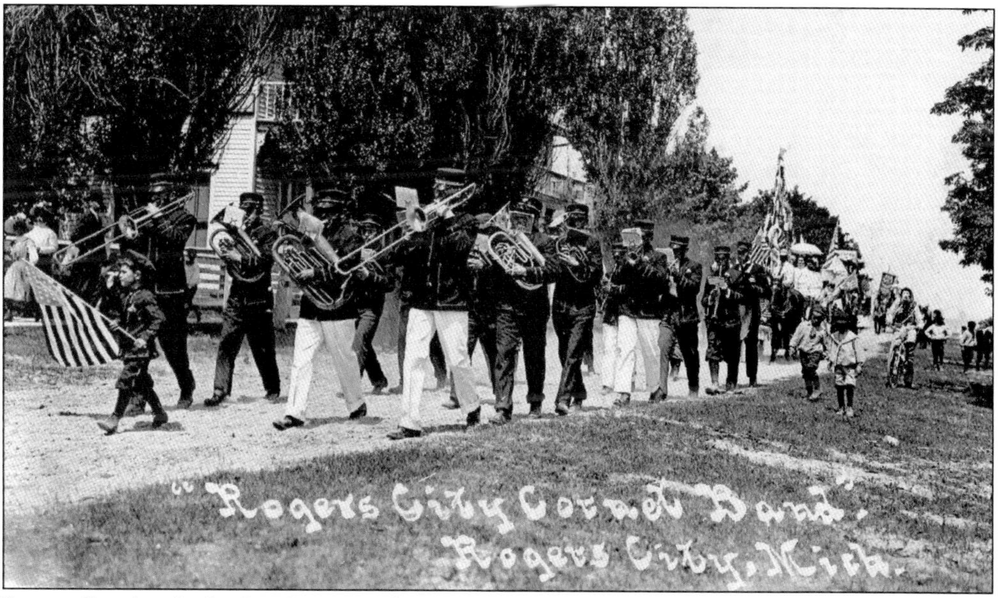

Rogers City has had a band since at least 1879. Since 1926, the band has been supported by a tax millage. The Rogers City Cornet Band is seen in this postcard view marching past the City Hotel on First Street around 1915.

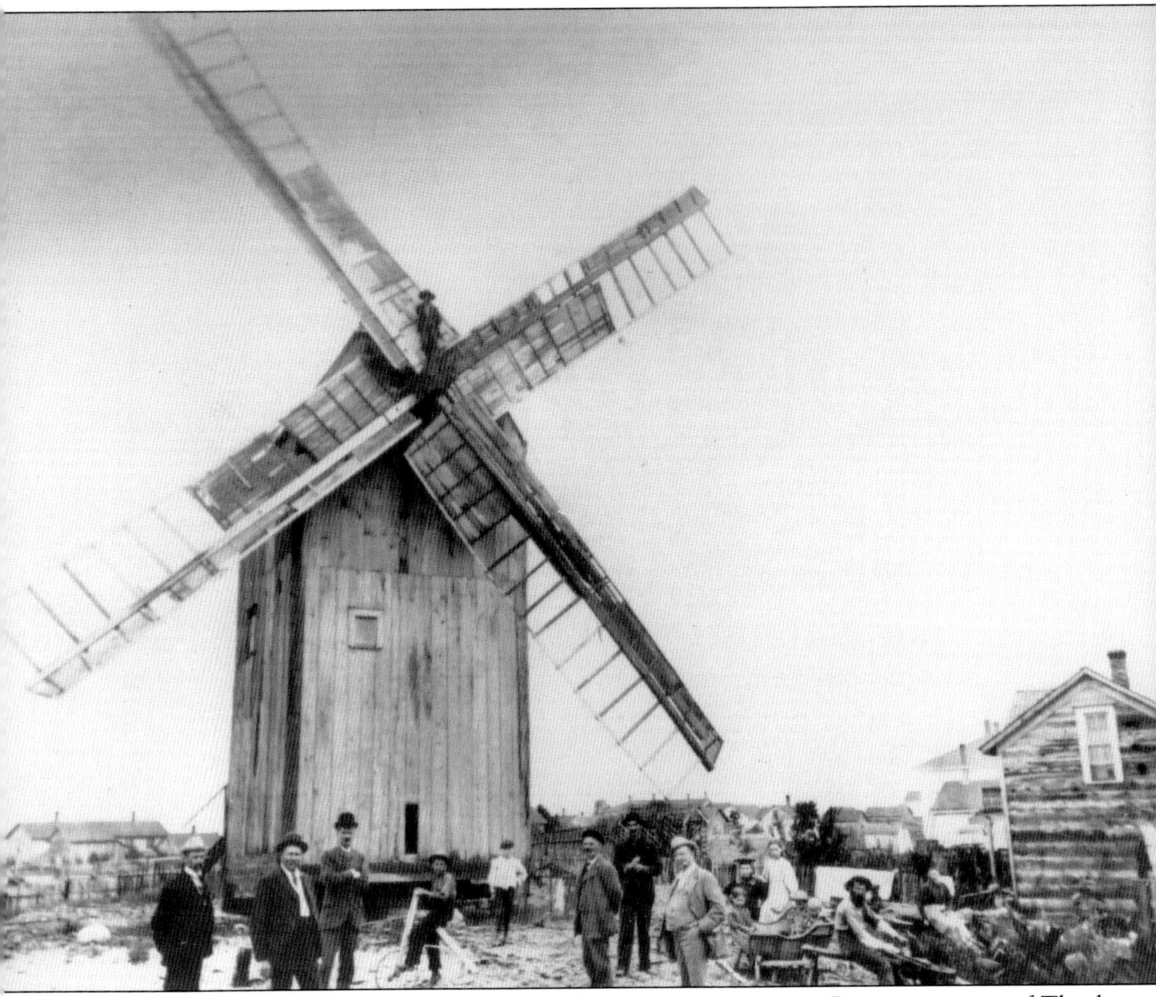

In 1892, August Kohnert built this windmill on Superior Street in Rogers, just east of Third Street, to grind grain. It could be seen from the waterfront, and steamer passengers often walked over to get a closer look at the European-style windmill. Two of Kohnert's sons are standing on the central hub of the windmill's giant arms in this c. 1900 photograph.

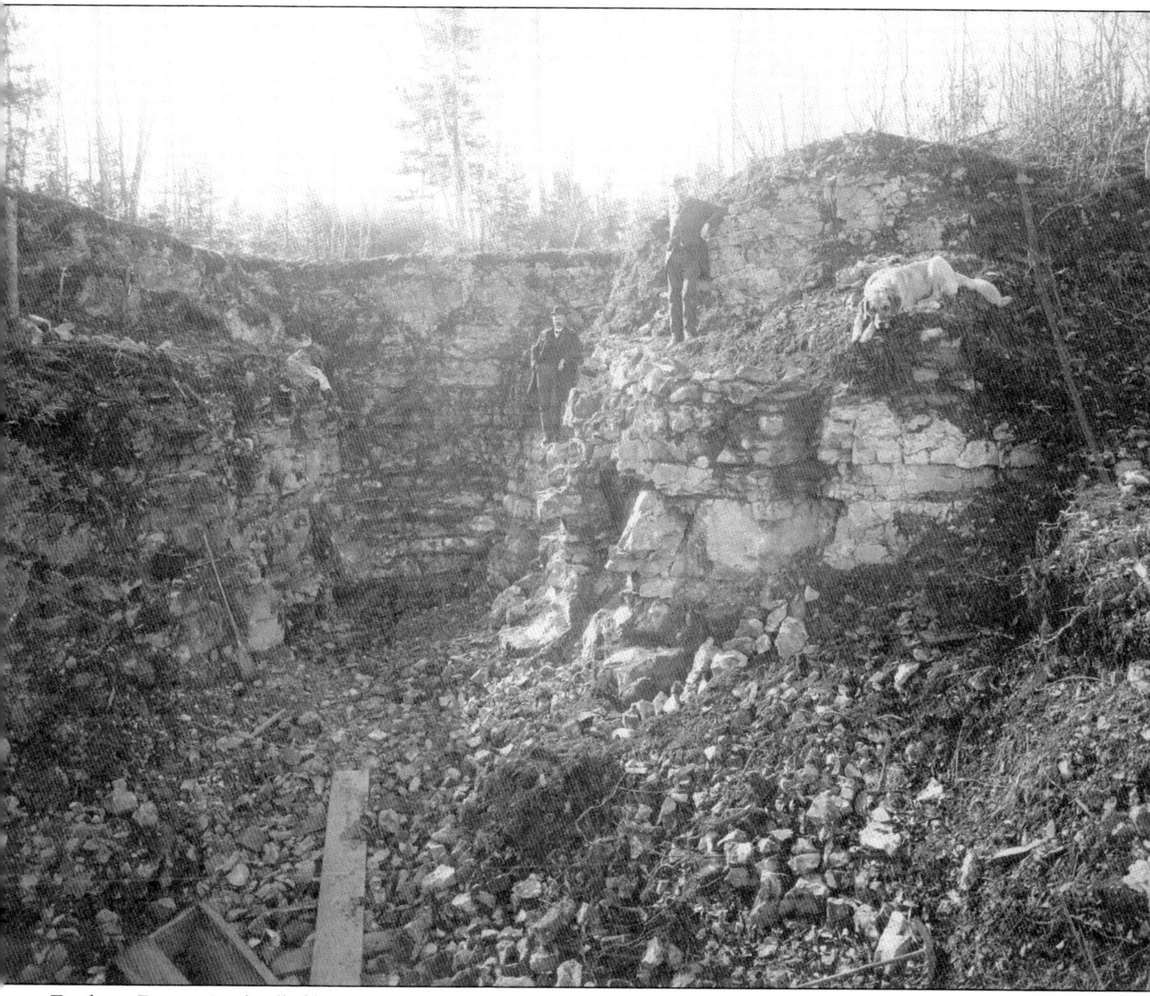

Frederic Denny Larke (left) and geologist O.S. Wood are seen here in the stone quarry at Crawford's Quarry in 1902. Larke and several other local leaders worked tirelessly to get someone to develop the quarry. Larke died in 1910, just months before Michigan Limestone announced plans to open a major limestone quarry on the site. Lying on a rock ledge on the right is Larke's massive dog Monarch.

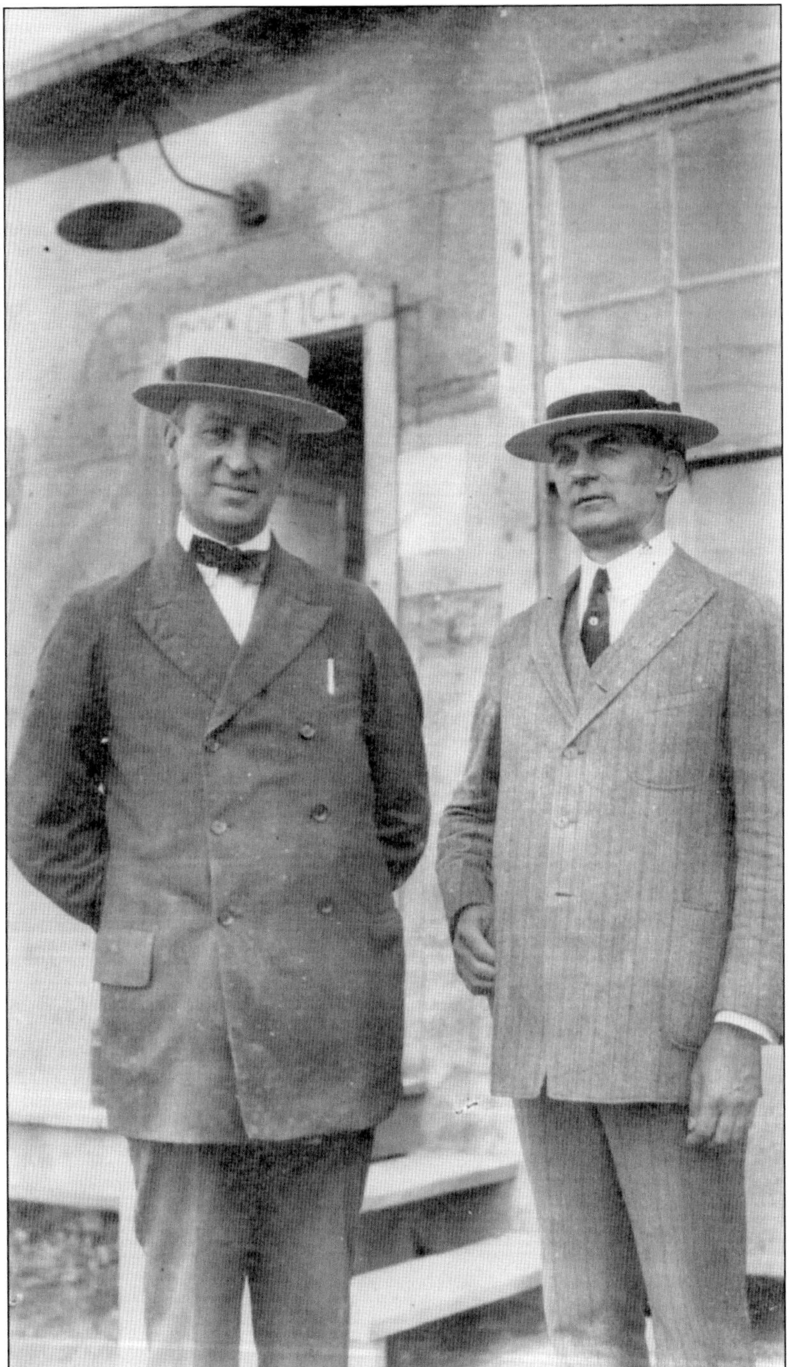

New York investment banker William F. White (right) organized the Michigan Limestone & Chemical Company in 1910 and began construction of the processing plant and quarry on 5,000 acres he purchased around Crawford's Quarry south of Rogers. In 1911, he brought in Carl D. Bradley (left) to serve as general manager of the Calcite Plant. In 1920, Bradley succeeded White as president of Michigan Limestone and its Bradley Transportation subsidiary.

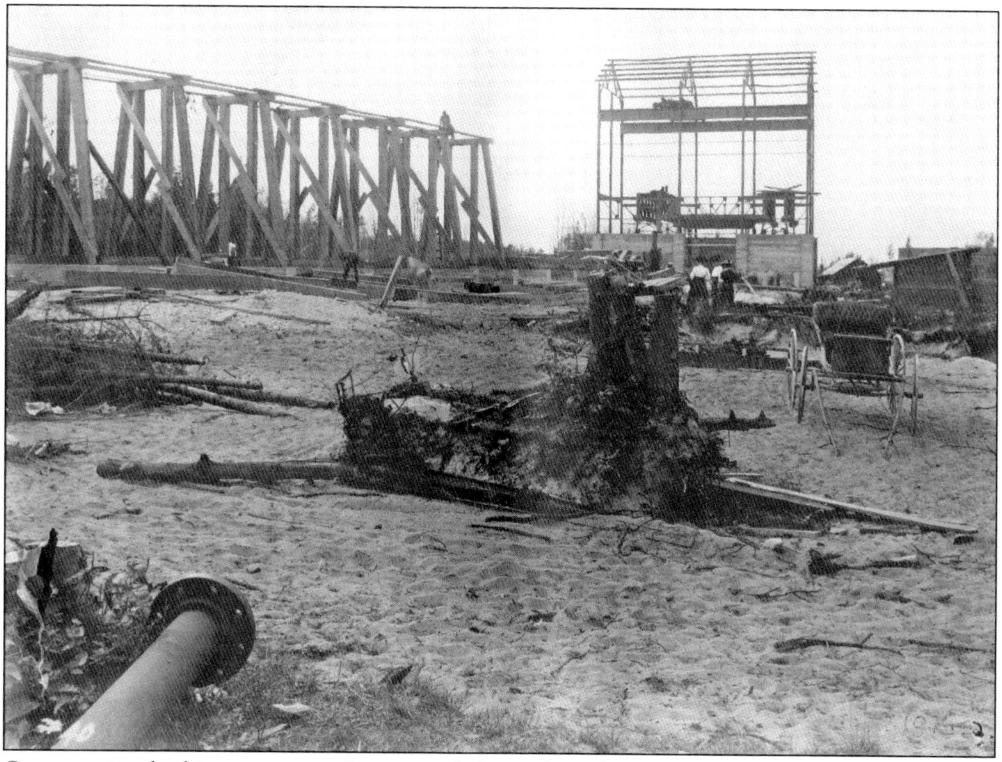

Construction had just gotten underway at Calcite when this photograph was taken in 1911. On the right is the steel framework for the two-story crusher building. The three well-dressed ladies are, in no particular order, Emma Bradley, the wife of Carl D. Bradley, the plant's general manager; Dorothea Hoeft, the wife of lumber baron and Michigan Limestone investor Paul H. Hoeft; and Francis Kemp, a friend of both couples from Alpena.

By the spring of 1912, construction of the Calcite Plant was nearing completion. Horses were used to move materials around the site, as the company had no trucks. The building on the left is the crusher, and the building on the right is the mill, or screen house, where stone went through its final processing and was sorted by size.

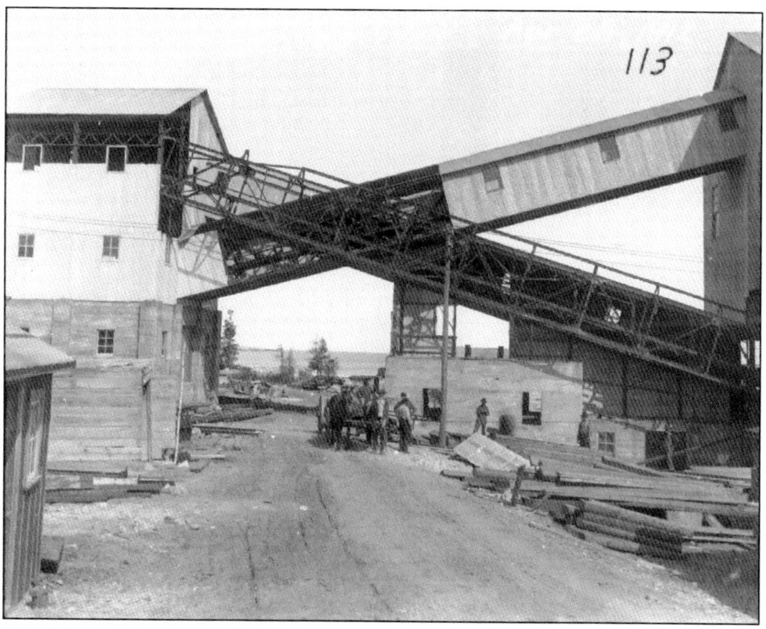

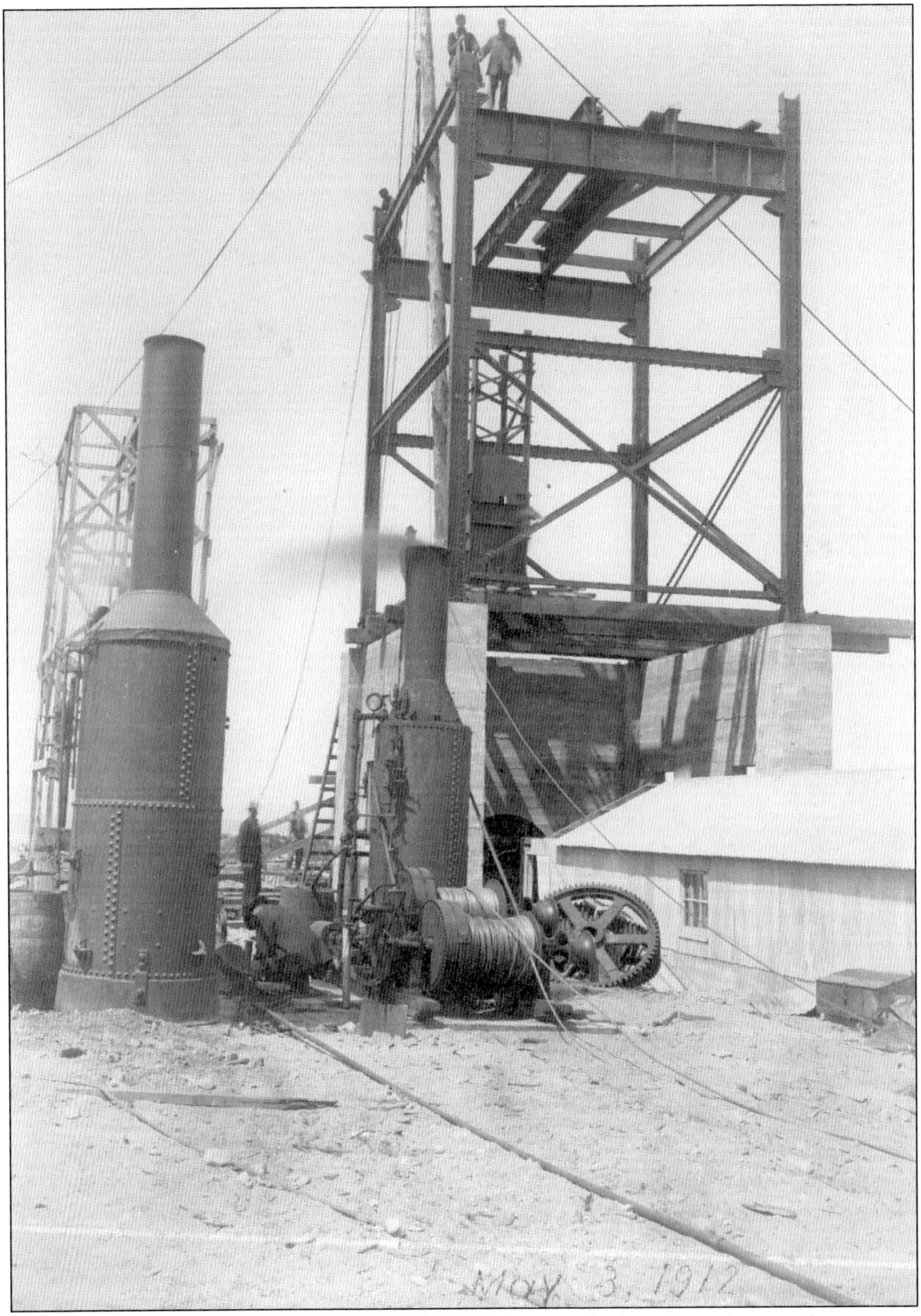

The Calcite Plant was a modern industrial facility, but it was built without the use of any cranes to lift steel beams and other materials into place. Lifting was done by a tall gin pole, clearly visible alongside the steel framework in this 1912 photograph. Hoisting was done with a steel cable that ran through a sheave on the top of the gin pole and down to the portable steam engine on the left.

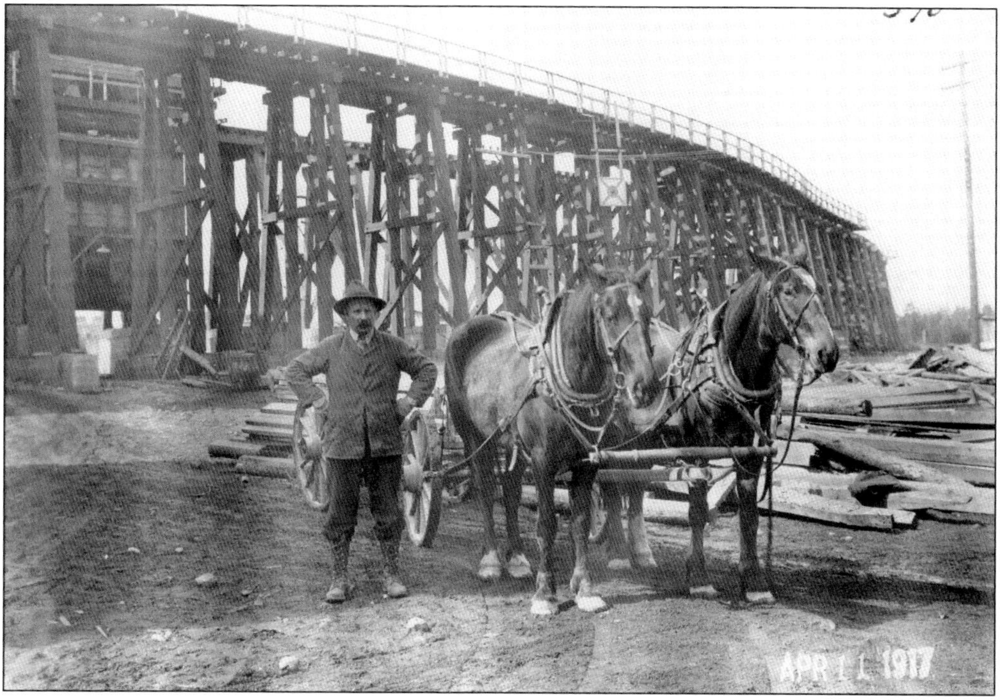

General manager Carl Bradley used a horse-drawn wagon to move around the property at Calcite. His team and wagon are seen here with Charles Pagels, Bradley's driver. In the background is the elevated railroad trestle that took trains to the second floor of the crusher to dump their loads of stone.

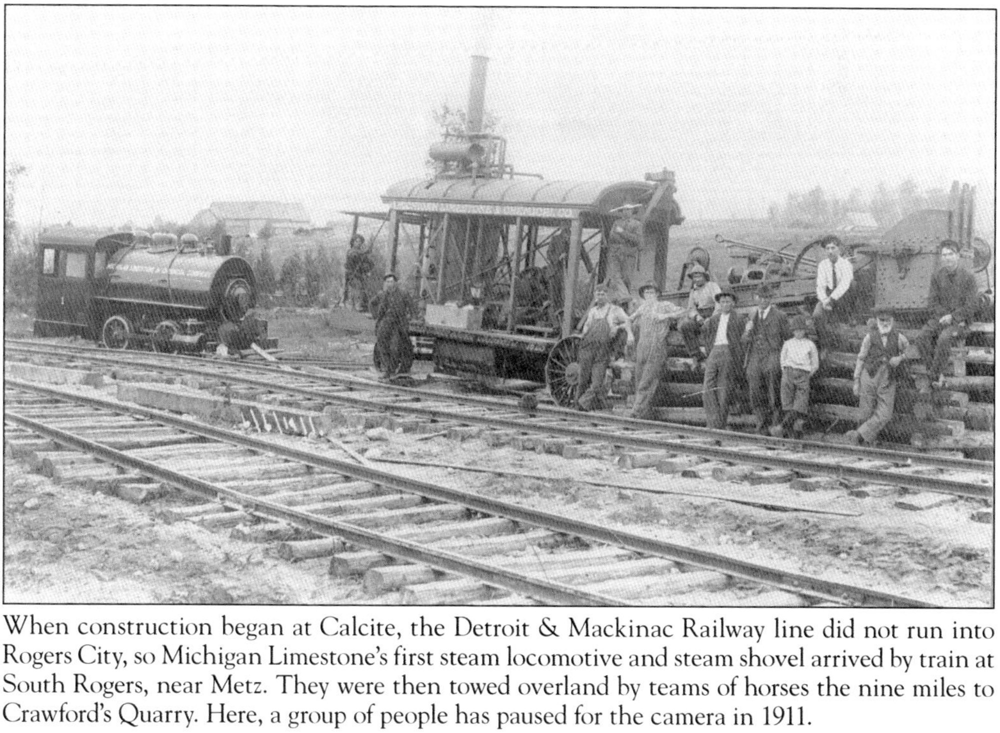

When construction began at Calcite, the Detroit & Mackinac Railway line did not run into Rogers City, so Michigan Limestone's first steam locomotive and steam shovel arrived by train at South Rogers, near Metz. They were then towed overland by teams of horses the nine miles to Crawford's Quarry. Here, a group of people has paused for the camera in 1911.

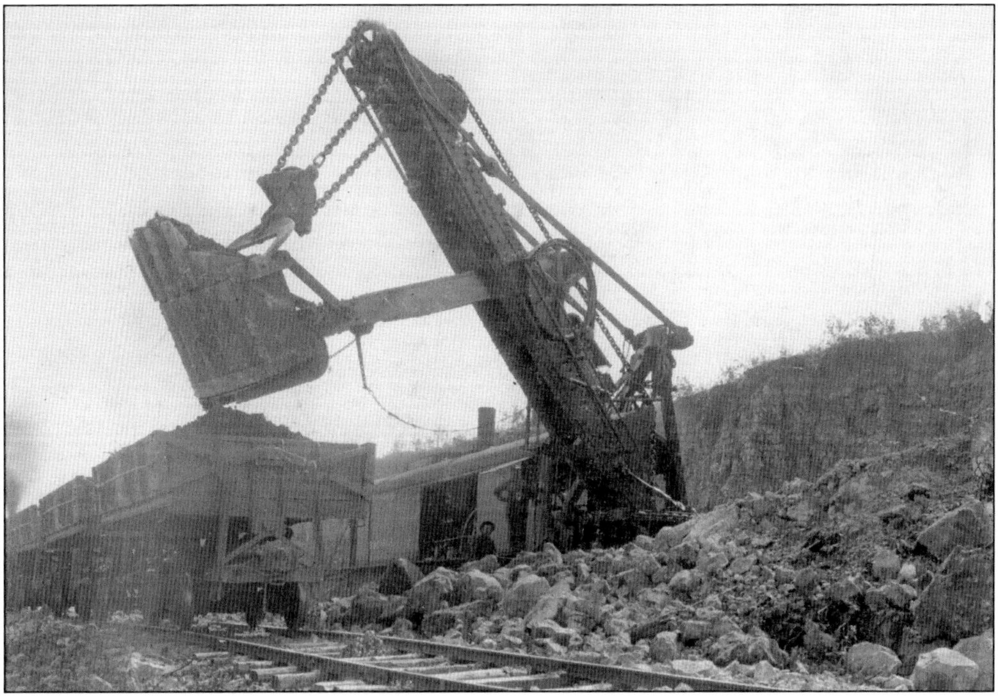

Here, one of the first production steam shovels loads railcars with stone in the summer of 1911. The shovels were mounted on rails so they could move along the quarry face.

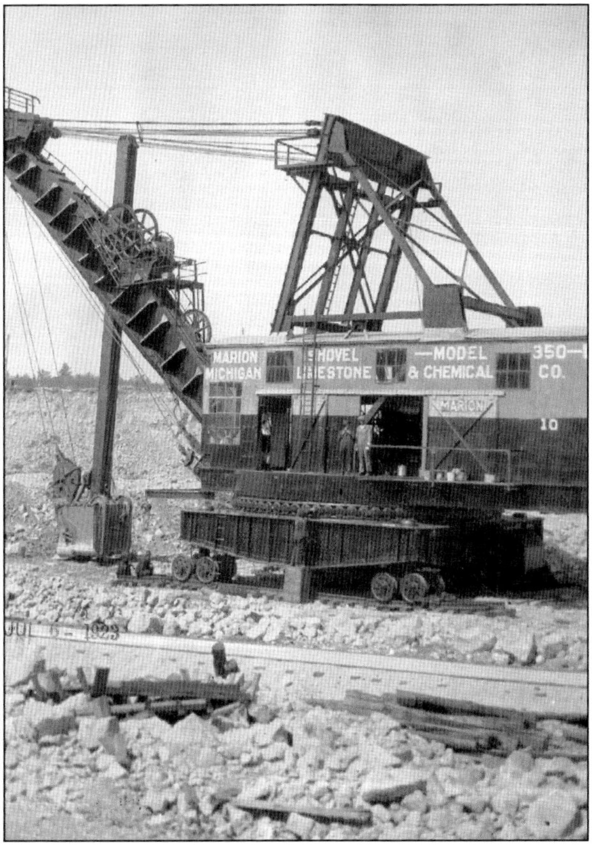

In 1920, Michigan Limestone began replacing its steam shovels with electric shovels like the one pictured, which were much larger and more powerful. Like the steam shovels, they operated on rails that ran parallel to the quarry face. Electricity was provided by a long, heavy extension cord that had to be moved frequently to keep up with the movement of the shovel.

A worker stands alongside the bucket of one of the plant's new electric shovels. The bucket was capable of scooping up 12 yards of stone. Three of the new electric shovels could do the same amount of work as eight steam shovels.

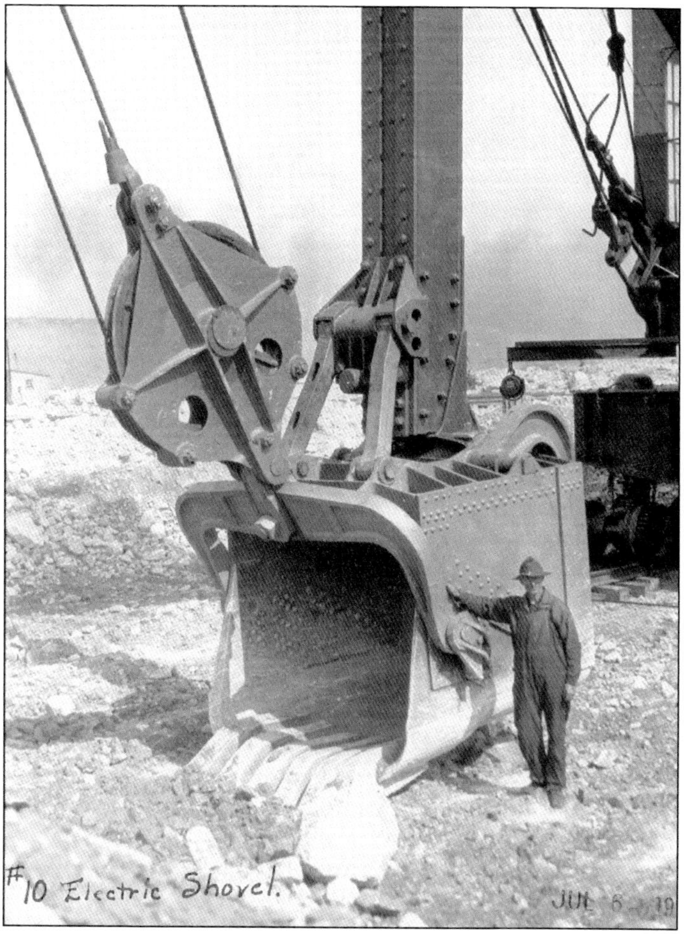

Construction of the Calcite Plant also involved the construction of a loading dock and the deepening of the harbor to accommodate large lake freighters. Much of the dredging of the harbor was done by the steam-powered *Majestic*, seen here scooping up a bucketful of mud.

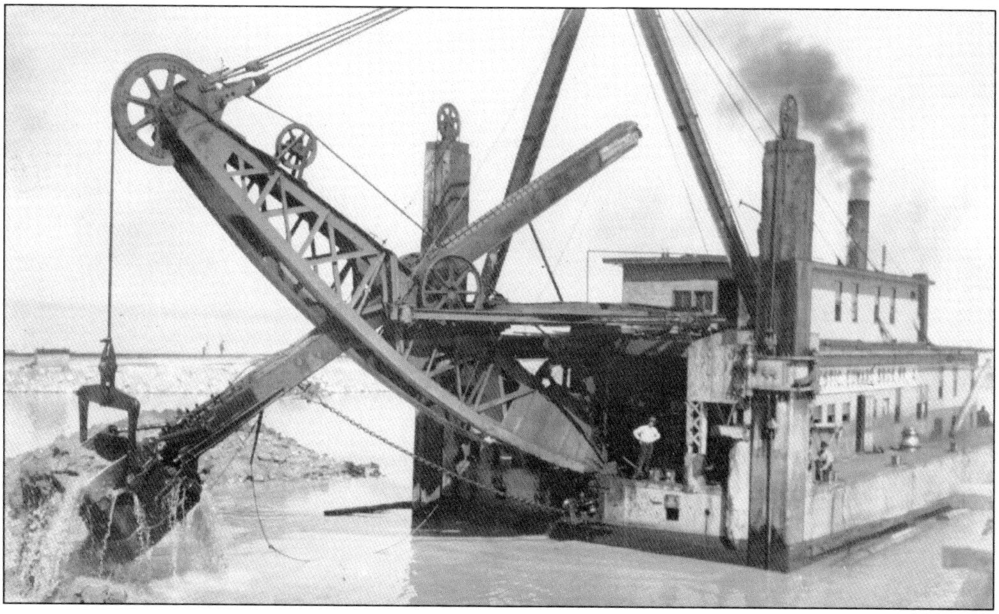

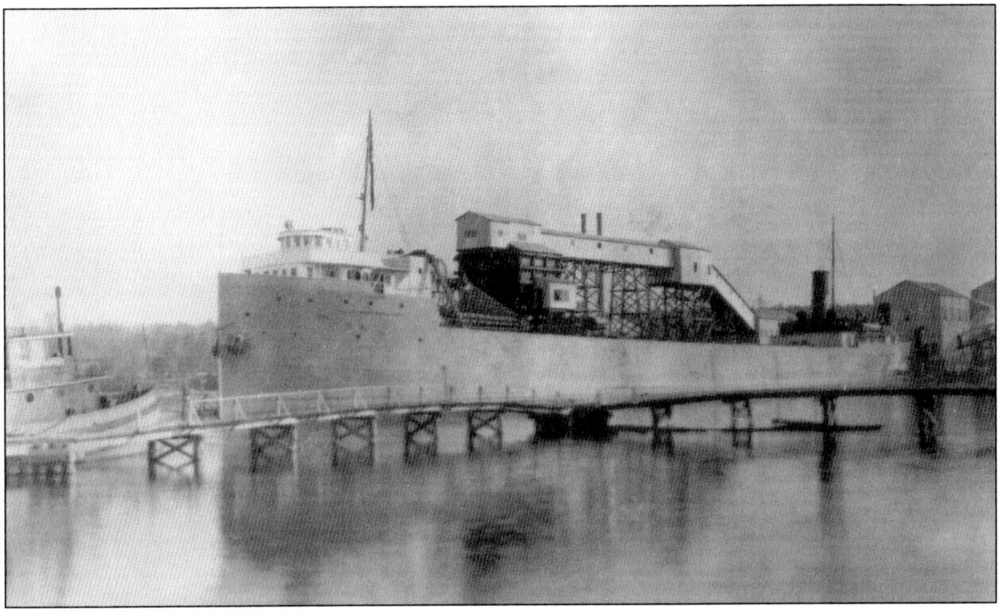

In addition to building the plant and quarry, Michigan Limestone also contracted with the Detroit Shipbuilding Company to construct a 416-foot, self-unloading bulk freighter for the company's use in delivering stone to customers around the lakes. Christened *Calcite*, it is seen here taking on its first load of stone at its namesake port on June 26, 1912. One of 11 ships that flew the Bradley Transportation flag over the years, it operated for the company until 1960.

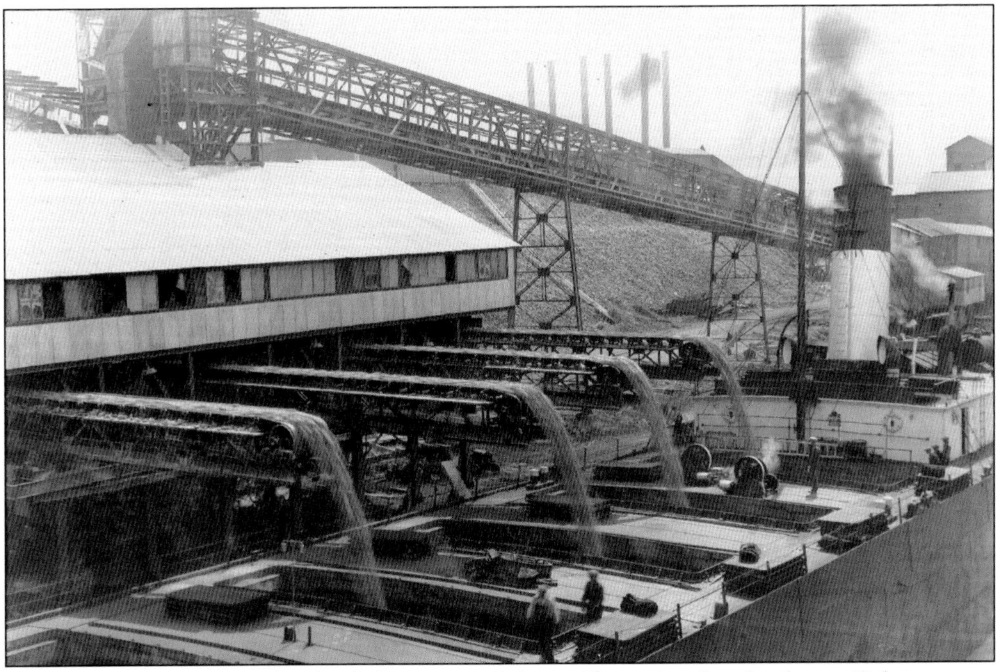

Ships from other fleets also loaded stone at Calcite. Here, the ship loader at Calcite pours limestone into the cargo hold of the United States Steel steamer *William E. Corey* in 1924. The giant steelmaker had purchased William F. White's controlling interest in Michigan Limestone and the Bradley fleet in 1920.

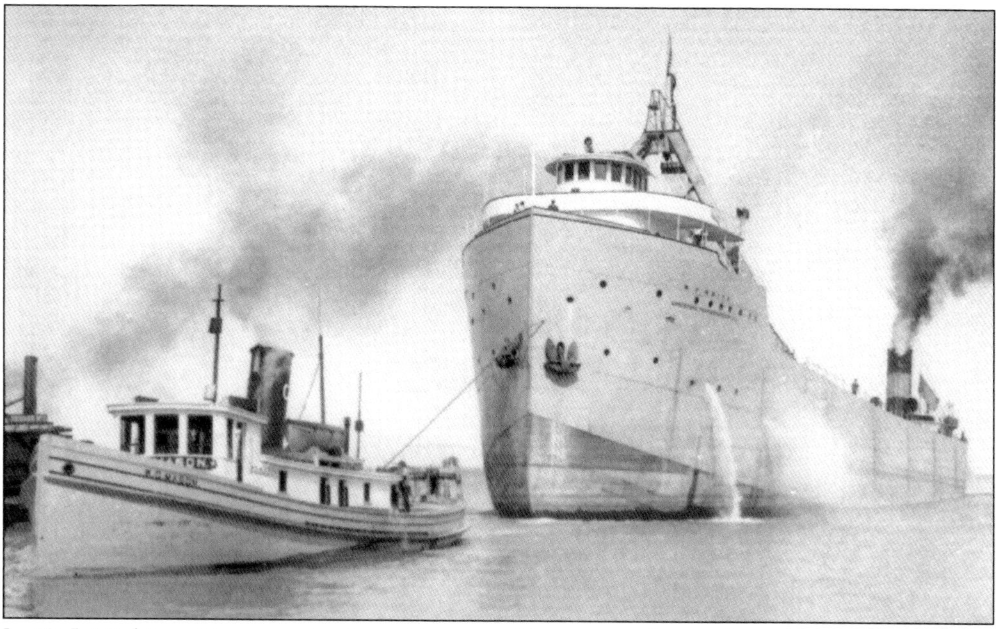

In 1915, Michigan Limestone had to add a second boat to its fleet to keep pace with increasing demand. The *W.F. White*, named for the founder and president of the company, arrived at Calcite on July 11, 1915, and was towed into the harbor by company tug *W.G. Mason*.

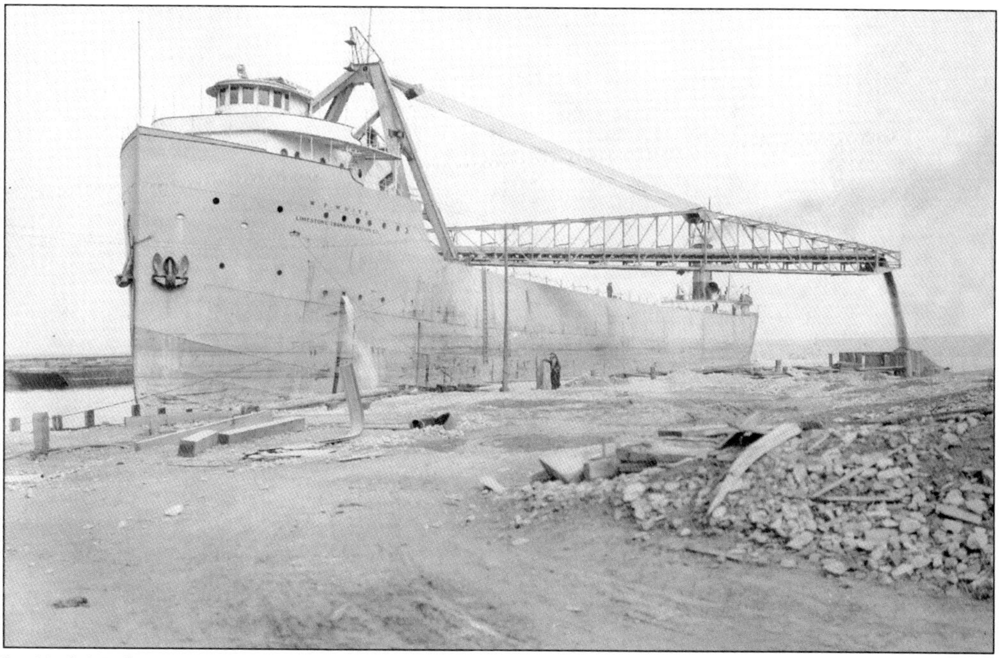

In 1915, Michigan Limestone found it necessary to extend its loading dock. To do that, the company developed a system Carl D. Bradley patented that was used in a great variety of applications around the Great Lakes. As seen in this photograph of the steamer *White*, when a Bradley freighter came in to load, it would first take on a partial load of large stone before shifting down the dock, swinging its boom out, and unloading it into a wooden crib that had been sunk in the area needing to be extended. It made quick work of lengthening the dock.

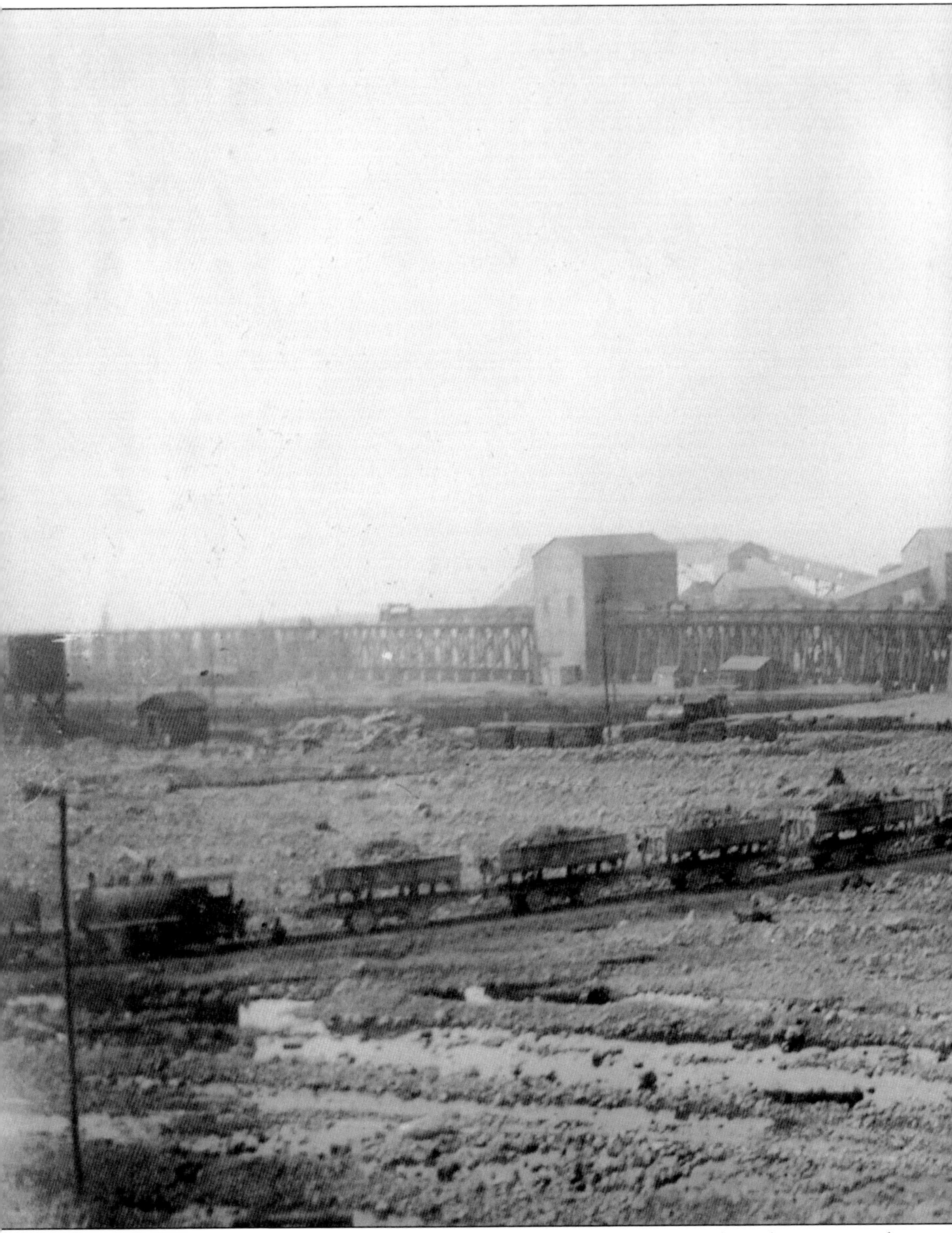

This panoramic view shows Calcite in 1914. The trains that hauled stone from the quarry to the crusher ran in a loop, as seen in the foreground. In the background, from left to right, are the

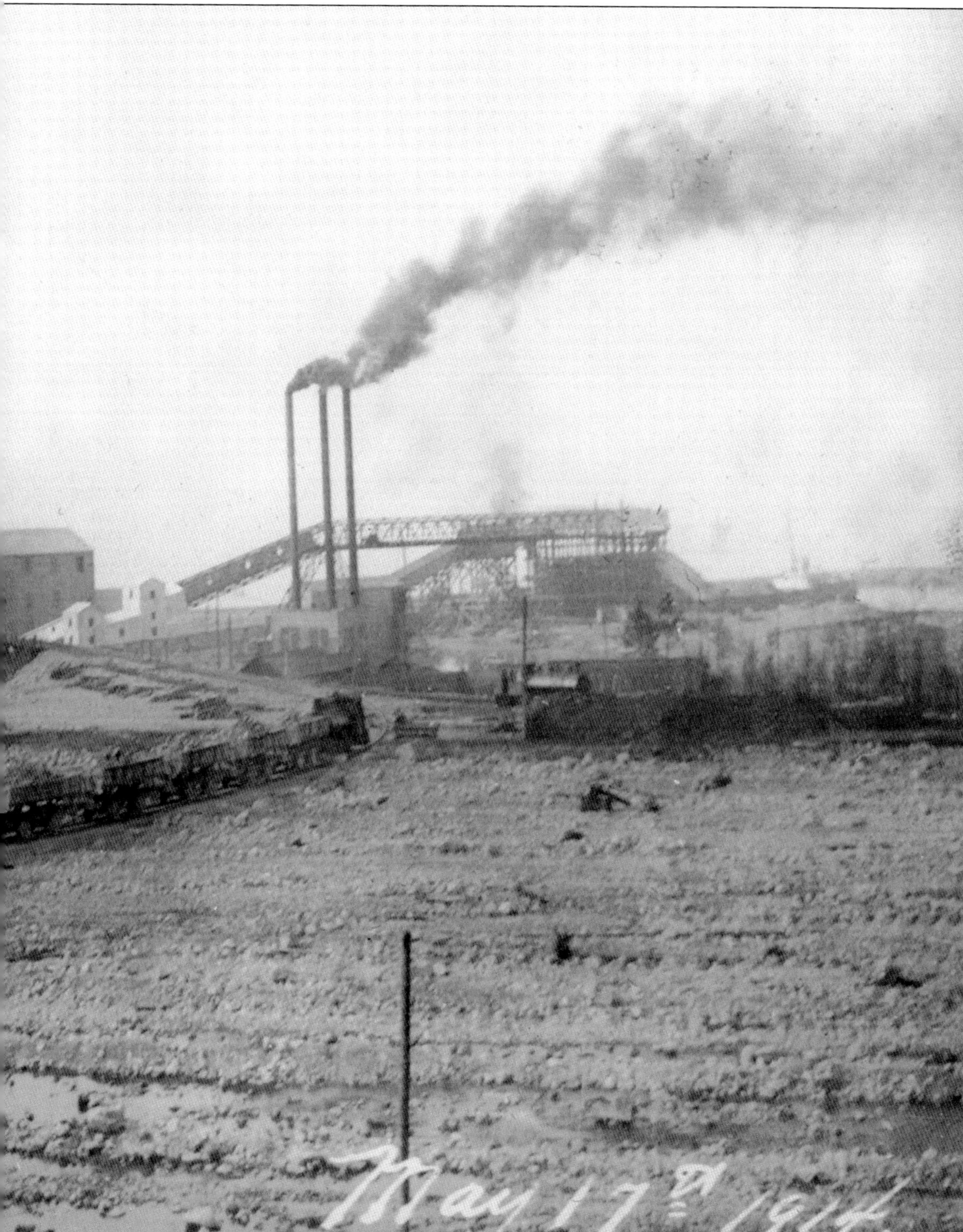

crusher, the mill, and the powerhouse. Behind the powerhouse is an overhead conveyor system that delivered stone from the mill to storage piles.

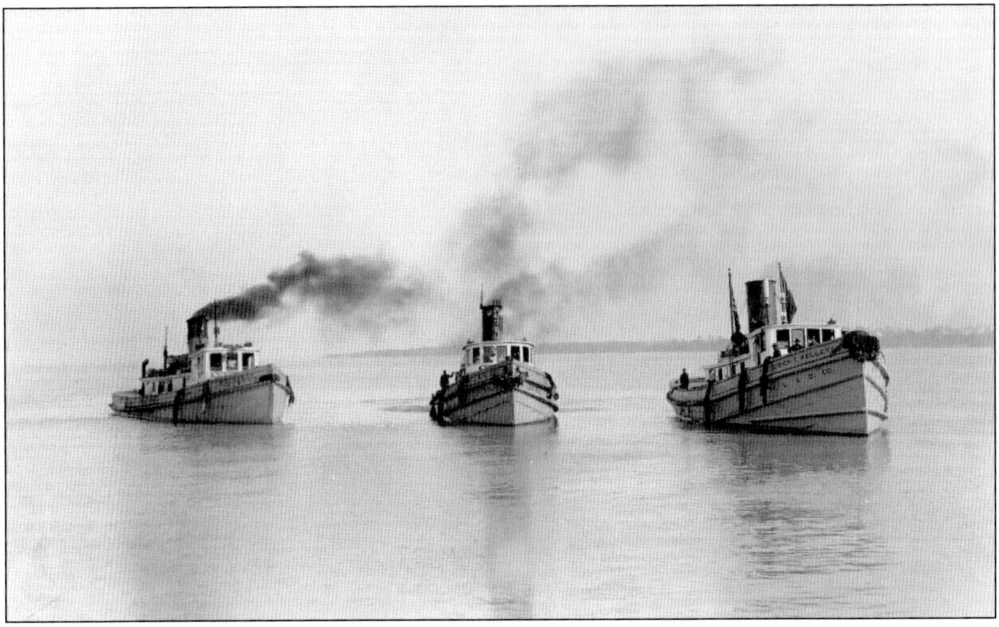

In order to assist ships maneuvering into the loading slip at Calcite, Michigan Limestone operated a fleet of tugs, including the *W.G. Mason*, the *Central*, and the *Frederick T. Kellers*. They have "posed" here, respectively, for a company photographer in 1924.

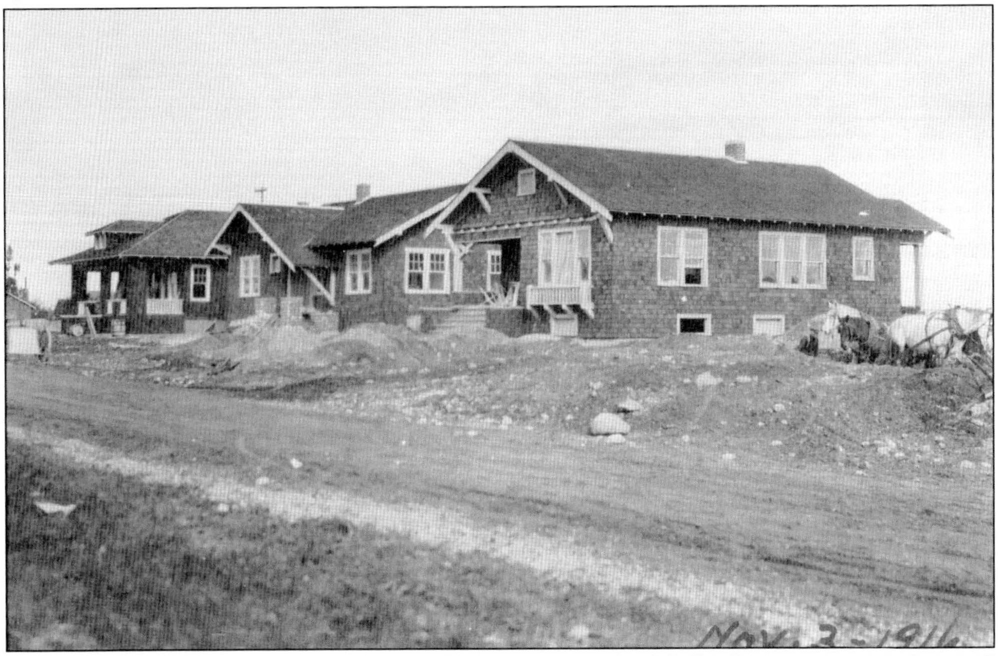

Throughout much of its early history, Michigan Limestone had difficulty recruiting professional and technical workers to relocate to Rogers, which was still very much a frontier village. In an effort to make employment offers more appealing, the company began building homes in 1916, which it offered to prospective employees at attractive rental rates. This neighborhood of Craftsman-style houses was occupied largely by the families of management personnel and skilled technical personnel.

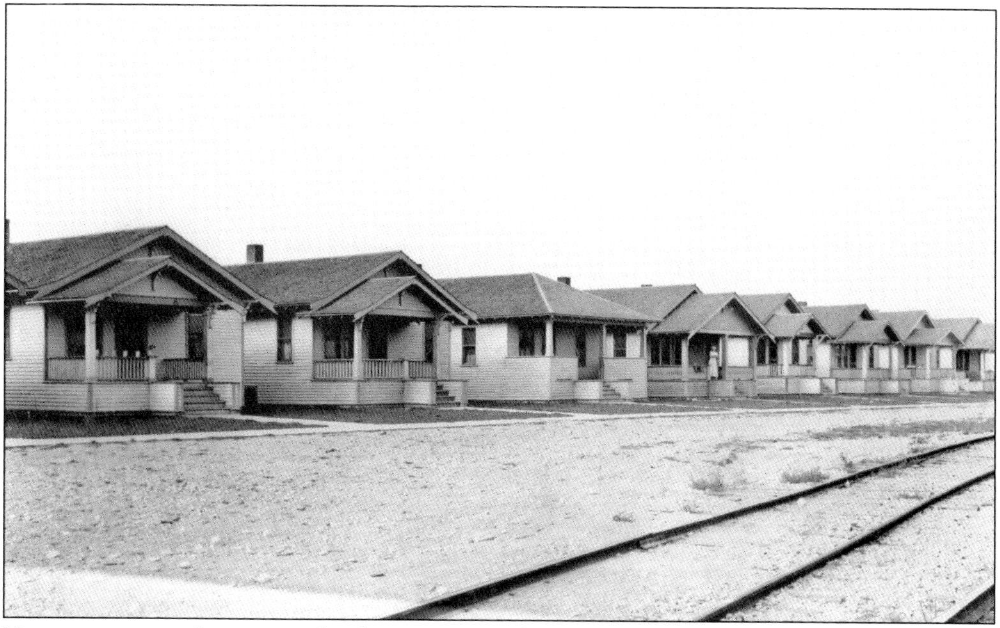

Homes in a second company development were slightly smaller and rented primarily to skilled workers and their families.

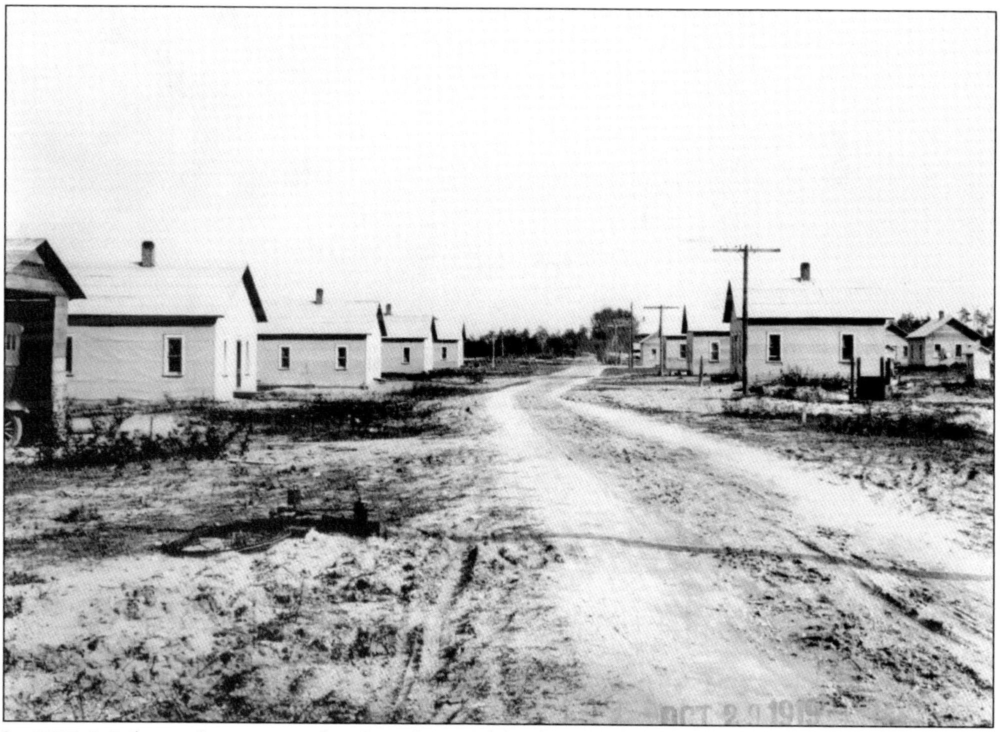

In 1919, Michigan Limestone developed a neighborhood of smaller, almost cottage-style homes that could be rented by any company employees. Eventually, the company got out of the real estate business, selling all of the homes to employees at attractive prices.

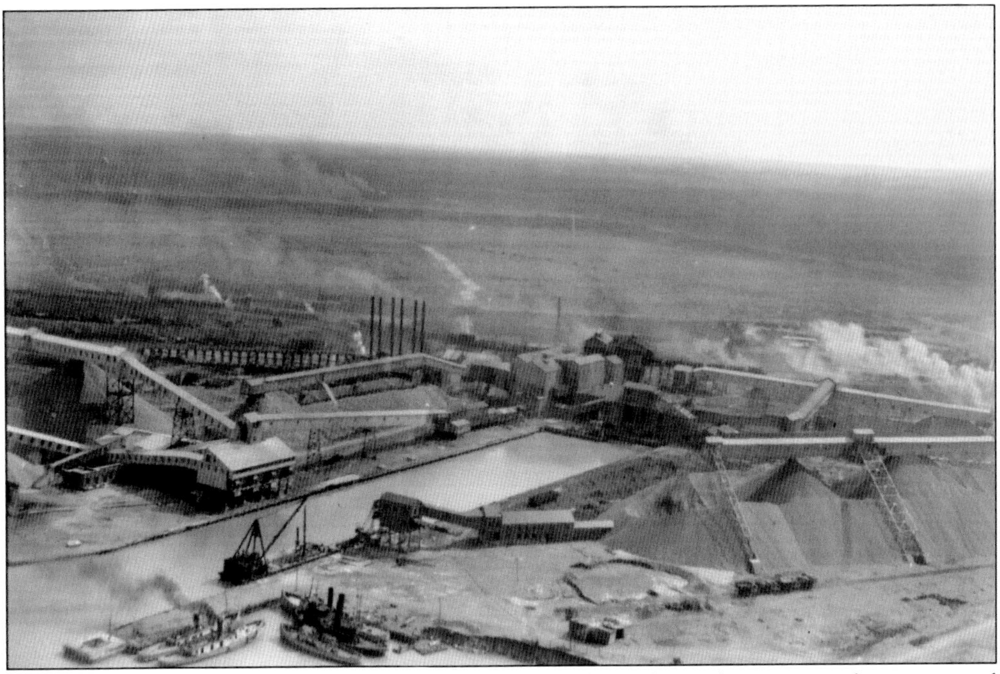

By the time this aerial photograph was taken in 1924, the Calcite Plant was producing around seven million tons of stone each year and was recognized as a world leader in the limestone industry. General manager Carl D. Bradley was often referred to as the "Limestone King," a title he probably deserved.

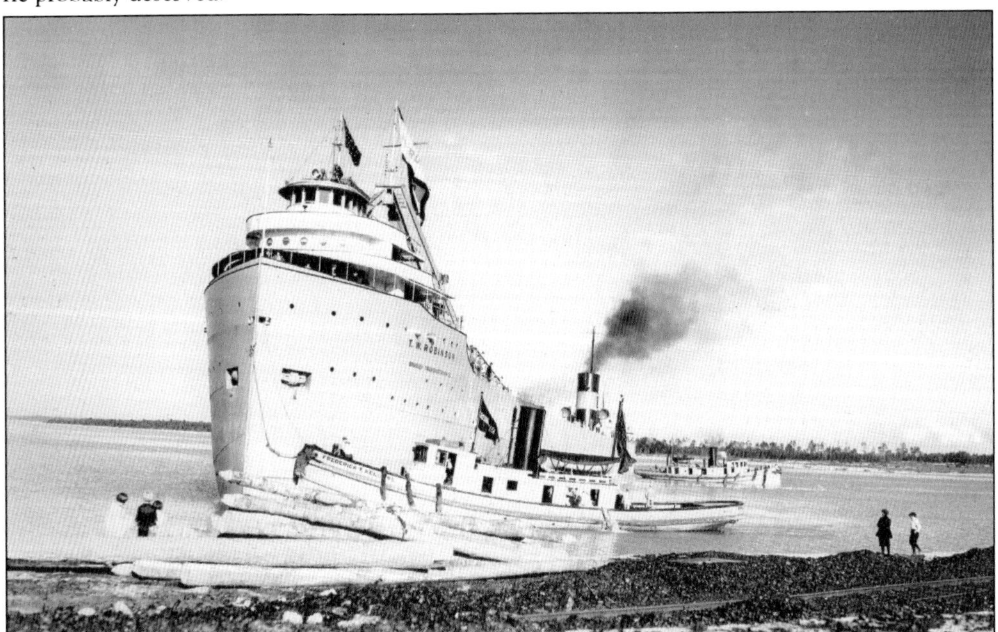

As production at Calcite increased to keep up with growing demand, the company had to continually increase its production and shipping capacities. New freighters were built in 1917, 1923, and 1925, including the *T.W. Robinson*, which was assisted by tugs when it arrived here at Calcite on July 12, 1925.

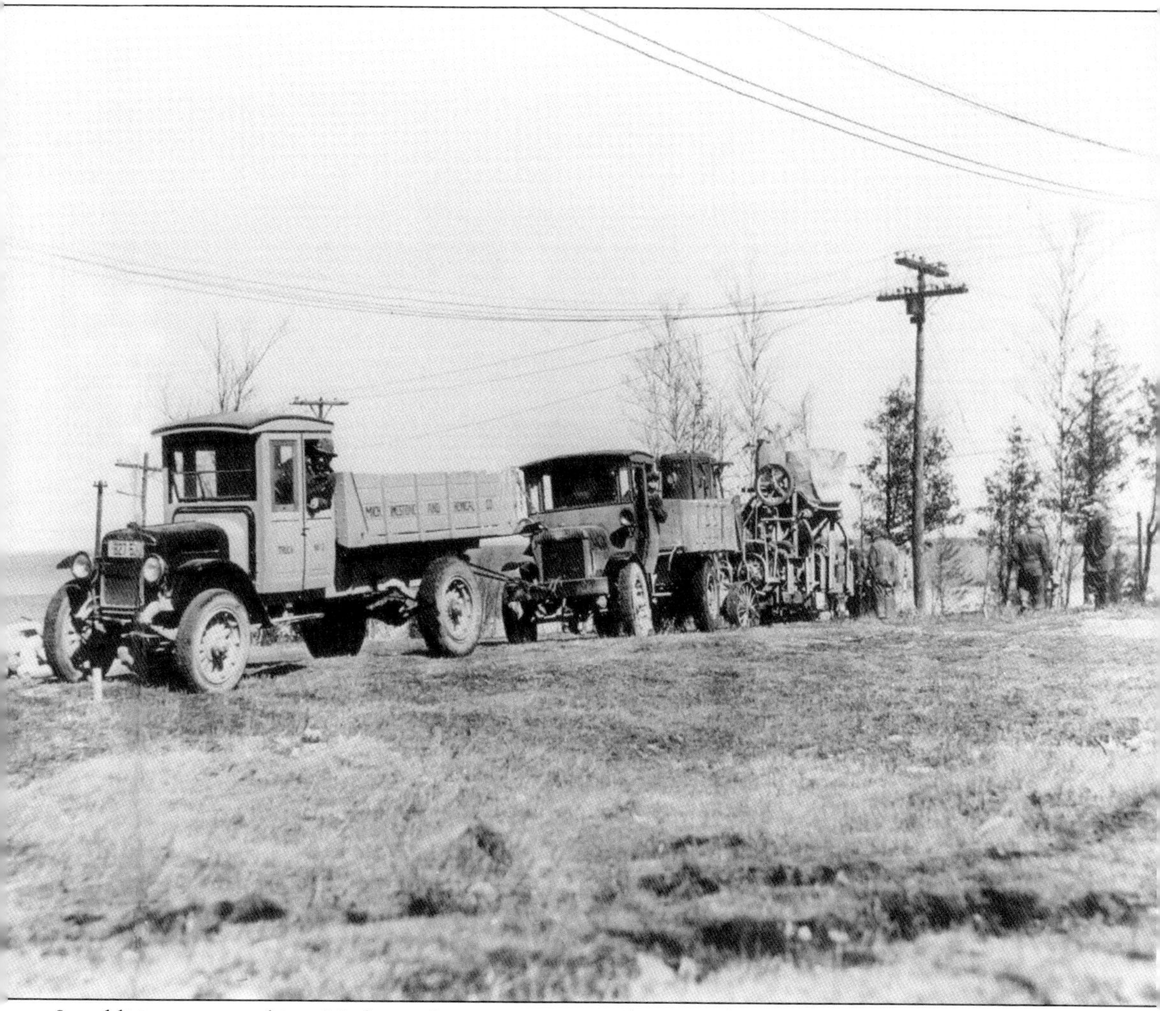

In addition to new ships, Michigan Limestone invested a great deal of money each year in new equipment, like the trucks and cement mixer in this 1925 photograph. They were the first trucks owned by the company.

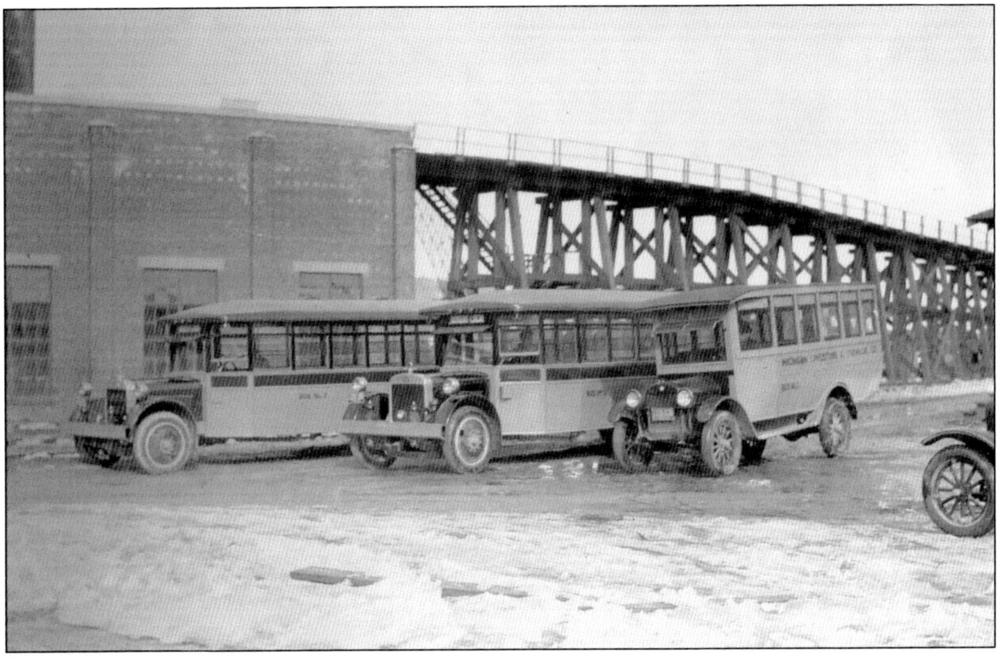

At a time when most company employees still did not own automobiles, Michigan Limestone initiated bus service between Rogers City and the quarry, which was several miles away. By 1926, it was operating these three buses. Company bus service continued into the 1950s.

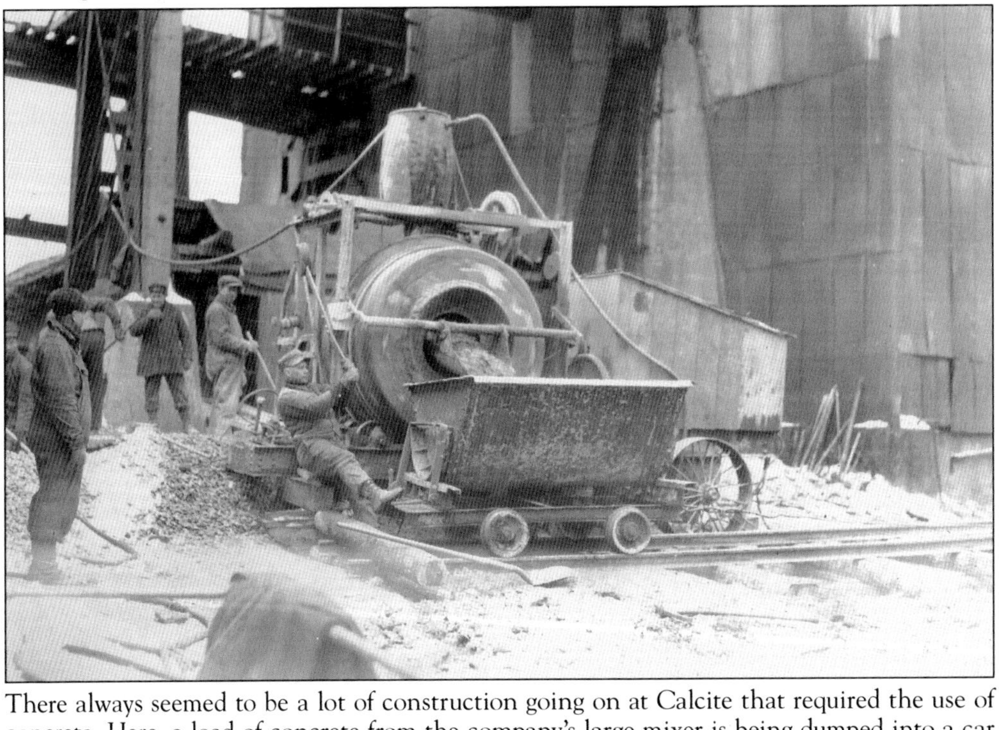

There always seemed to be a lot of construction going on at Calcite that required the use of concrete. Here, a load of concrete from the company's large mixer is being dumped into a car that rolls on tramway rails. Both the mixer and the system of rails could be moved to job sites as necessary.

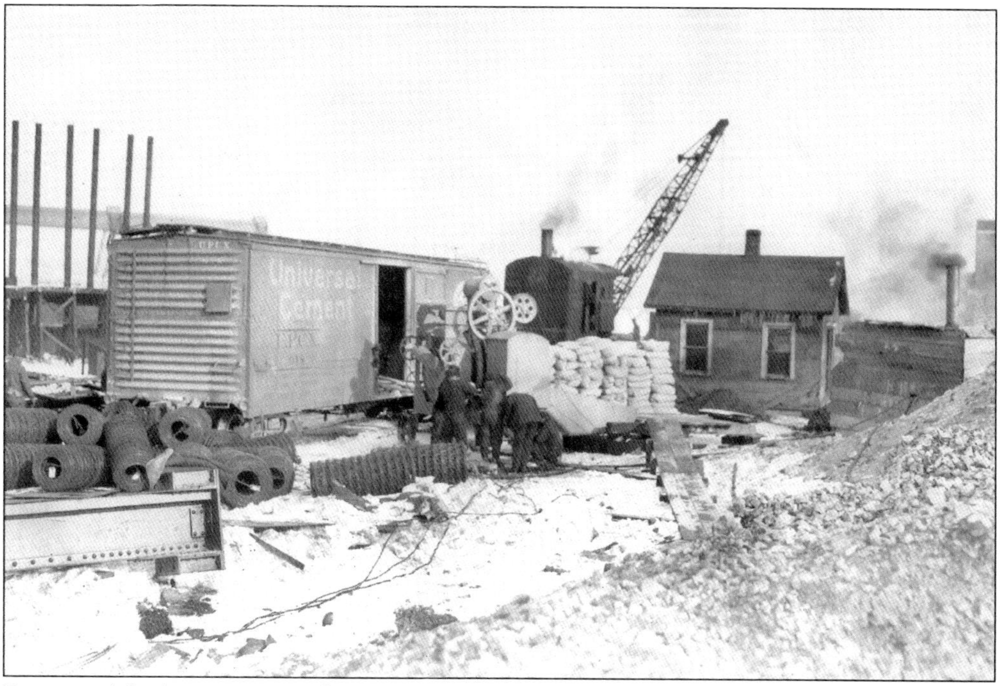

Because of the large amount of construction at Calcite, the company purchased bagged cement by the railcar, like this load from Universal Cement in 1927.

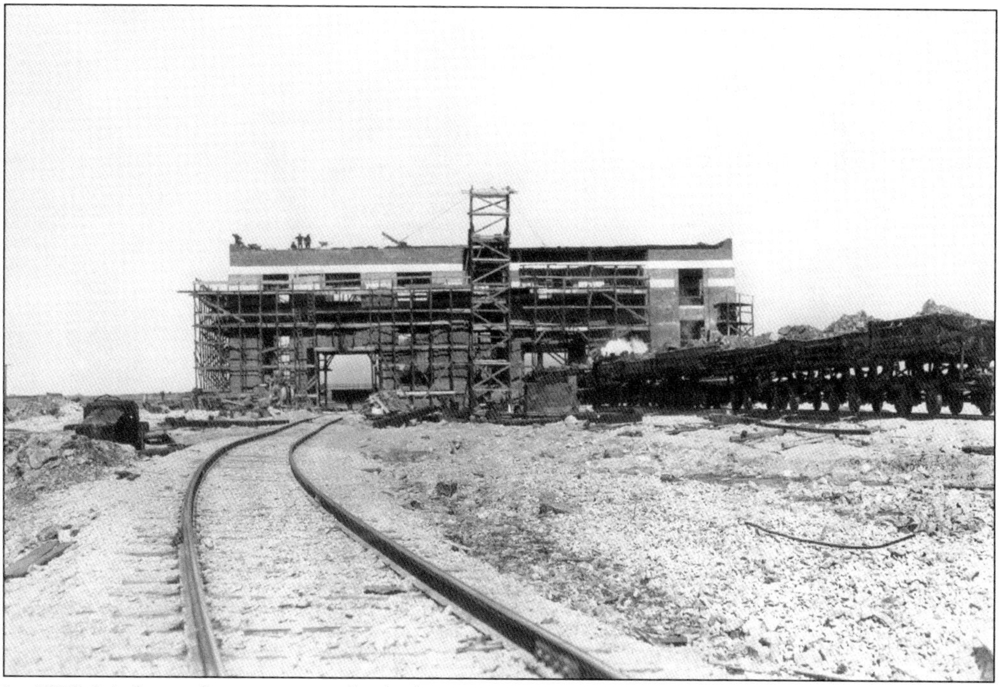

In 1927, Michigan Limestone embarked on a construction program that essentially rebuilt the entire plant from the ground up. The first major project was the construction of this new crusher in 1927. While trains had already begun to dump in the crusher when this photograph was taken, work was still underway on the building's redbrick exterior.

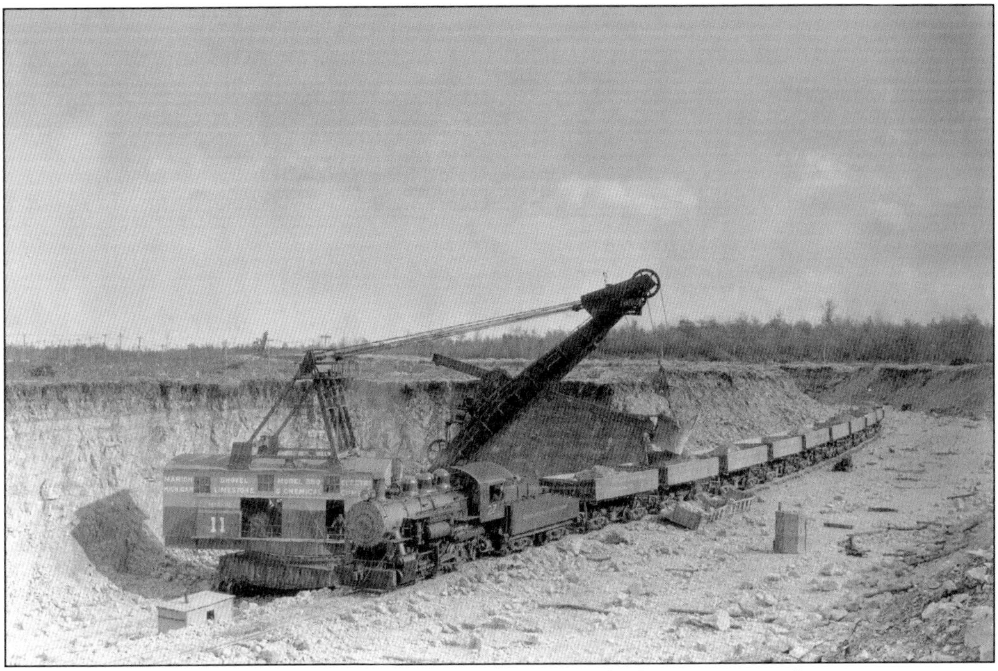

Another of the company's massive electric shovels loads dump cars in the growing quarry in 1927.

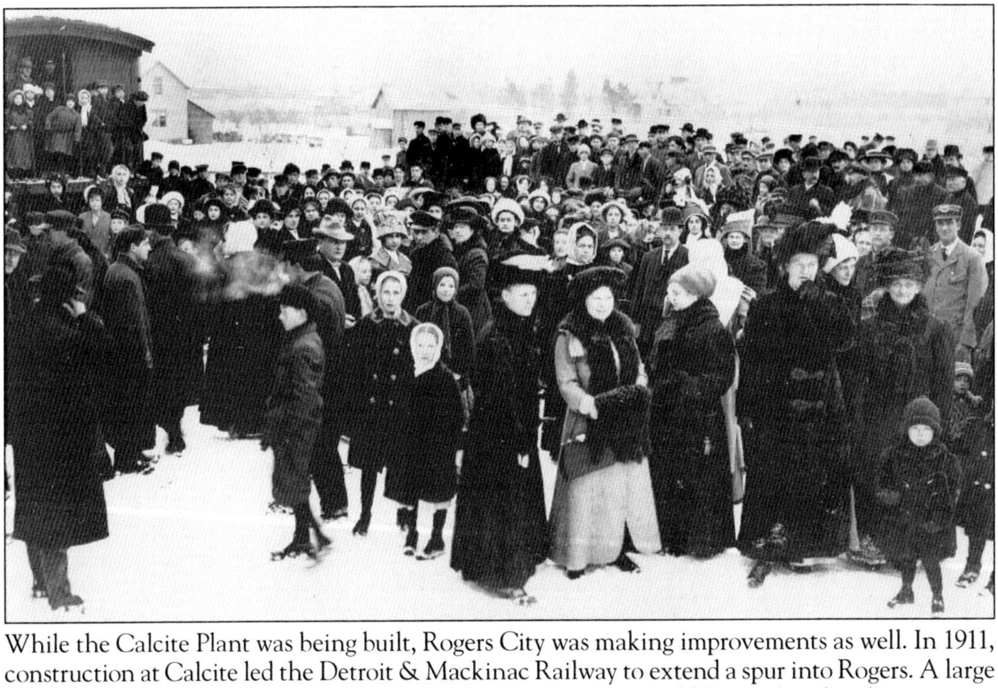

While the Calcite Plant was being built, Rogers City was making improvements as well. In 1911, construction at Calcite led the Detroit & Mackinac Railway to extend a spur into Rogers. A large crowd of local residents is on hand to greet the first train on a cold December day that year.

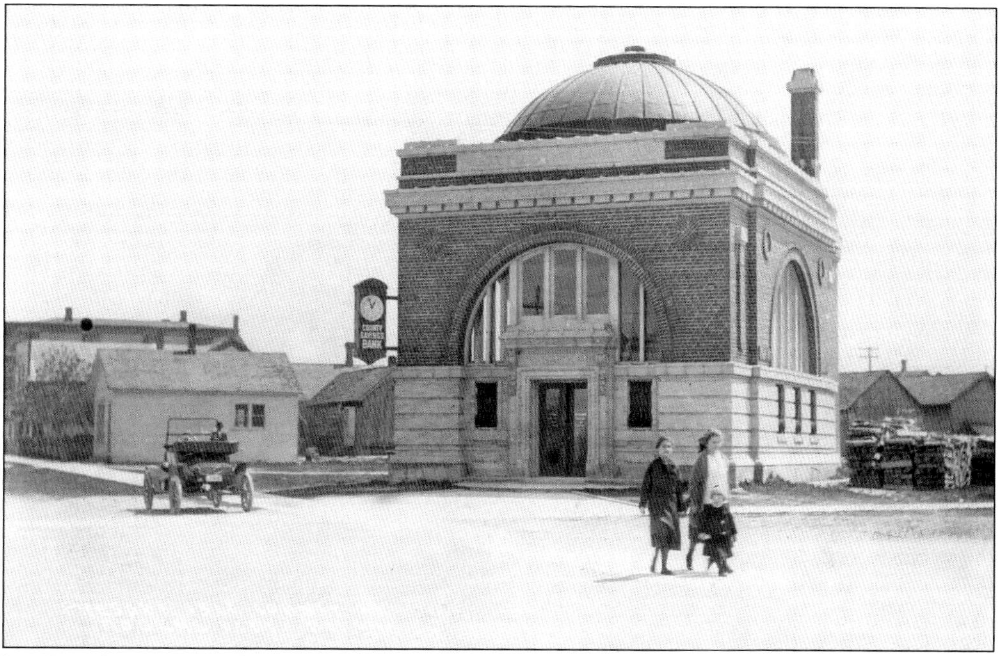

In 1911, the Presque Isle County Savings Bank built an imposing new facility at the corner of Third Street and Michigan Avenue under the supervision of Paul H. Hoeft. The domed structure was reportedly modeled after a bank in Cleveland. It served the community until 1964, when it was demolished to make room for the construction of a modern bank building.

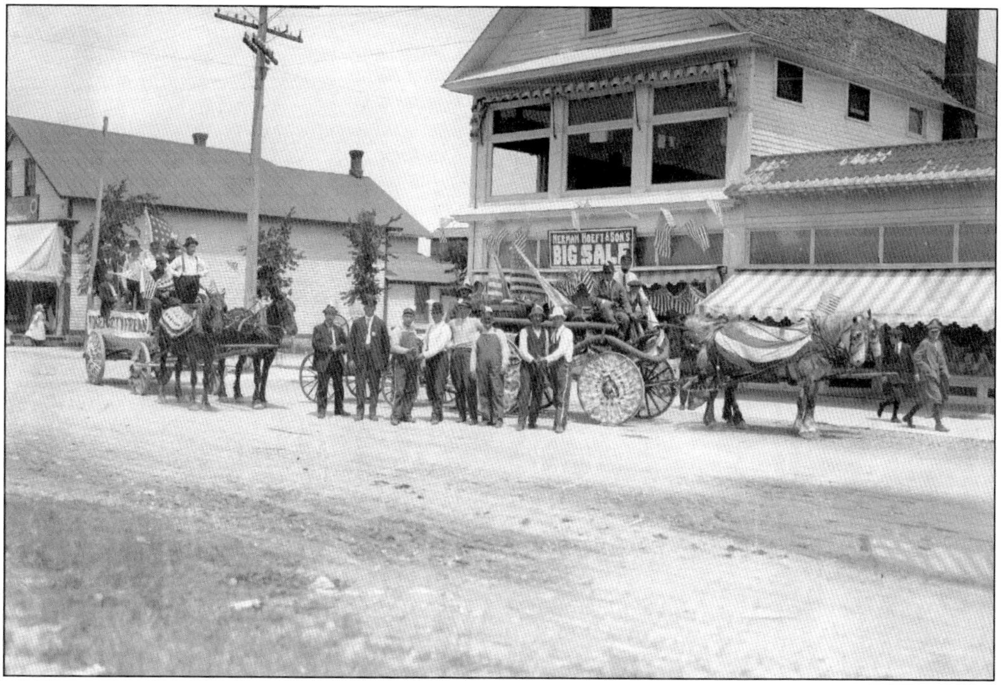

Michigan Limestone aided the community in many ways, including contributing to the purchase of better equipment for the village's volunteer fire department, which is seen here getting ready for a Fourth of July parade around 1915.

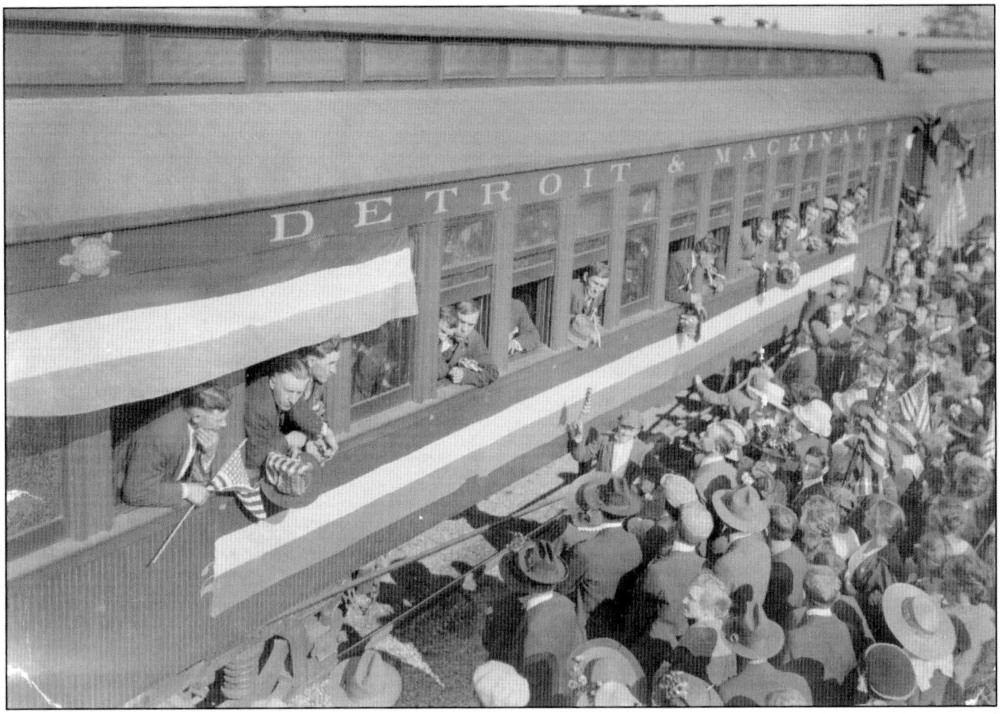

When the United States became embroiled in World War I, many county residents volunteered to serve their country, including this trainload of recruits leaving Rogers City on September 21, 1917. A large crowd was on hand to send off the recruits.

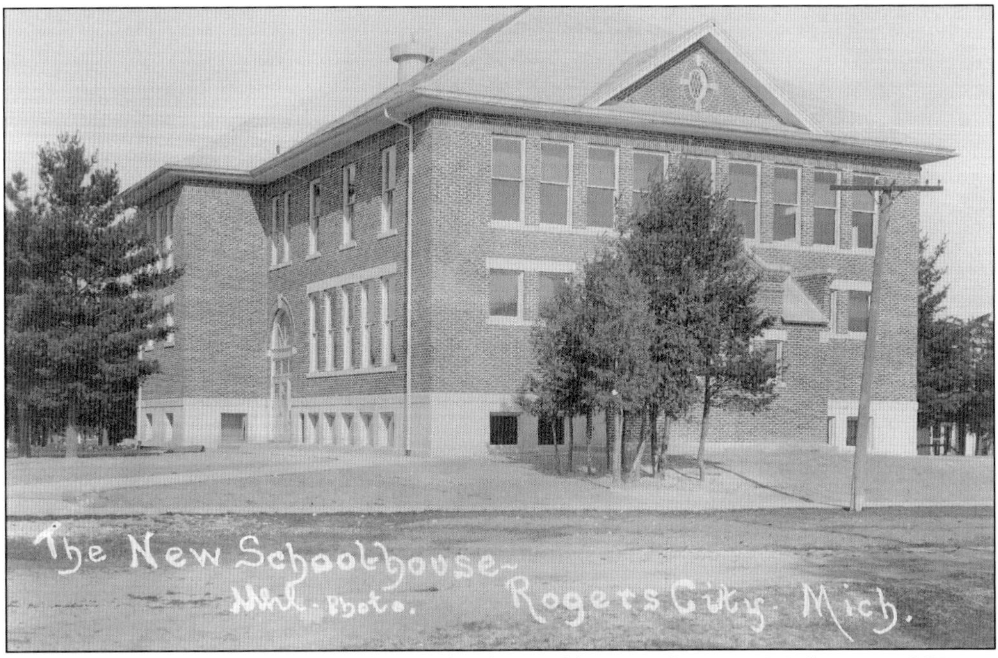

In 1918, Rogers City built its first high school on Fifth Street between Michigan and Huron Avenues. Prior to the construction of the two-story redbrick building, local schools had only gone through eighth grade.

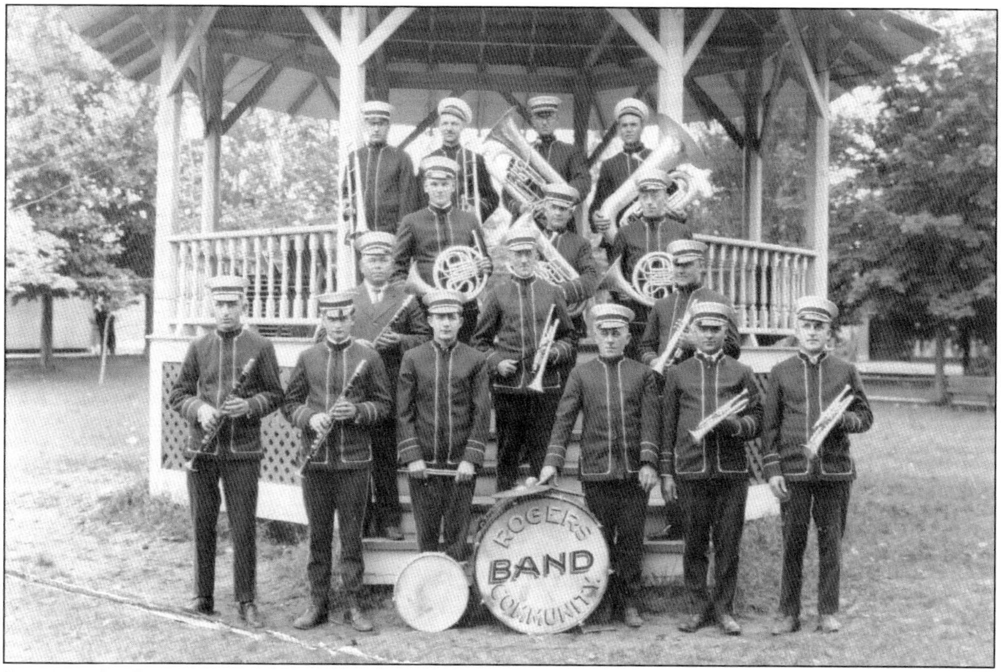

In 1918, the Rogers City Band received its first bandstand. Built for the community by workers at Calcite, it was initially located on the courthouse lawn just off Third Street. When the village hall, now city hall, was built in 1934, the bandstand was moved across Michigan Avenue and placed next to the new building. Now known as the gazebo, it is the centerpiece of Westminster Park.

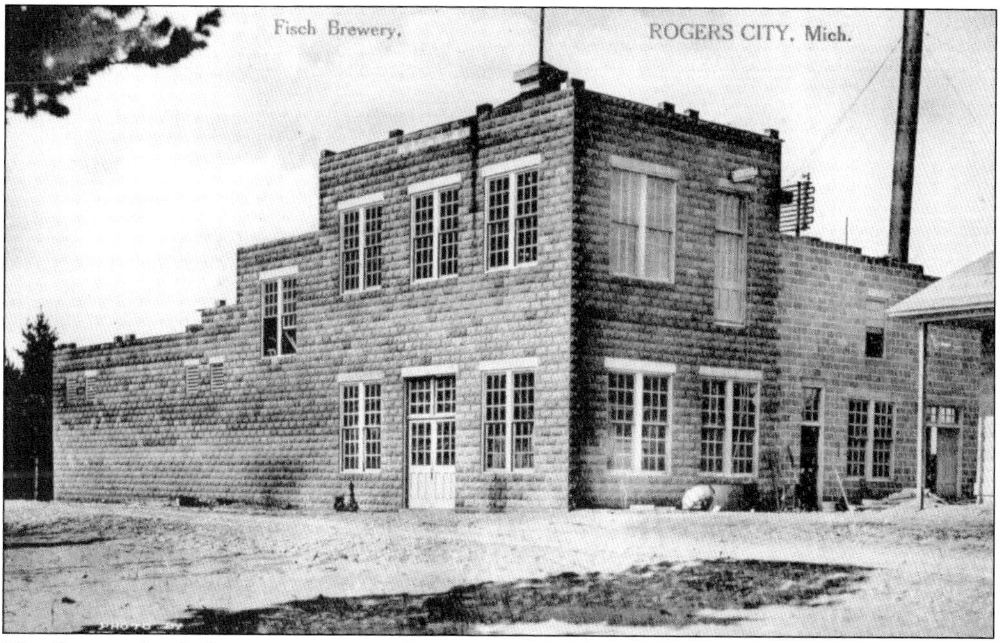

The Bittner family began operating a brewery at Crawford's Quarry in the 1870s. In 1909, the brewery was purchased by Fred Fisch Sr. It was still operating when production began at Calcite in 1912, but Michigan Limestone soon bought the property, prompting Fisch to erect this building, on Third Street in Rogers City, to house the brewery.

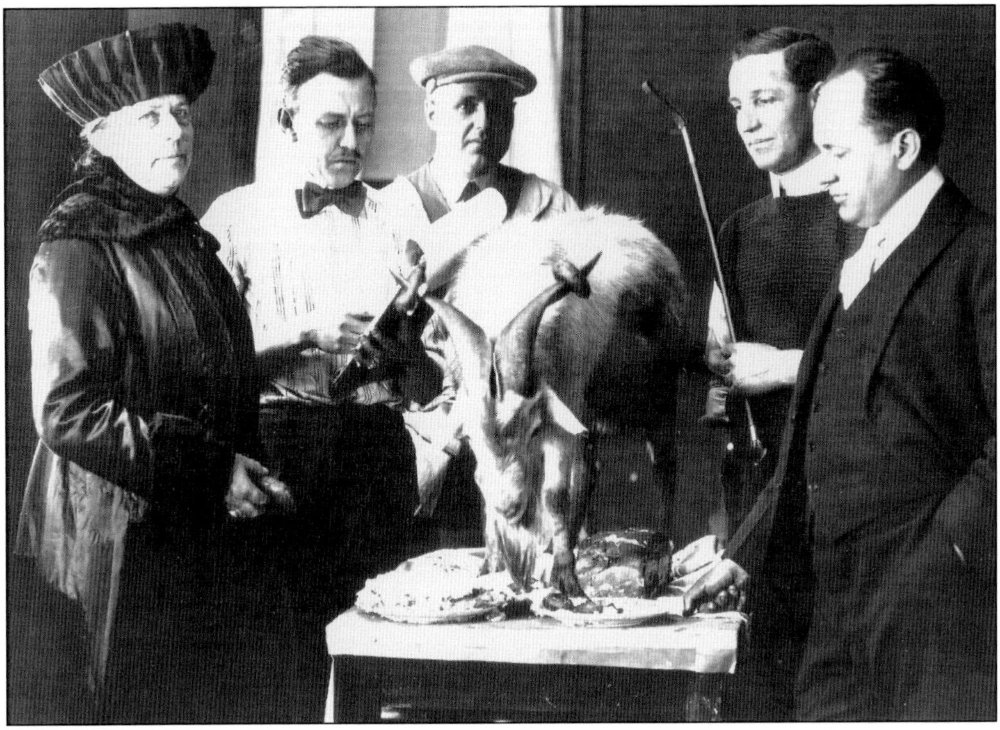

A frequent visitor to Rogers City in its early years was Francis Trego Montgomery, the author of the popular Billy Whiskers series of 32 books that had a goat as the main character. Seen here on the left in a promotional photograph, Montgomery spent many summers visiting her daughter in Rogers and writing at her retreat on Larke's Hill. She died in Hong Kong while on a world tour in 1925.

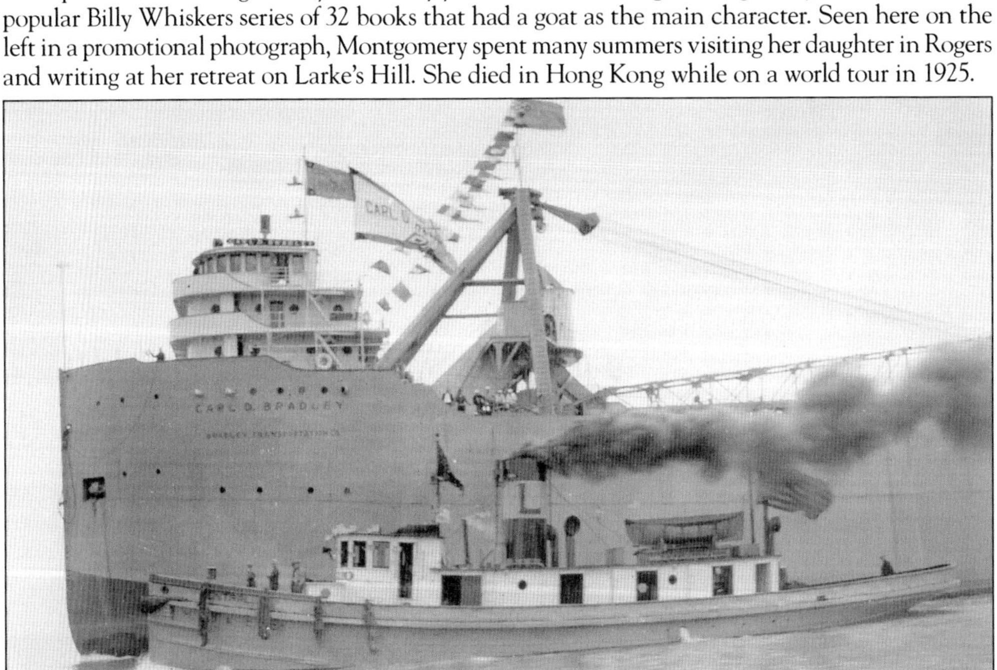

Michigan Limestone added another ship to its fleet in 1925. The 639-foot *Carl D. Bradley* was built in Lorain, Ohio. From 1927 until 1949, the *Bradley* held the title of "Queen of the Lakes," an honor bestowed on the longest ship operating on the Great Lakes.

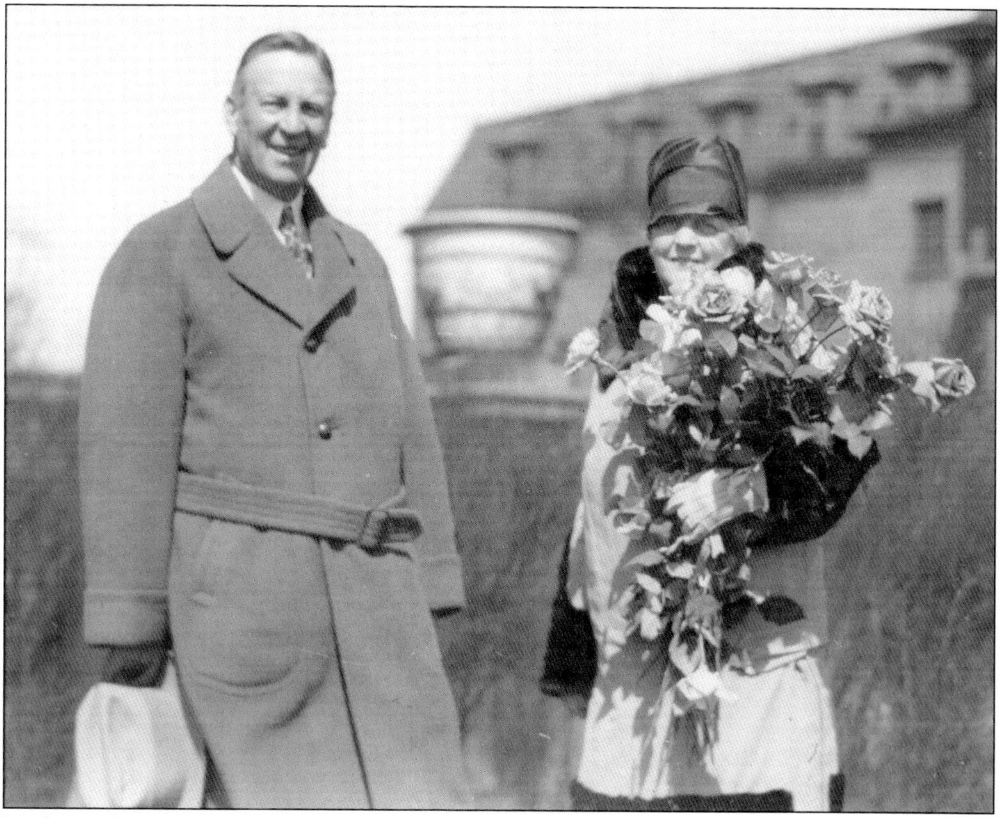

Michigan Limestone and Bradley Transportation president Carl D. Bradley and his wife, Emma, were on hand at American Ship Building in Lorain, Ohio, for the launching of the giant new ship that bore his name. Emma had the honor of christening the big freighter with a bottle of water from a spring in the quarry at Calcite.

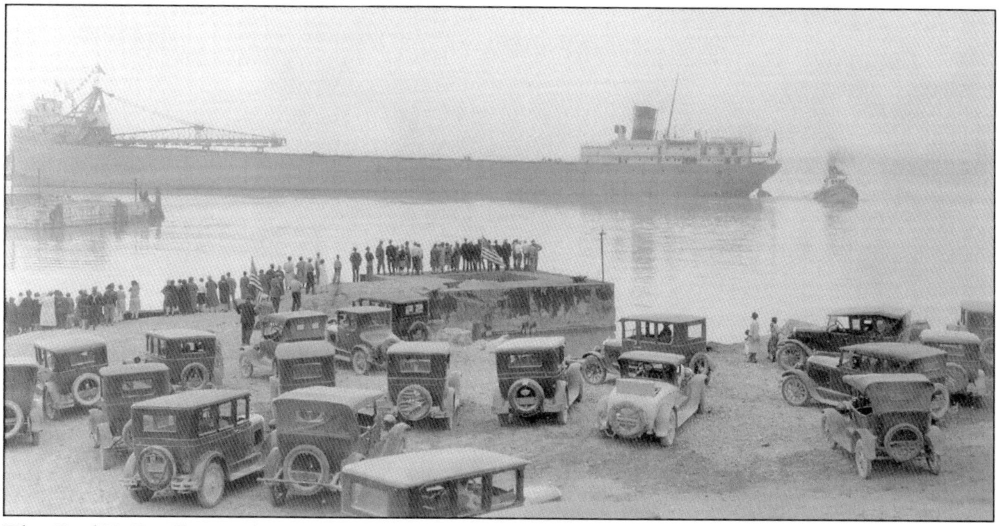

The *Carl D. Bradley*, with its namesake aboard, arrived at Calcite on July 28, 1927. A large crowd of company officials, customers, and local residents was on hand to welcome the ship and the popular Mr. Bradley home.

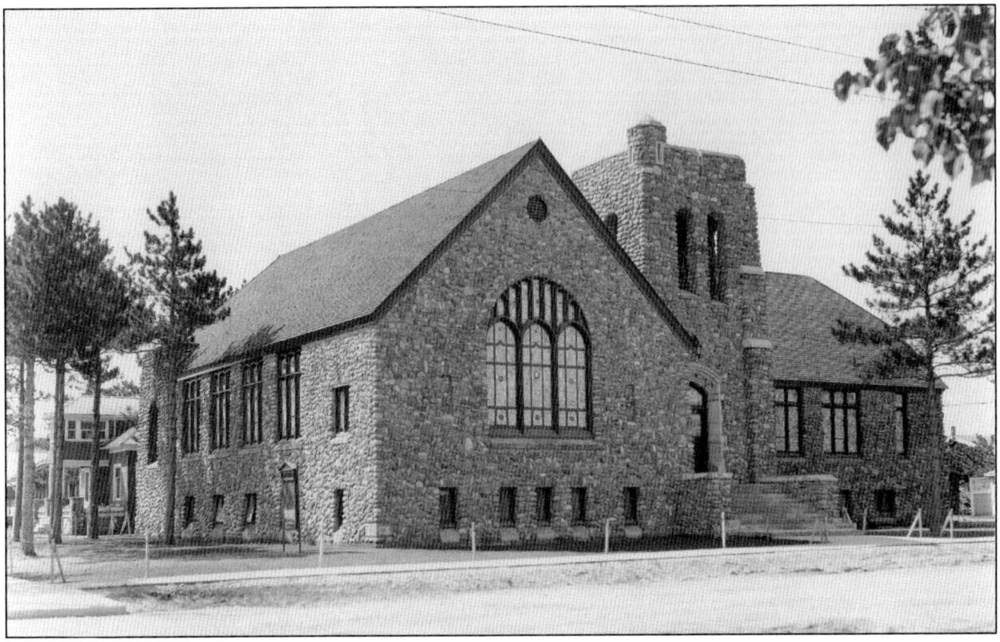

Carl D. Bradley was the biggest promoter and supporter of Rogers City, the community he adopted when he was brought in to run Calcite. He was involved in many community activities and served on the board of directors of Presque Isle County Savings Bank and Rogers City Light and Power. He is also credited as the founder of Westminster Presbyterian Church, seen here, which was built in 1924 and known as the stone church.

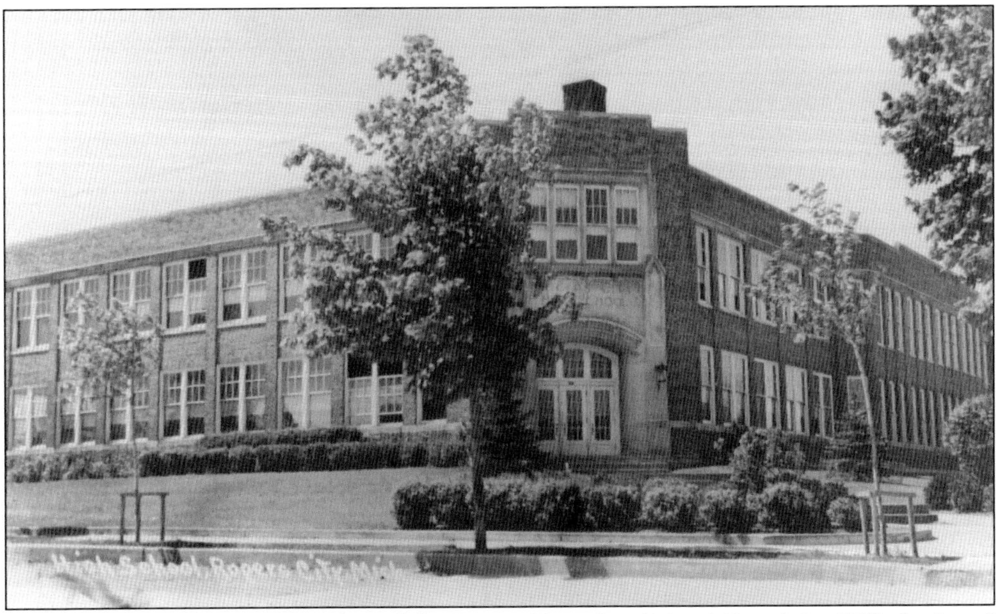

Carl D. Bradley was also a member of the Rogers Township School Board. In 1927, the board was overseeing construction of a new high school on Huron Avenue, seen here after completion. Bradley did not live to see the building finished. He died on March 19, 1928, while vacationing with his wife in Pasadena, California.

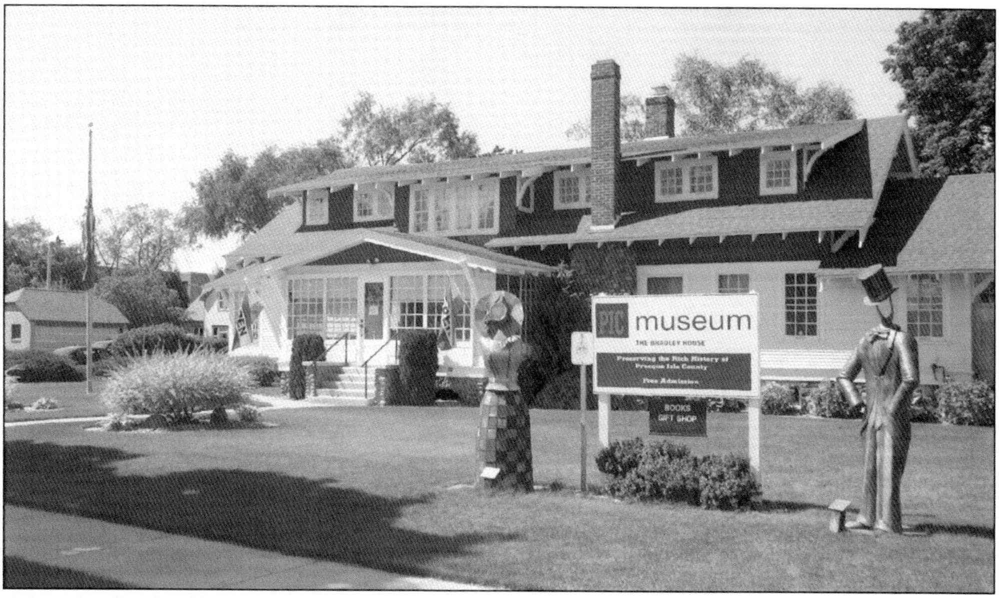

After the death of her husband, Emma Bradley sold their Rogers City home and moved back to New York. Purchased by Michigan Limestone, the Bradley's sprawling Craftsman-style bungalow served as the residence of the next three heads of the Calcite Plant: John G. Munson, Irvin L. Clymer, and Joseph Valentin. In 1960, the house was donated to the city and served as the community's library for the next 20 years. When the library outgrew the building, it was given to the nonprofit Presque Isle County Historical Museum, which opened in the building in 1981 and is still in operation today. The building is still referred to as the Bradley House.

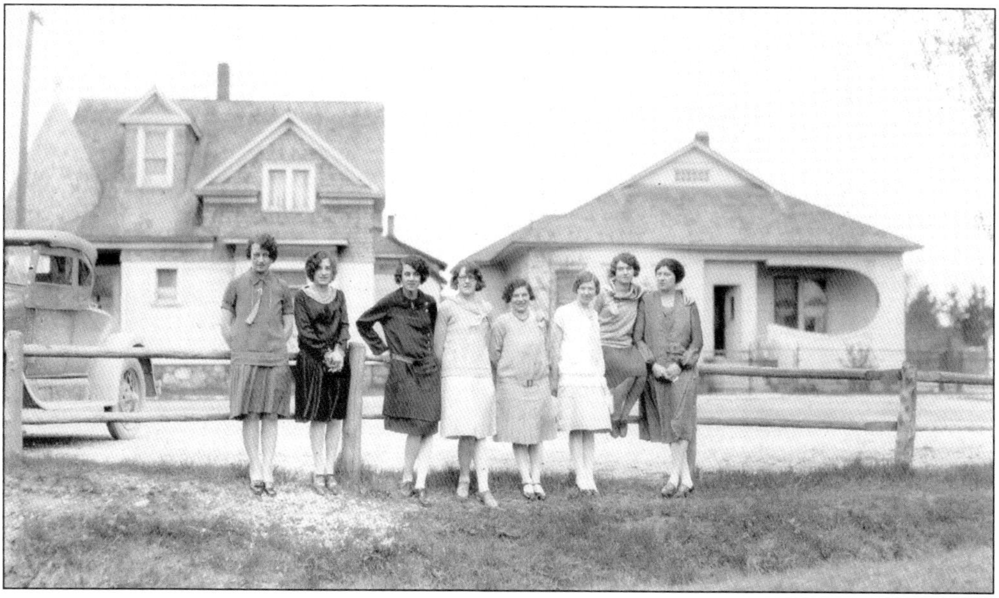

A Calcite company photographer assembled the "office girls" for this photograph in front of the company's main office in the spring of 1928. Calcite's original office building at the plant burned in 1925, and the company took over the former Rogers City Light and Power building on Woodward Avenue. Referred to as the temporary office, it served the company until a new building was constructed at Calcite in 1953.

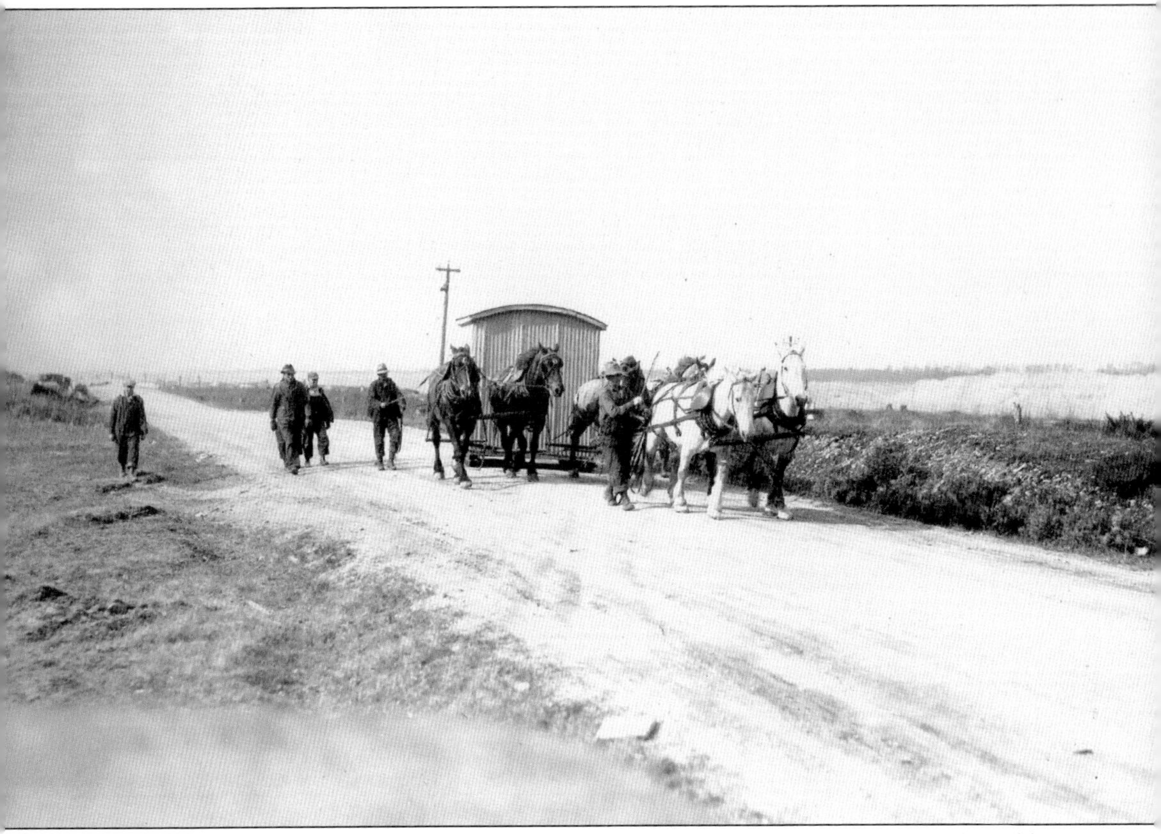

Seen in 1929, workers in the blasting crew use teams of horses to move the small building in which they stored blasting caps. The blasters used horses in their dangerous work until around World War II, when they finally began using trucks.

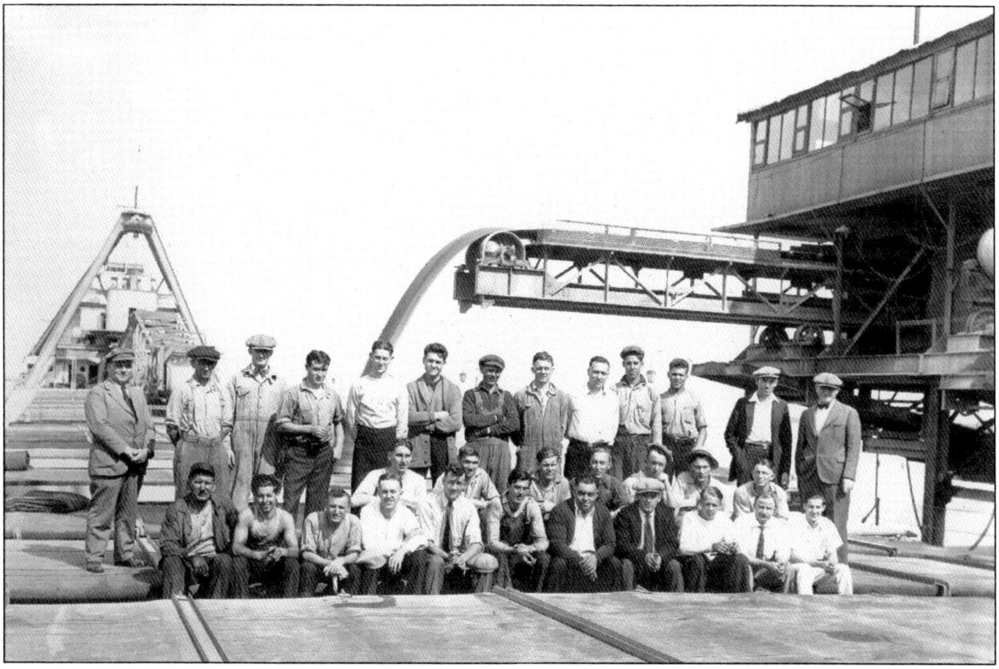

Crew members of one of the Bradley Transportation boats pose on deck for a Calcite photographer while their ship was being loaded in August 1929. Each of the Bradley ships had a crew of 30 to 35 sailors.

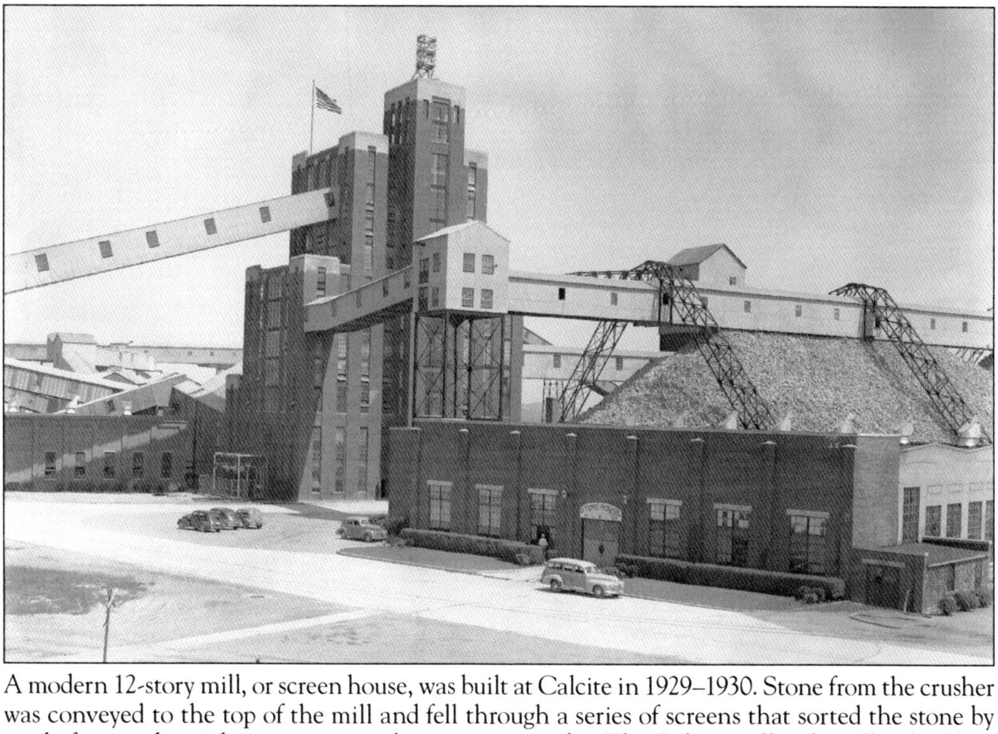

A modern 12-story mill, or screen house, was built at Calcite in 1929–1930. Stone from the crusher was conveyed to the top of the mill and fell through a series of screens that sorted the stone by size before sending it by conveyor to adjacent storage piles. The Calcite mill is the tallest building in Presque Isle County.

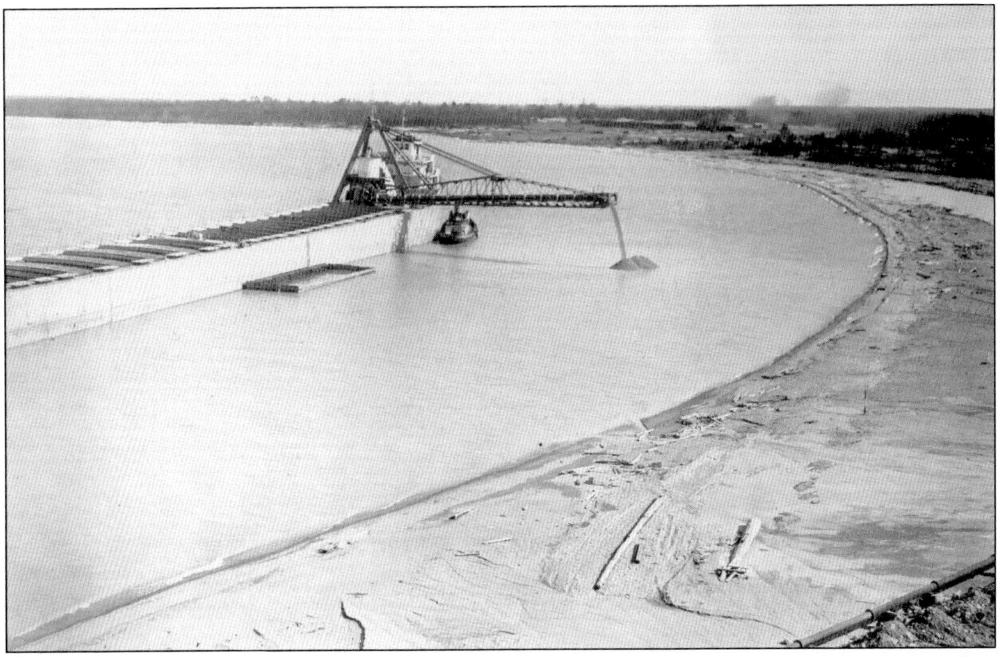

In 1929, Calcite began work on a new powerhouse along the shore just south of the loading slip. There was not enough property along the shore to accommodate the structure, so the first task was to fill in a large section of the lakeshore. Bradley boats that came in to load at Calcite, like the *T.W. Robinson* seen here, would receive a partial load of stone, and then a tug would assist them to the area that had to be filled. With the tug helping to hold them in place, they would swing their boom over and dump their cargo into the water.

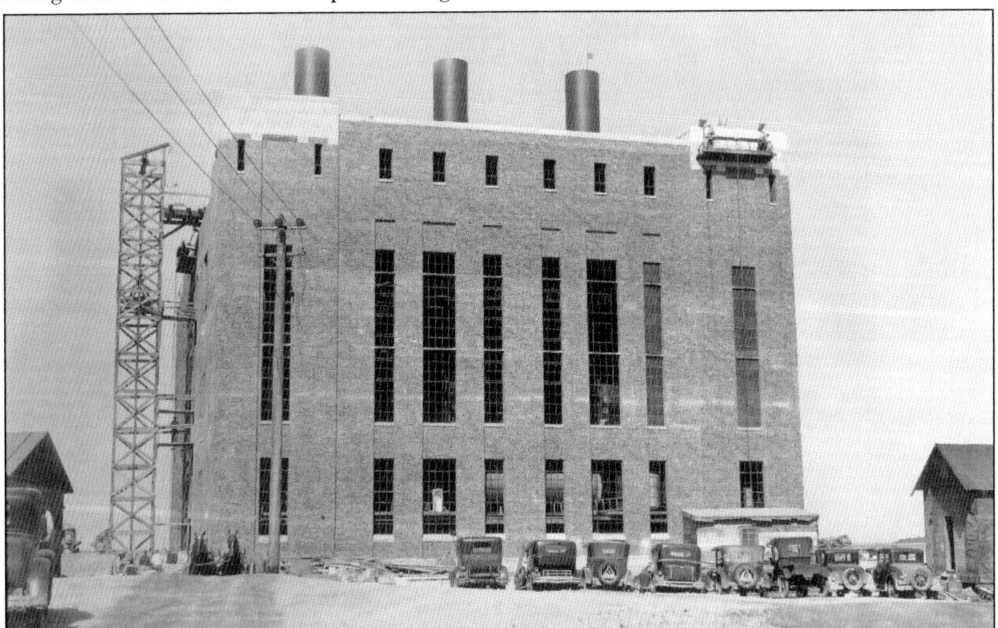

The new powerhouse was nearing completion in the summer of 1930. While many company employees owned automobiles, teams of horses were still used for many tasks around the plant.

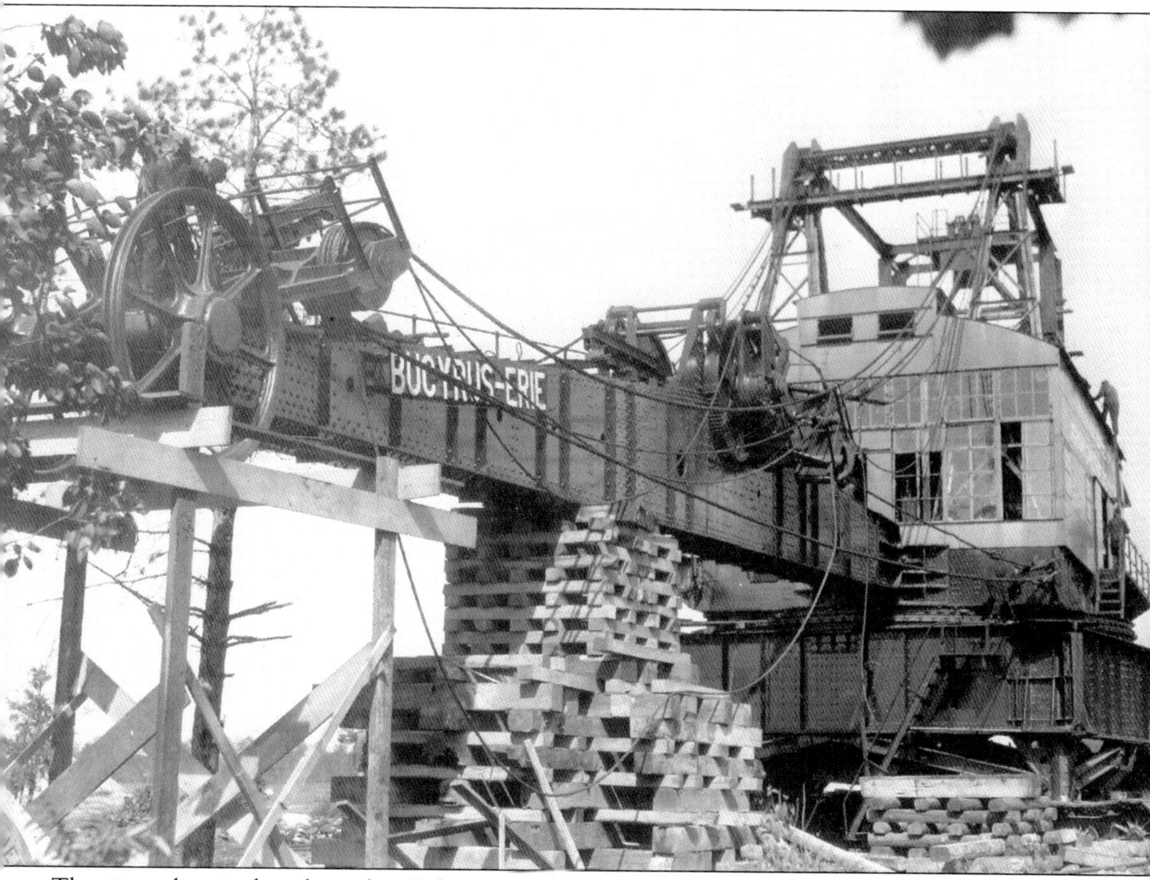

The giant electric shovels used at Calcite were shipped in by train in pieces, like a huge erector set, and had to be assembled by plant workers. This photograph shows a boom being installed on a new shovel in 1930.

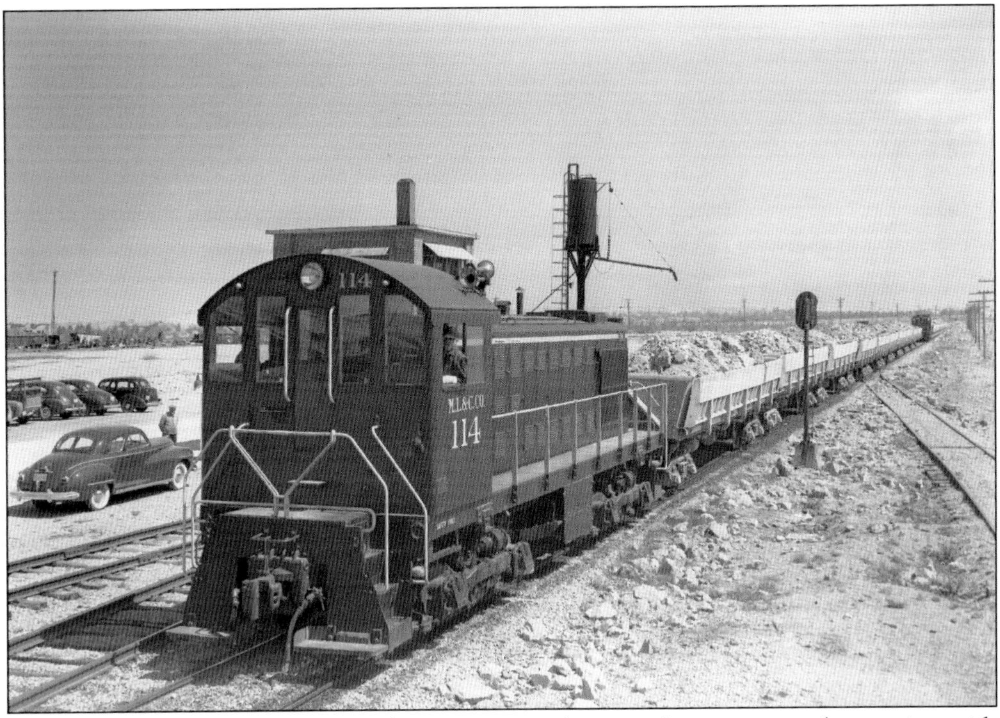

Beginning in the summer of 1937, Michigan Limestone began replacing its steam locomotives with diesel locomotives that were more powerful and less expensive to operate. Each diesel locomotive cost more than twice as much as their steam counterparts then in use in the quarry.

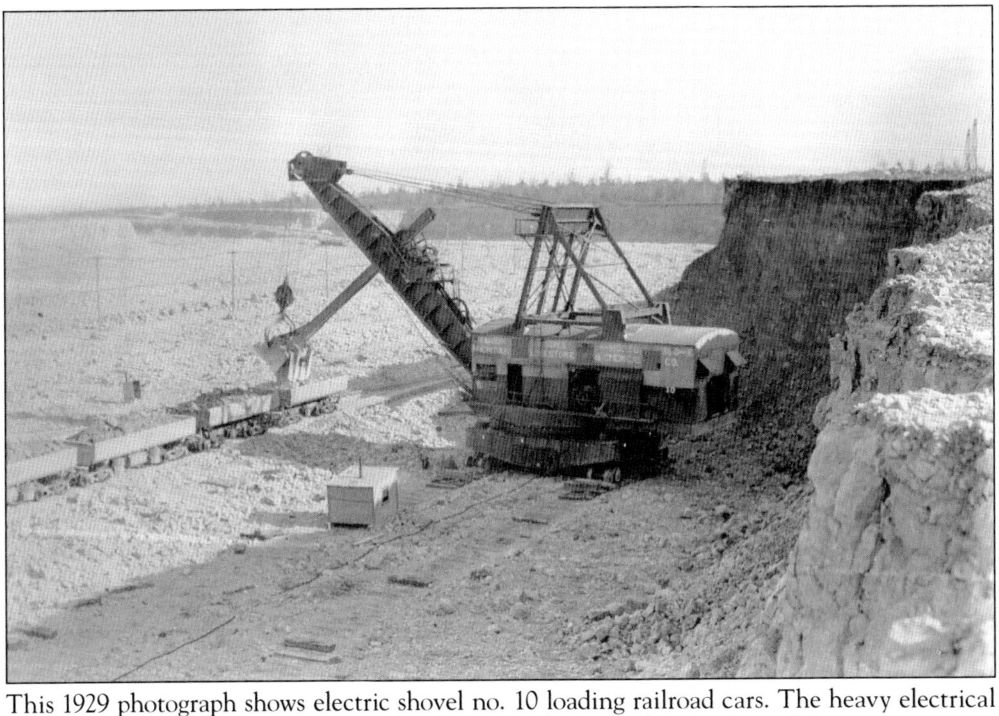

This 1929 photograph shows electric shovel no. 10 loading railroad cars. The heavy electrical cable that supplied power for the shovel is lying on the ground in the lower left.

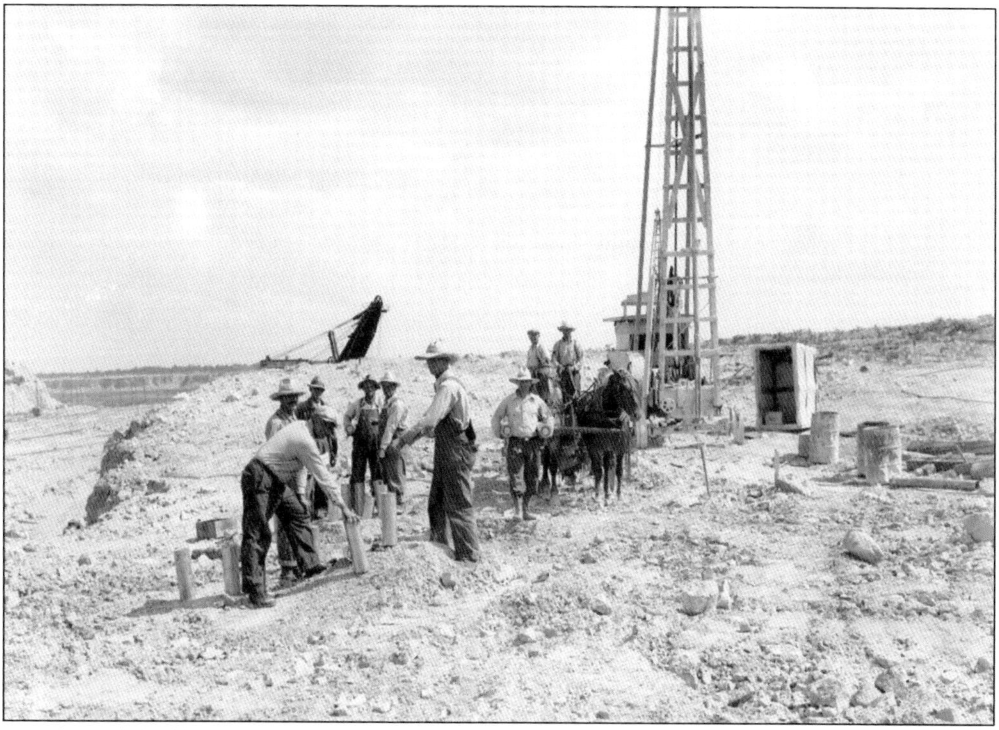

Members of the blasting crew load drill holes with a new type of explosive for tests in the summer of 1935. The explosives were taken to the site on top of the quarry in a horse-drawn wagon. The boom of an electric shovel is just over the edge of the quarry bank. On the right is a drill unit used to drill the blast holes.

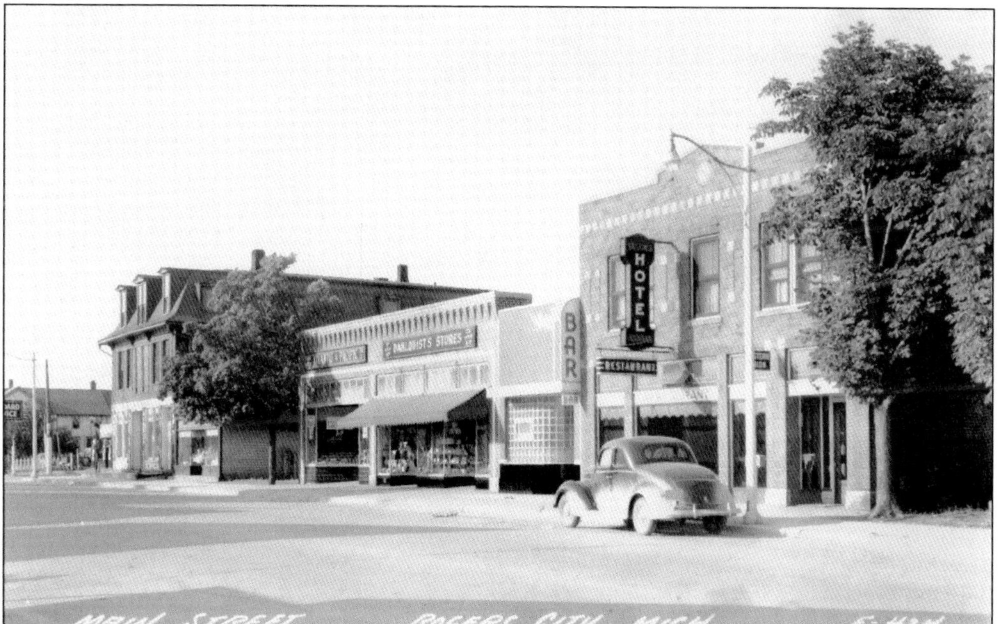

Third Street in Rogers City is seen here around 1940. The historic three-story Bertram Building is on the left.

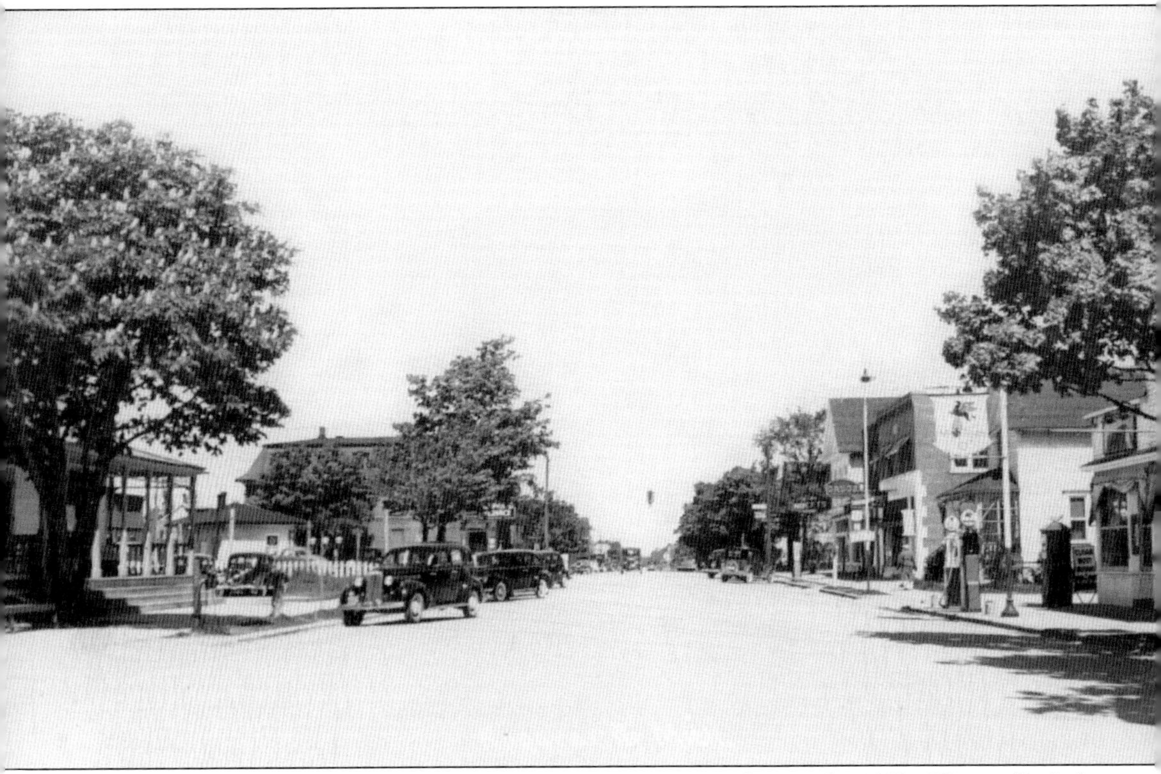

This photograph of South Third Street in Rogers City was taken in the 1930s. The traffic light in the center is still the only traffic light in Presque Isle County.

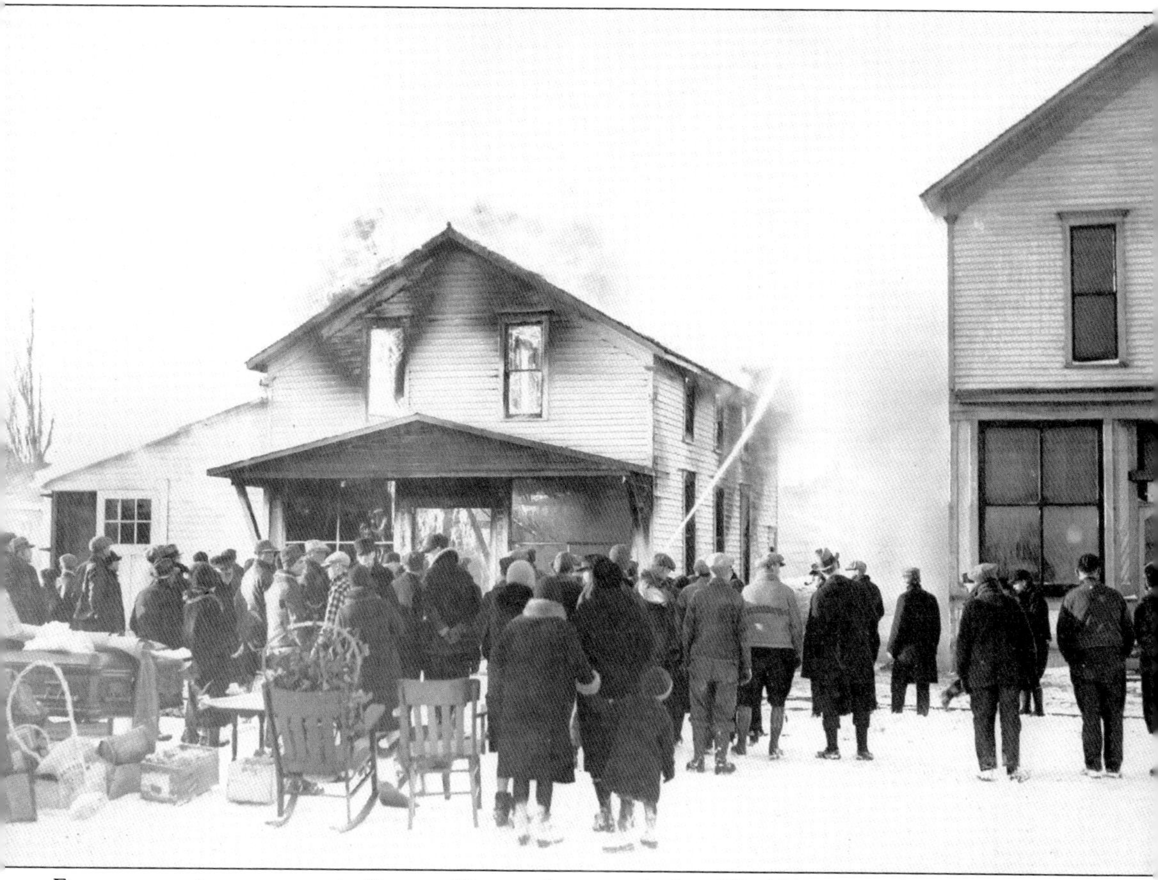

Fires were quite common in Rogers City in the years before World War II, when available firefighting equipment was rather rudimentary. Here, a large crowd gathers to watch a fire at the E.K. Shirtum Funeral Home in January 1930. Much of the furniture from the building, including several caskets, had been removed. The fire eventually destroyed the entire building as well as the adjacent structure.

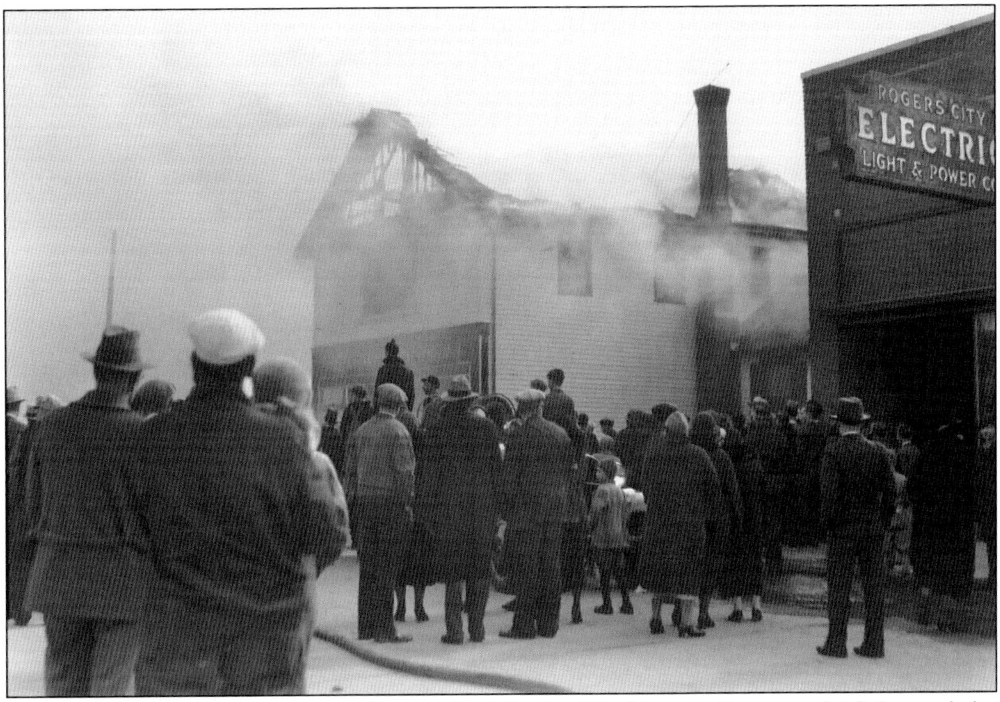

In April 1935, there was a serious fire at the Lehndorf Building in Rogers, which housed the local A&P store. The fire destroyed much of the second floor of the building, which was occupied by the American Legion hall. The building, constructed in 1873 as Herman Hoeft & Son's general store, still stands today and is believed to be the oldest surviving commercial structure in the community.

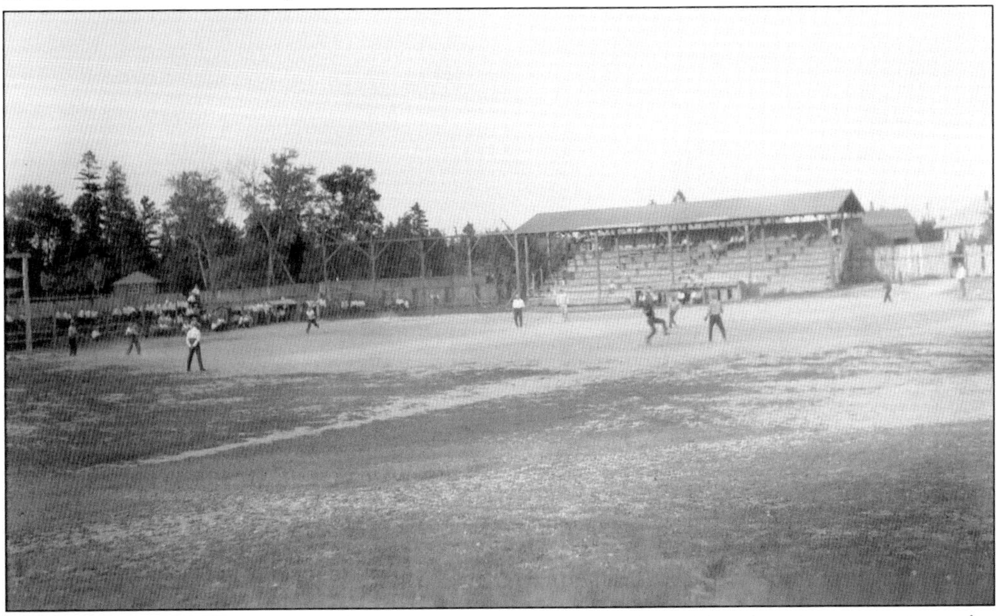

The property now known as Westminster Park was purchased by the city in 1918, and a baseball field, complete with covered bleachers and a tall wooden fence along Second Street, was constructed.

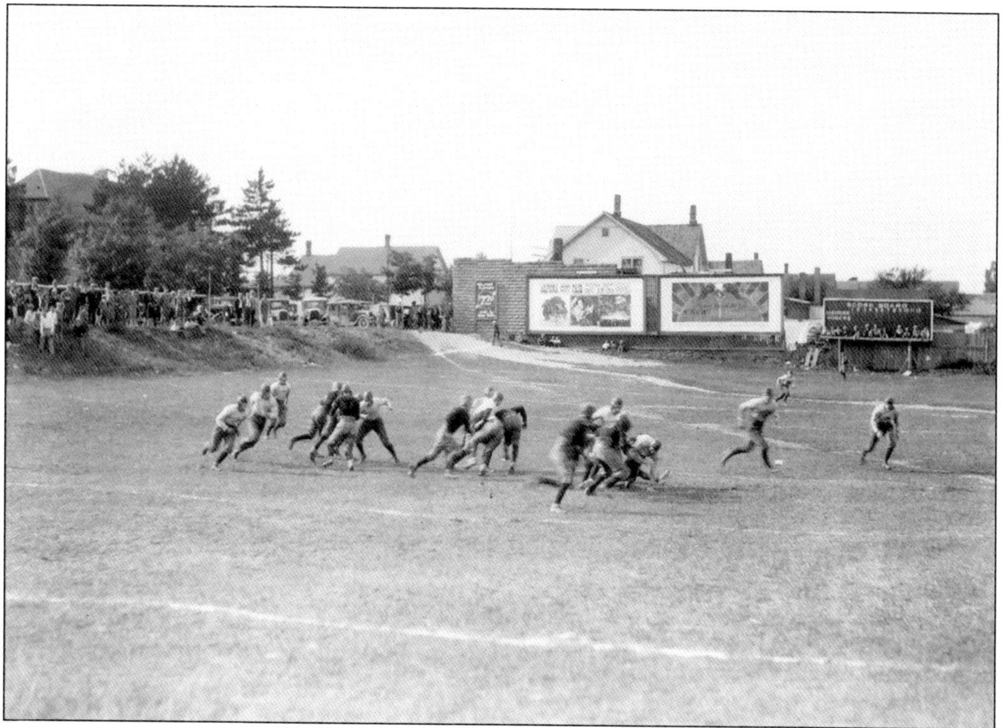

The Rogers City High School football team also played its games on the Third Street side of Westminster Park even though the field was only 80 yards long.

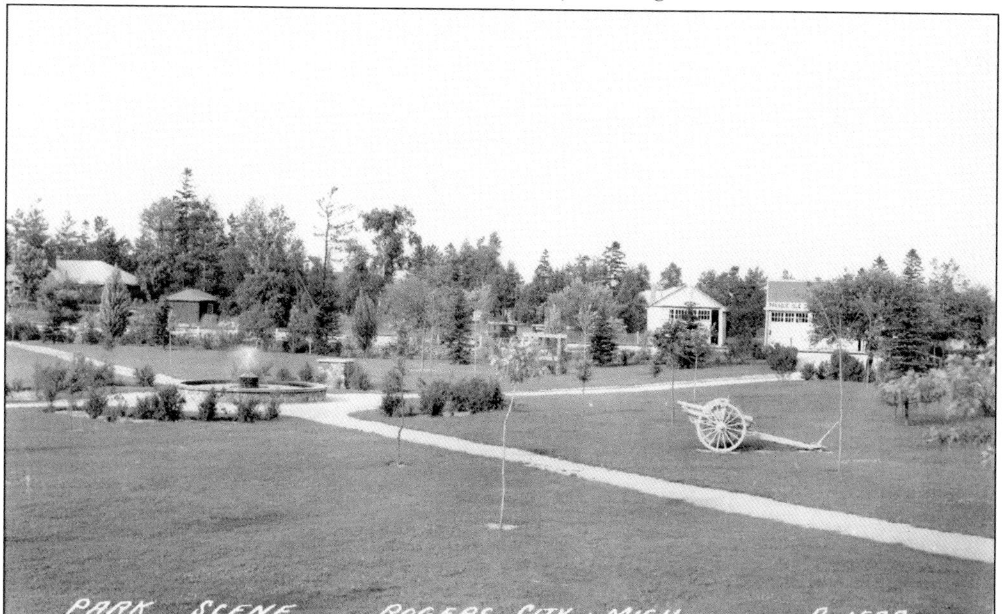

After Gilpin Field was developed as the school's sports park in 1932, Westminster Park was converted into an attractive urban-type park with a central fountain, as seen in this 1938 postcard. It remains a park today, but the fountain has been replaced by the city's 1918 bandstand, now referred to as the gazebo.

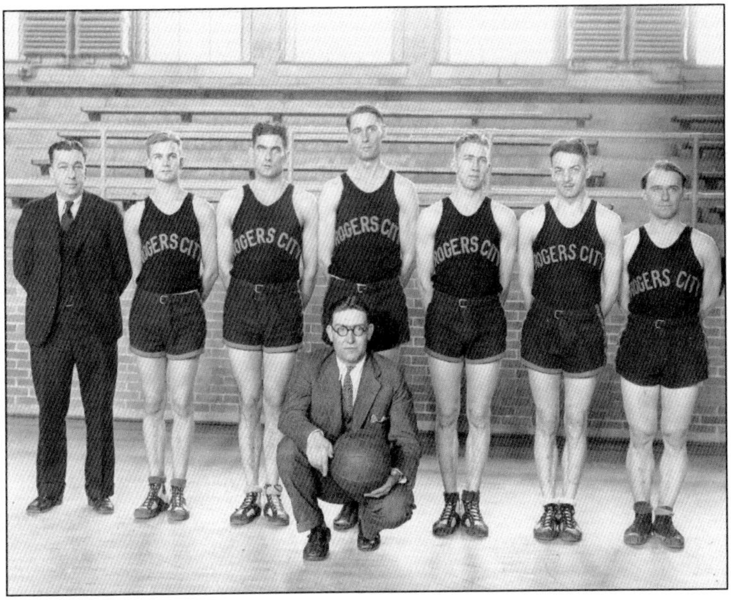

Sports have always been important to the residents of Rogers City. This photograph shows one of eight teams in the basketball league sponsored by Calcite in 1930. The team manager, kneeling in front, is Fred Bradley, the son of Carl D. Bradley. After working at Calcite for 18 years, the younger Bradley was elected to the US House of Representatives, serving from 1939 until his death in 1947.

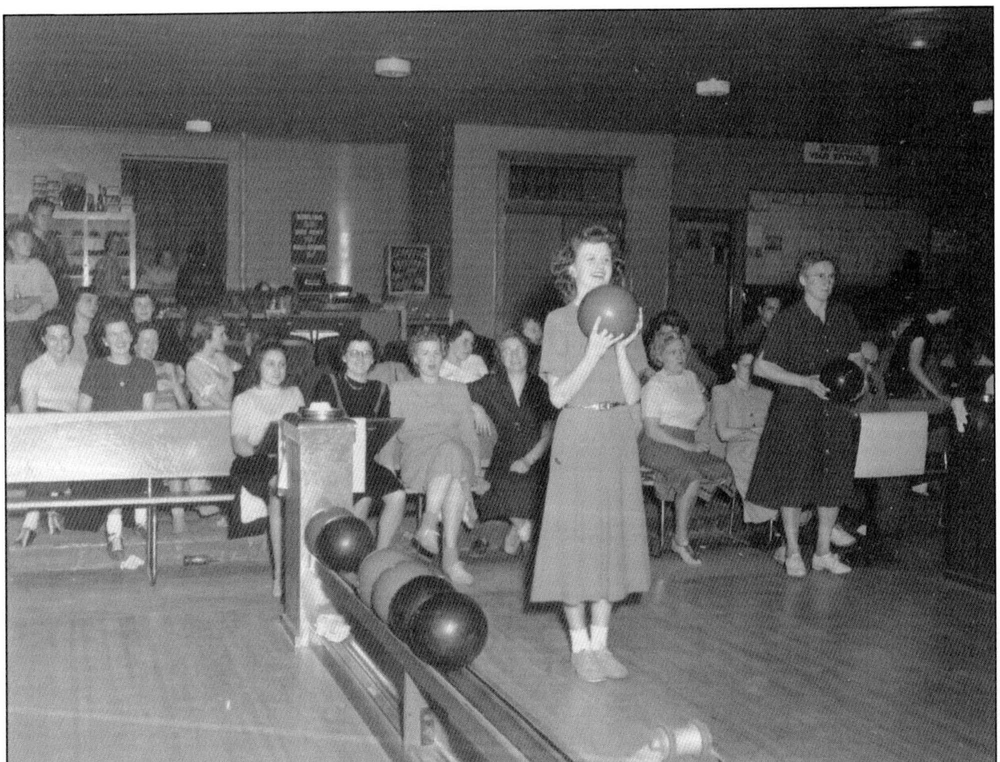

The first bowling alleys built in Rogers City were in 1916, but the popularity of the sport really skyrocketed in the years following World War II. Unlike baseball and basketball, which had dominated men's sports for years, bowling was also enjoyed by women. The women's bowling league at Lucky Strike Lanes is seen in action in 1949. Donna Tosch is ready to bowl in the center lane, while Kate Lamb waits her turn on the right.

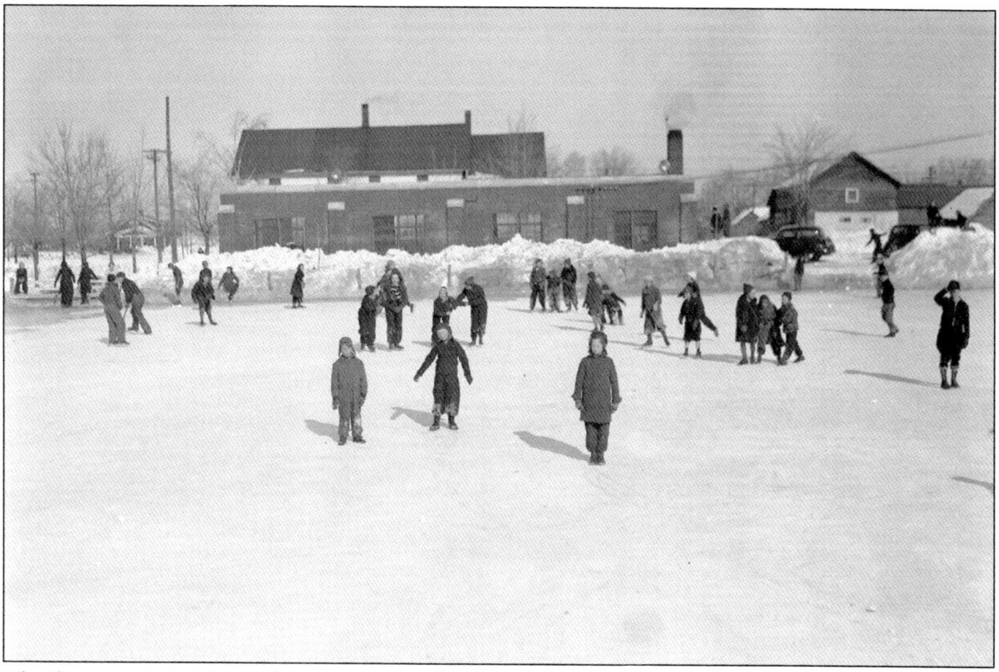

The first municipal ice rink in town, seen here in 1936, was next to the village hall on Michigan Avenue. Skating was a popular winter activity for the younger set.

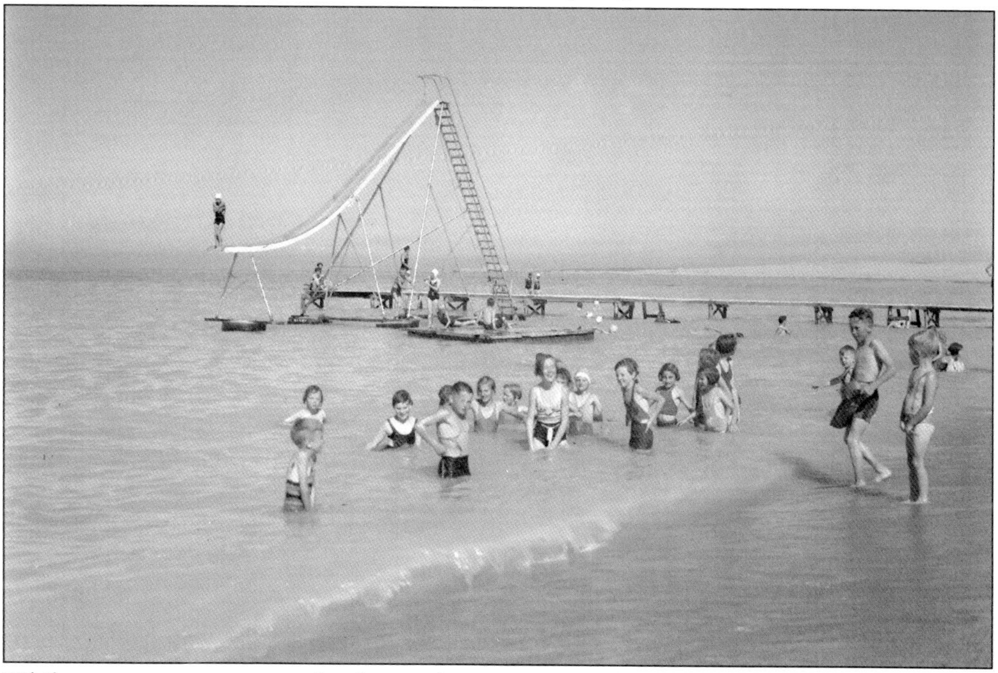

While many sports were popular during the summer months, swimming seems to have topped the list. The first bathing beach developed in Rogers City was along Calcite Road, near where the Little League fields are today. The bathing beach featured a tall slide that shot people into the water from a height of about eight feet. In the 1950s, the public beach was moved to what is now Lakeside Park on a stretch of waterfront that was once dominated by three lumber docks.

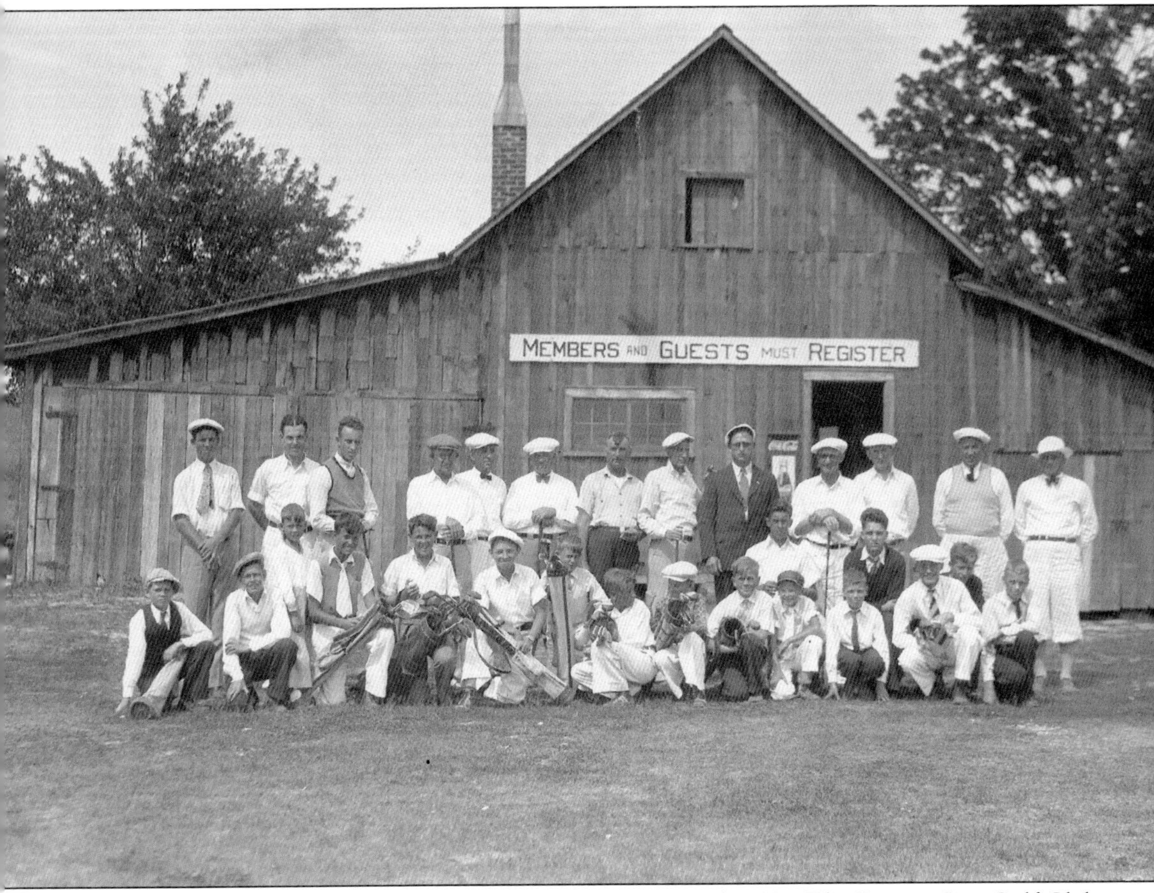

Golf increased significantly in popularity in the 1920s and 1930s. The Rogers City Golf Club was formed in 1933, supported in part by financial assistance from Michigan Limestone. This photograph shows early club members and caddies in front of the clubhouse on Highway 451 on the grounds of today's Knights of Columbus Hall.

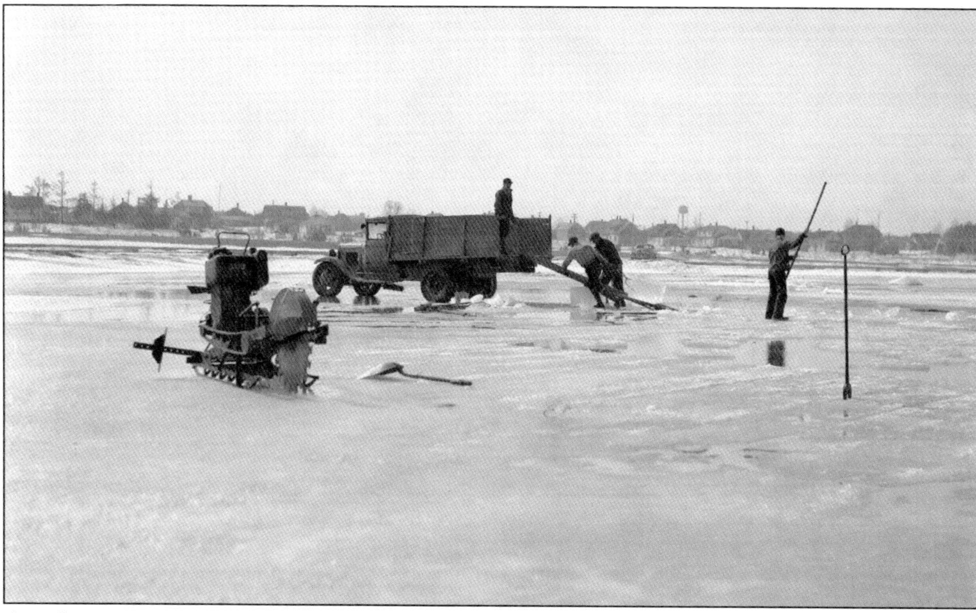

Another winter activity was the harvesting of blocks of ice from Lake Huron and the county's inland lakes. This 1936 photograph shows workers on Lake Huron loading ice onto a truck. On the left is a gasoline-powered saw used to cut the ice into blocks. In the background is Rogers City. The ice was used in people's iceboxes and by commercial fishermen to ice down their catches in the summer months.

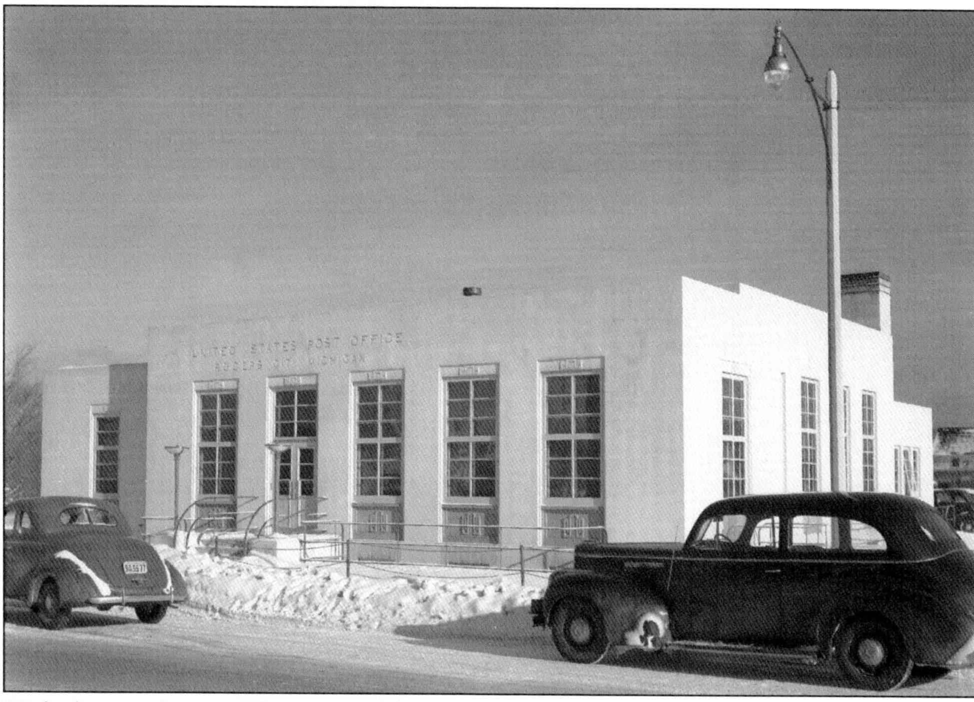

With the population of Rogers steadily increasing, the federal government constructed a new post office at the corner of Michigan Avenue and Third Street in 1940, seen here that year. The art deco-style structure is still in use today.

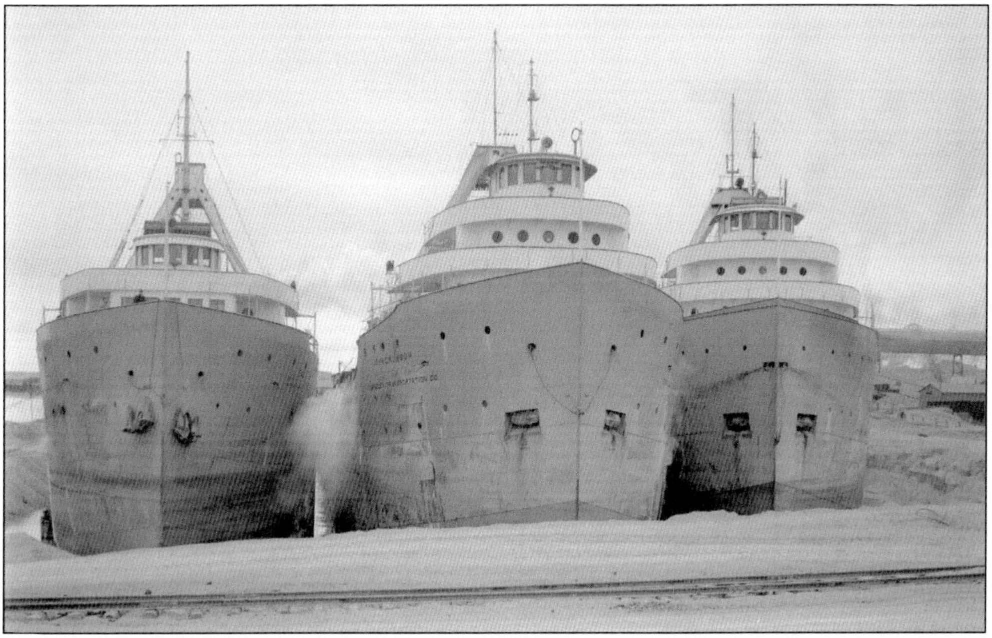

From left to right, Bradley steamers *Calcite, John G. Munson*, and *T.W. Robinson* are laid up for the winter of 1939–1940 in the enlarged tug basin, known as the frog pond, at Calcite. Prior to 1939, all of the Bradley boats spent their winters laid up in the Cheboygan River or at shipyards around the Great Lakes. Having the ships laid up in Rogers City made it easy for Calcite and Bradley employees to do repair work on them during the winter months.

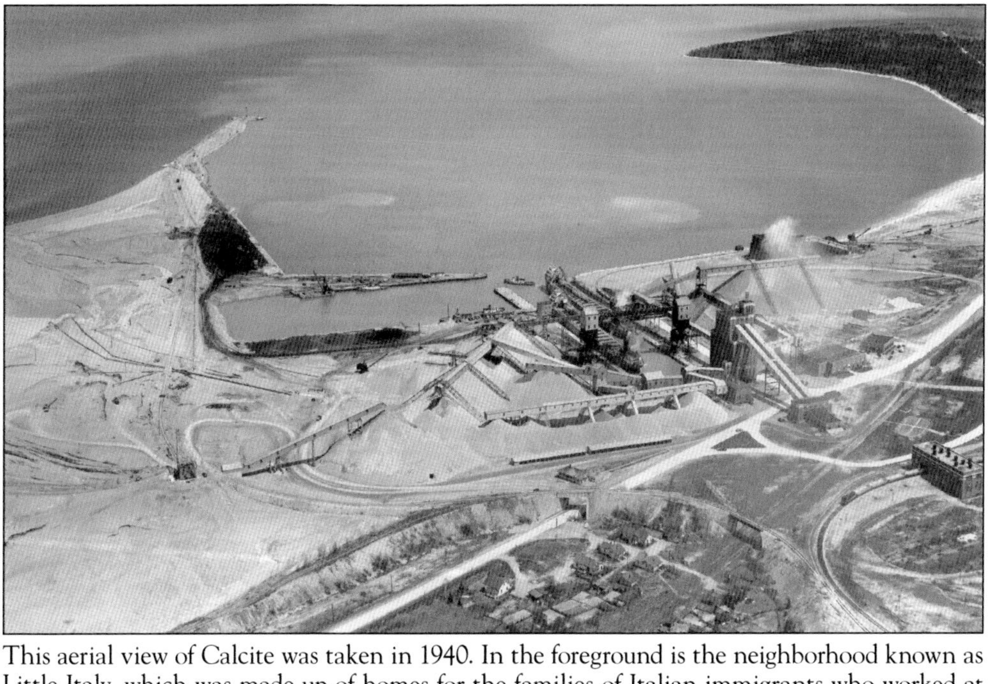

This aerial view of Calcite was taken in 1940. In the foreground is the neighborhood known as Little Italy, which was made up of homes for the families of Italian immigrants who worked at Calcite. In the left center is the rectangular tug basin that had been enlarged so that ships from the Bradley fleet could be laid up there in the winter. Two ships are loading in the slip.

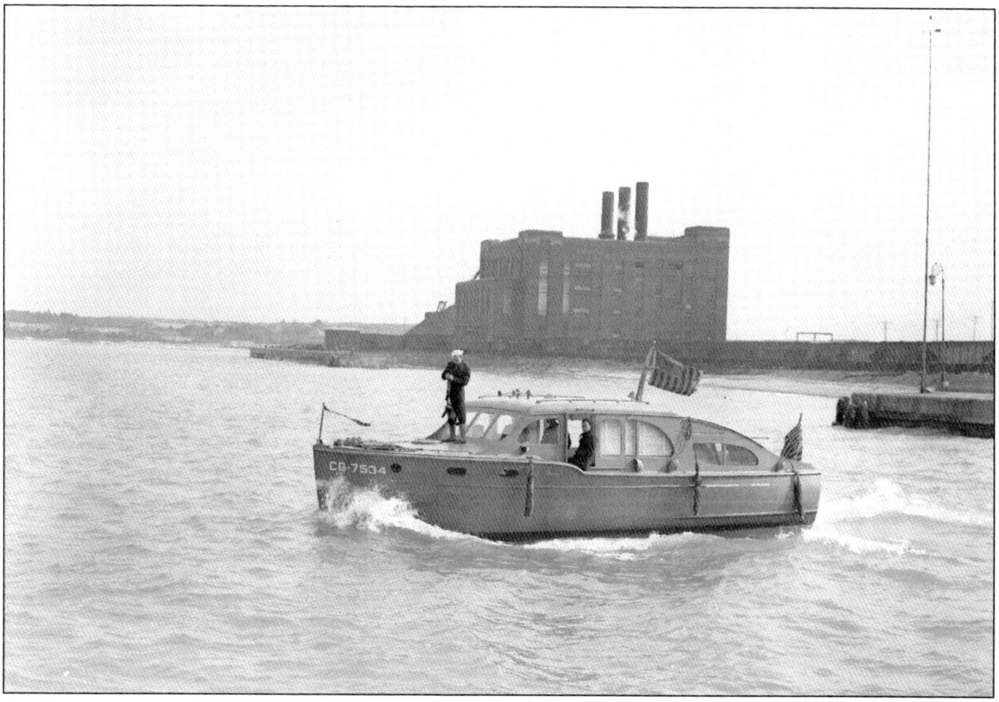

As America entered World War II in December 1941, security was dramatically increased at Calcite. A detachment of Coast Guard personnel was assigned to guard the plant, including patrolling the waters off Calcite with this Coast Guard cutter. The Calcite powerhouse is in the background.

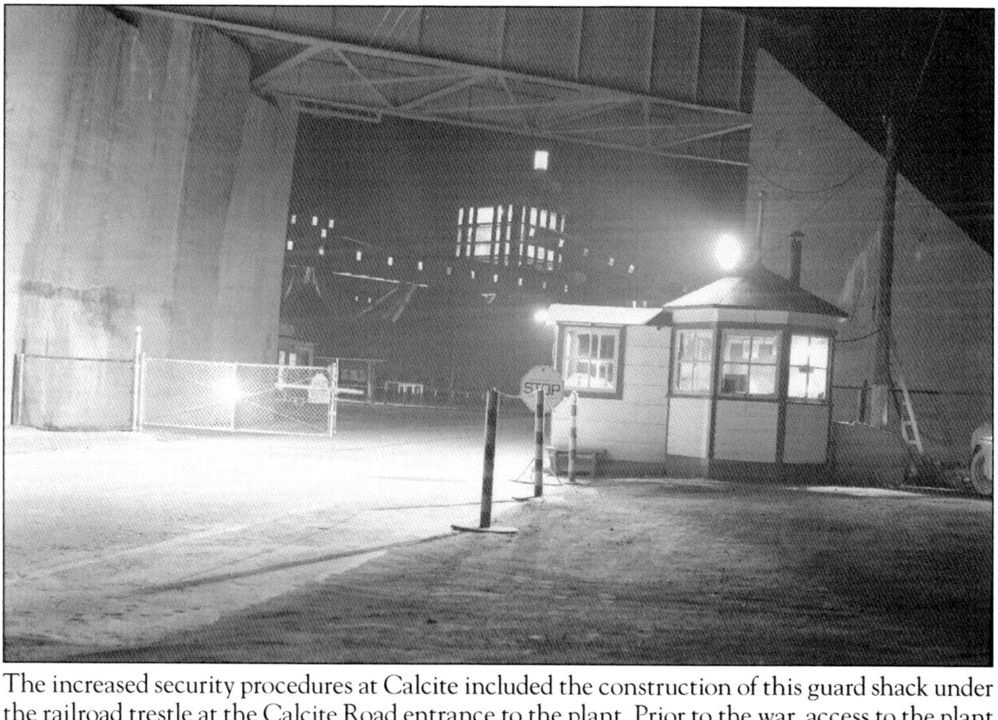

The increased security procedures at Calcite included the construction of this guard shack under the railroad trestle at the Calcite Road entrance to the plant. Prior to the war, access to the plant was essentially unrestricted.

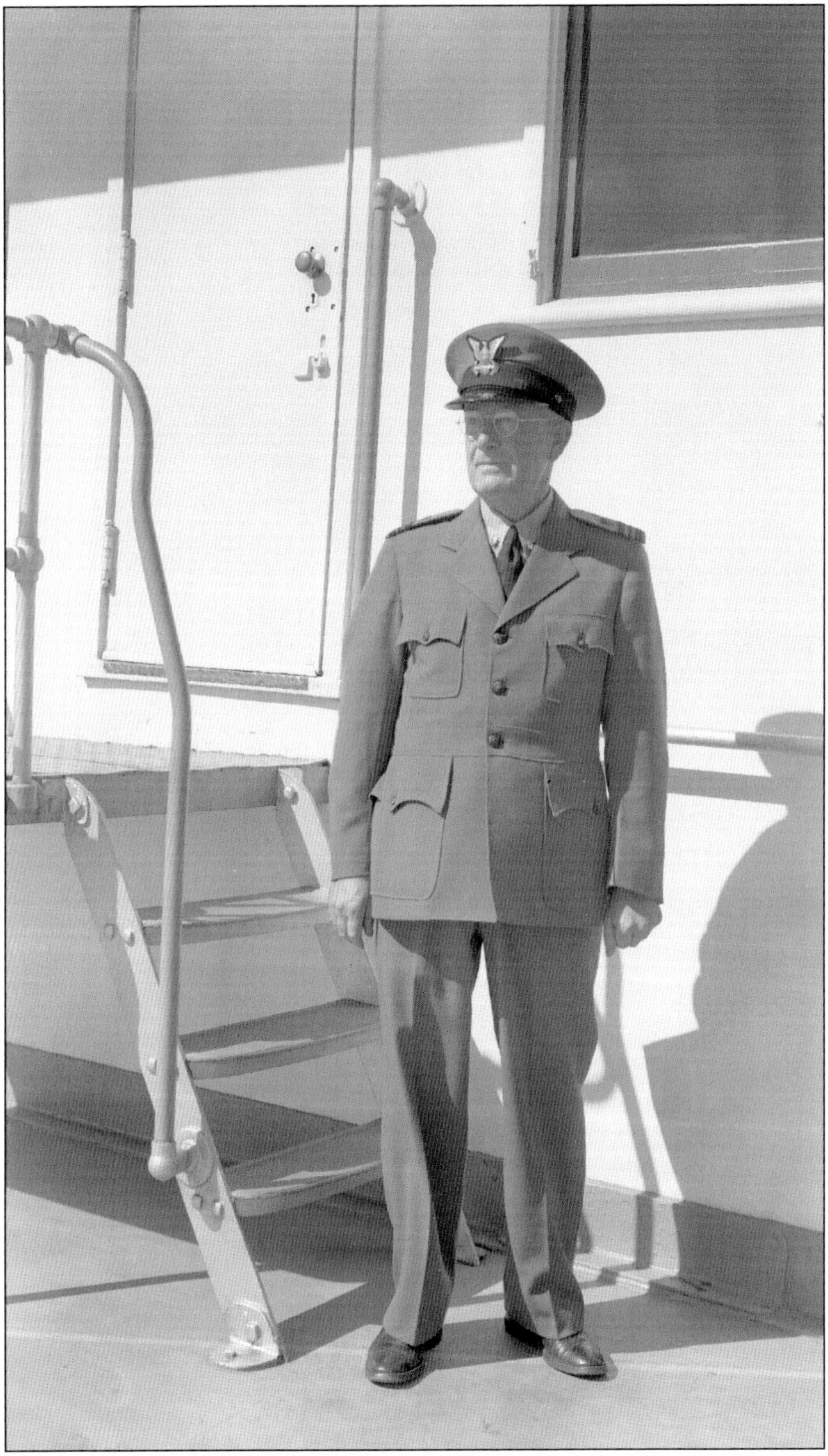

Deck and engine officers in Great Lakes fleets were commissioned in the Coast Guard Reserve during the war years. Capt. Malcolm MacLean of the Bradley fleet, seen here, and the other officers were even issued military uniforms, although they usually only wore them for special occasions.

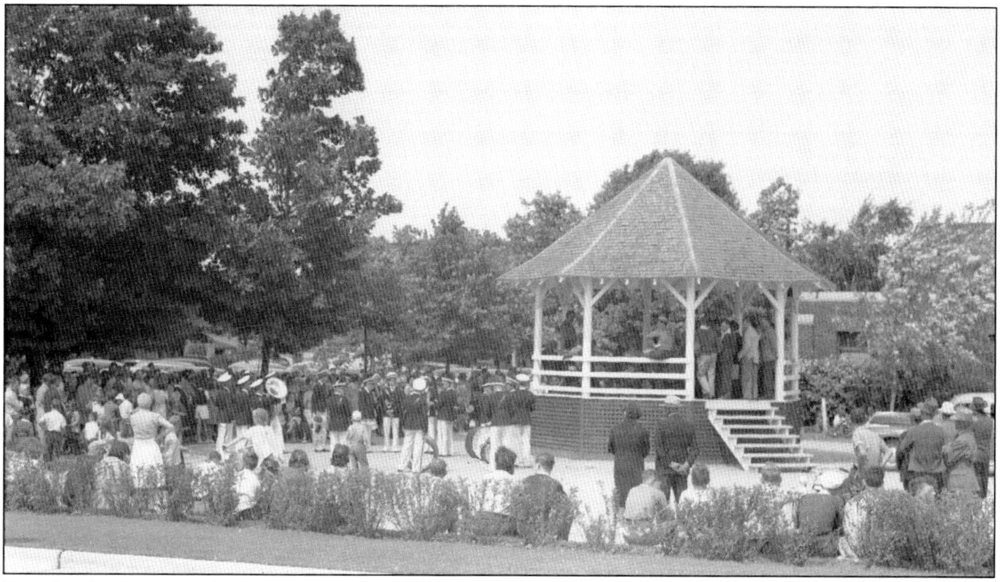

Hundreds of men and a few women from Presque Isle County were drafted or volunteered for service in the military during World War II. As had been the case during World War I, groups leaving for the service were often feted at send-off ceremonies. This 1942 celebration was held at the bandstand next to city hall and included speeches by community leaders and music by the city band.

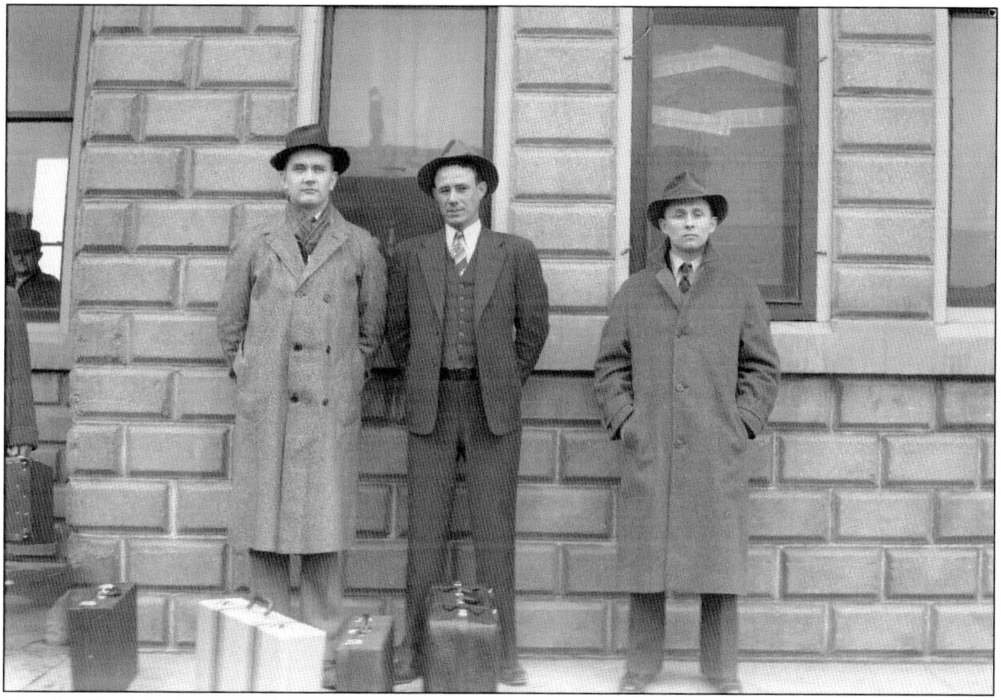

Hundreds of employees left Calcite for the service during the war years. Here, from left to right, Herman Stienke, Clarence Eldridge, and Paul Mulka wait at the depot in Rogers City for a train to take them to Detroit for induction in the spring of 1941. While the United States did not enter the war until December 1941, the Selective Service Act was passed in December of that year, and men began to be drafted. All three returned to work at Calcite following the war.

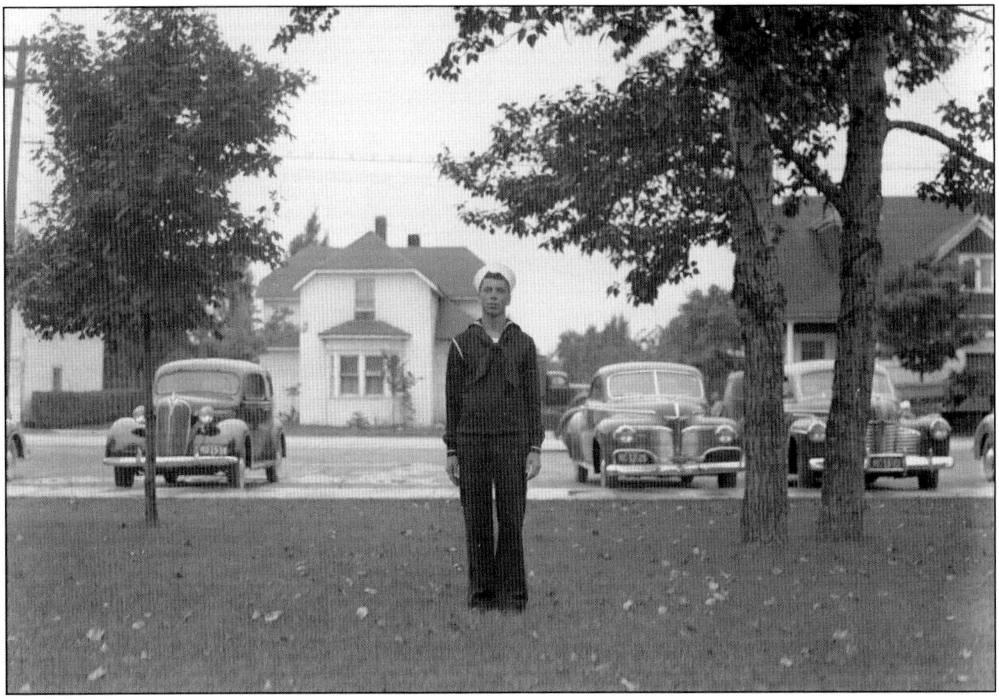

In addition to taking photographs of most of the company employees who entered the military during the war, Calcite photographers also took shots of former employees who were home on leave, including this image of Otto Ross posing in front of Calcite's main office in his Navy uniform.

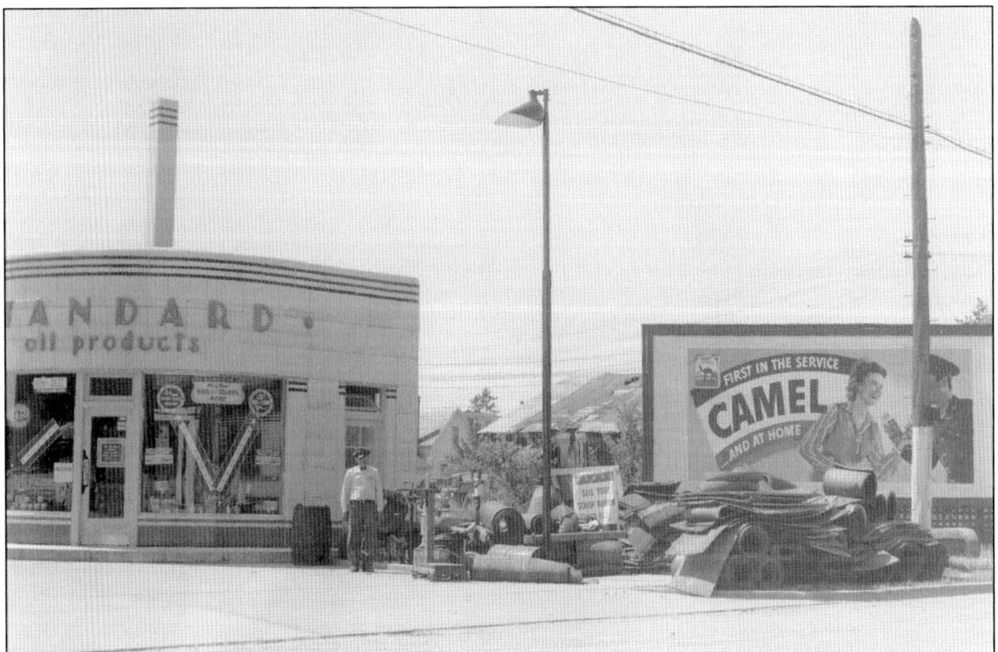

People in the community who stayed behind also supported the war effort in a variety of ways. This 1944 photograph shows scrap rubber being collected at Hopp's Standard Service in Rogers. Posing next to the growing pile is Paul Hopp.

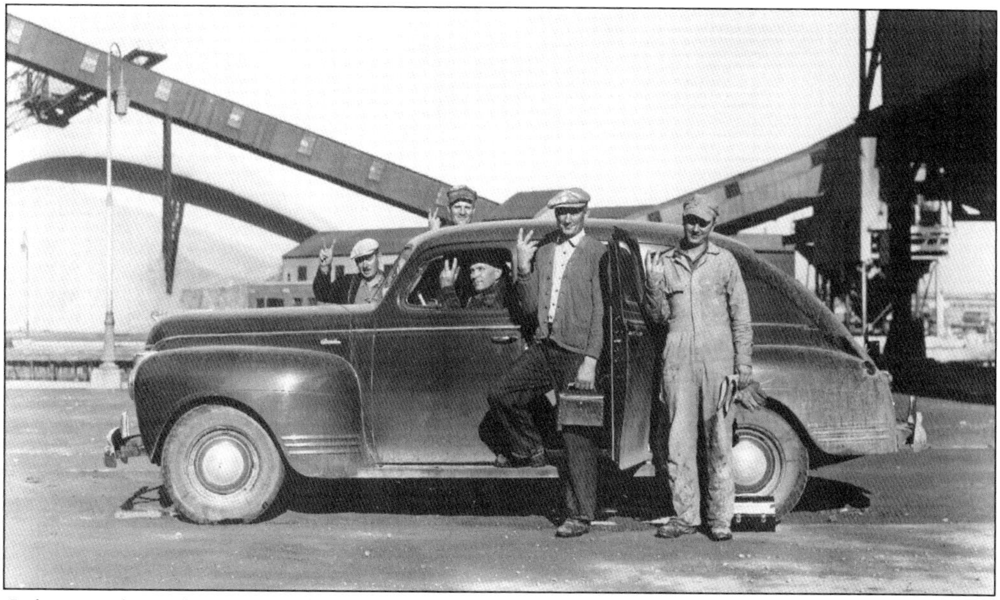

Calcite workers who remained on the job also contributed to the war effort through participation in the Share-Ride program by carpooling to save on gasoline and tires, commodities badly needed by the military. A group of workers poses here in 1944.

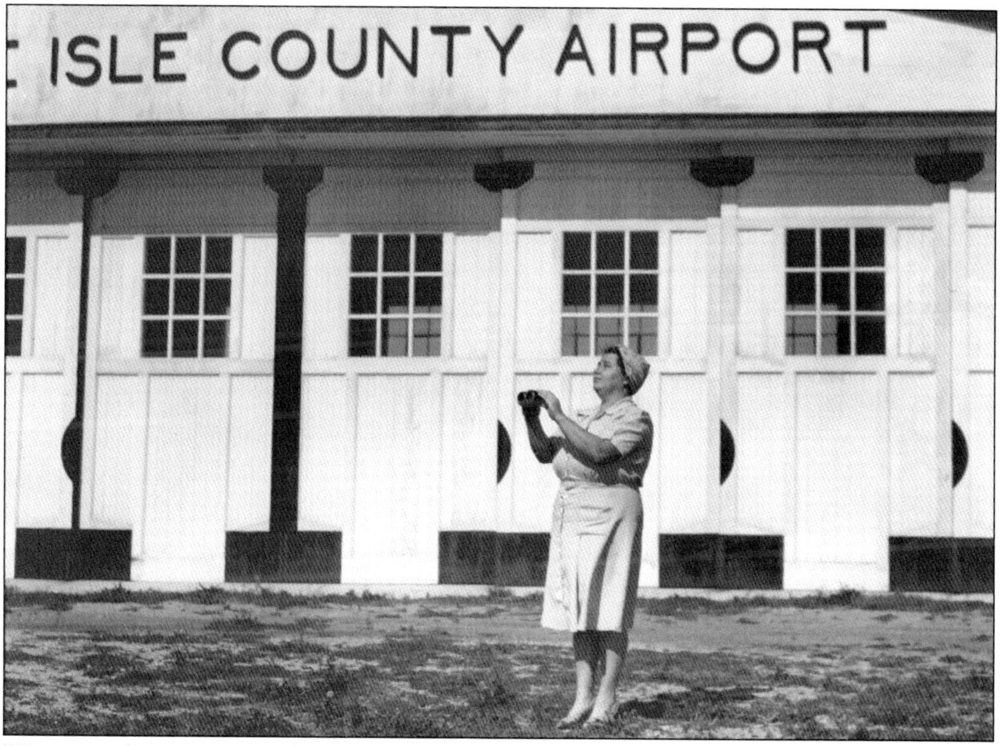

Women in the community also contributed. This woman, posing in 1943 in front of the hangar at the Presque Isle County Airport, was trained as an airplane spotter to watch for enemy airplanes passing overhead. There was great concern during the war that Calcite would be a target for enemy bombers.

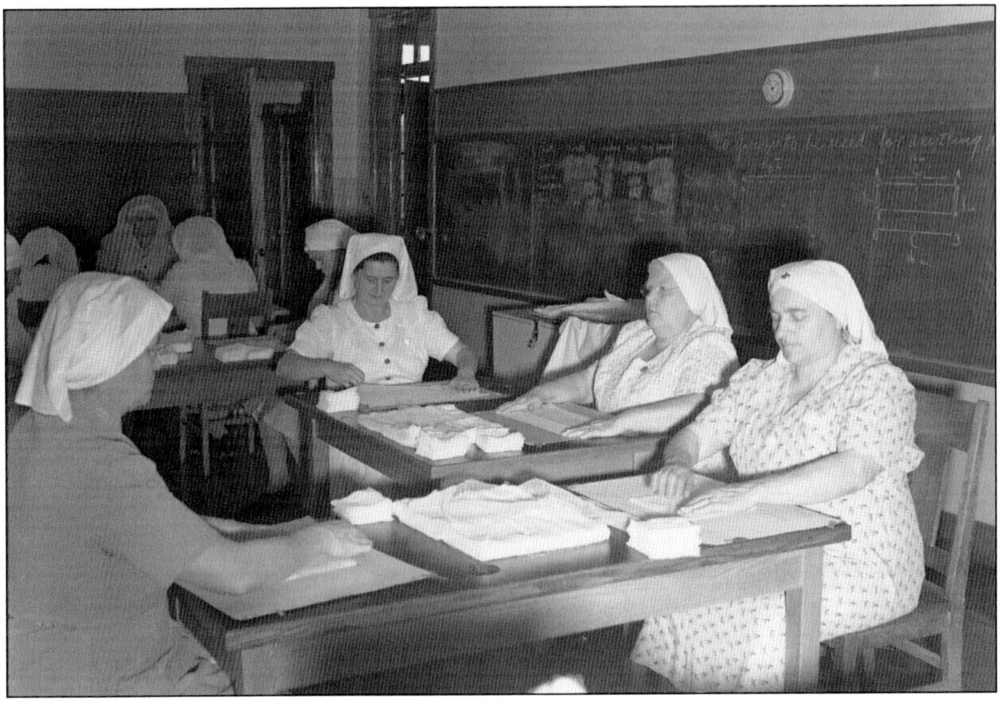

Many local women participated in Red Cross programs during the war, including this group that made surgical dressings. Seen here in 1944, they appear to be working in a classroom at the high school.

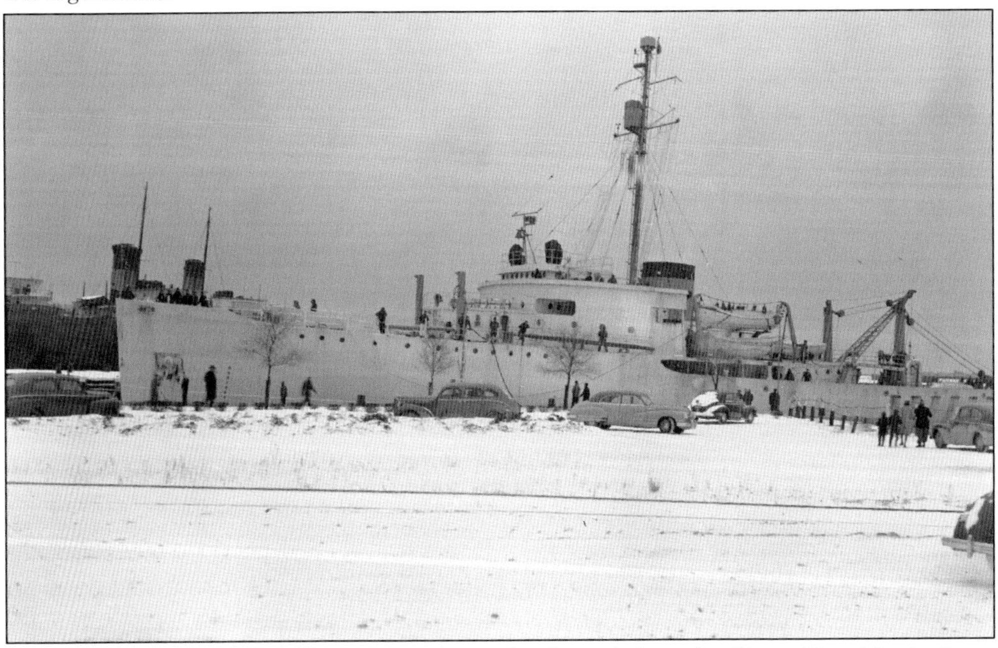

In an effort to extend the shipping season on the Great Lakes, the Coast Guard had a large icebreaker built for service on the lake. The icebreaker *Mackinaw* is seen here on its first visit to Calcite in December 1944. In the background are the smokestacks of Bradley freighters laid up in the tug basin.

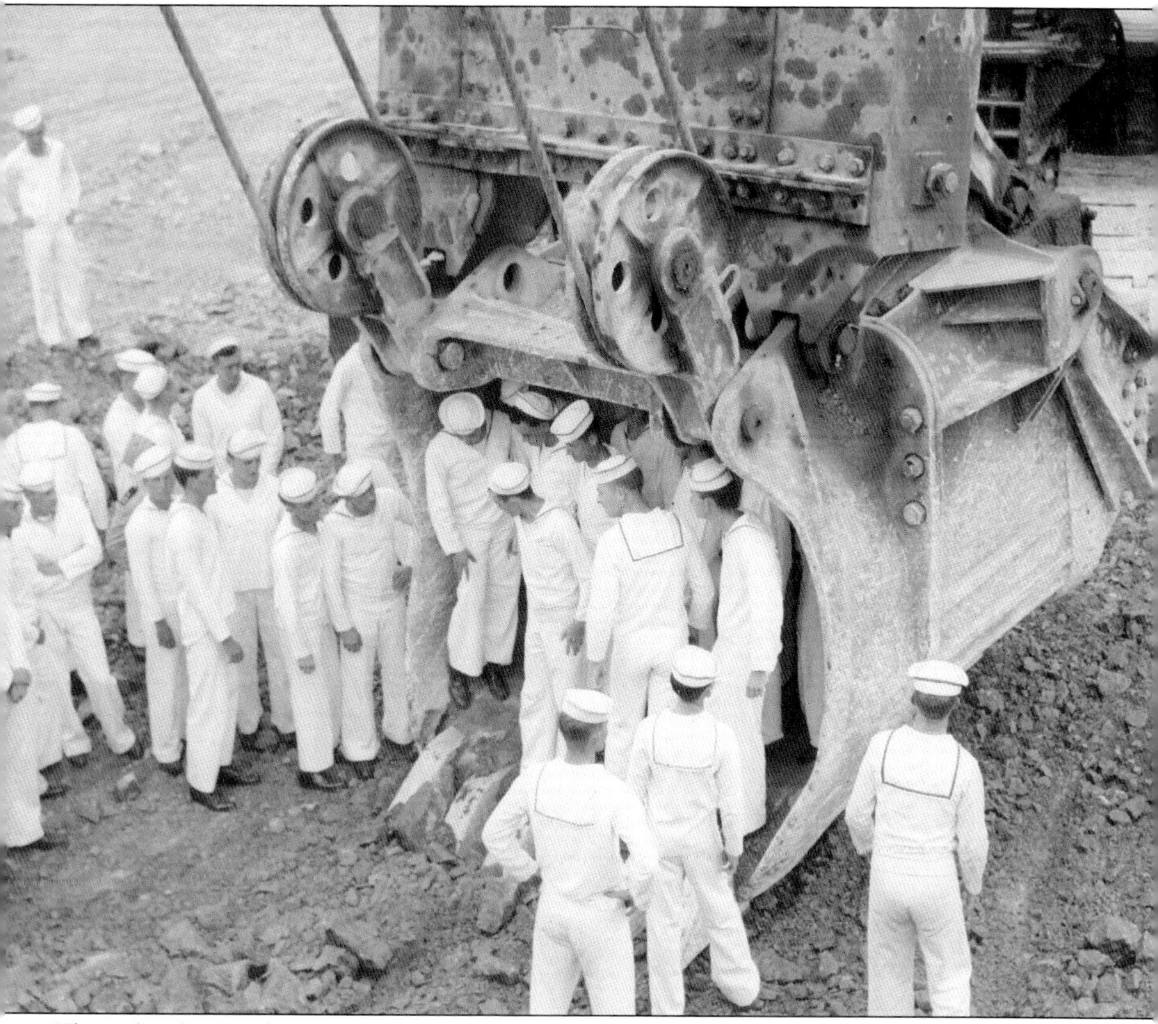

The icebreaker *Mackinaw* was a fairly frequent visitor to Calcite. During a visit in 1946, cadets from the Coast Guard Academy serving aboard the *Mackinaw* had an opportunity to tour the plant. Their visit included determining how many cadets they could squeeze into the massive bucket of one of Calcite's electric shovels.

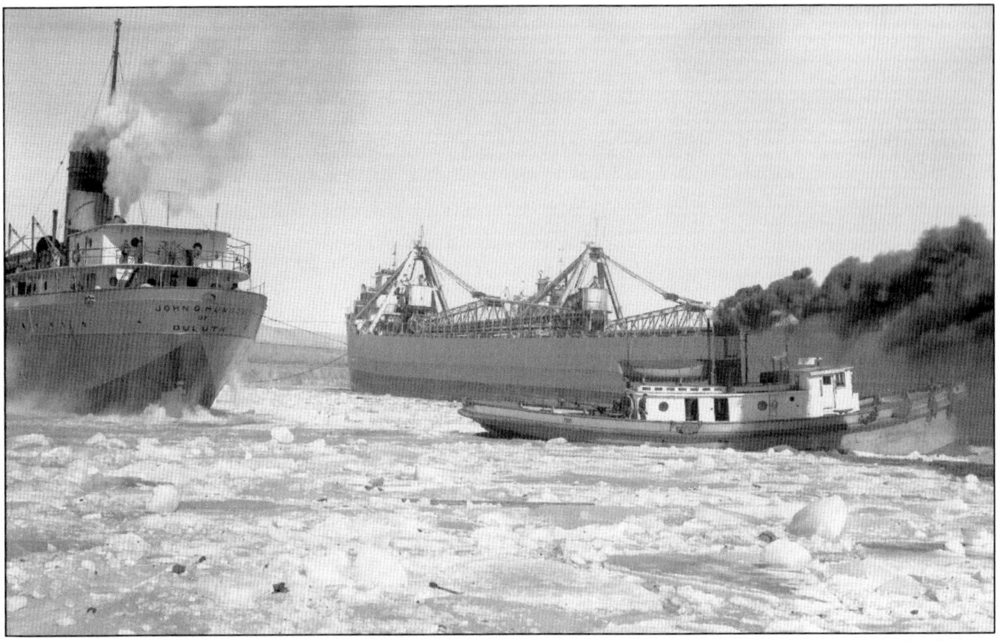

While icebreakers like the *Mackinaw* were tasked with keeping shipping lanes open on the lakes, Michigan Limestone's tugs were pressed into service each spring to break ice at the start of the shipping season. This 1948 photograph shows the tug *Frederick T. Kellers* breaking ice for the *John G. Munson* and two unidentified Bradley freighters.

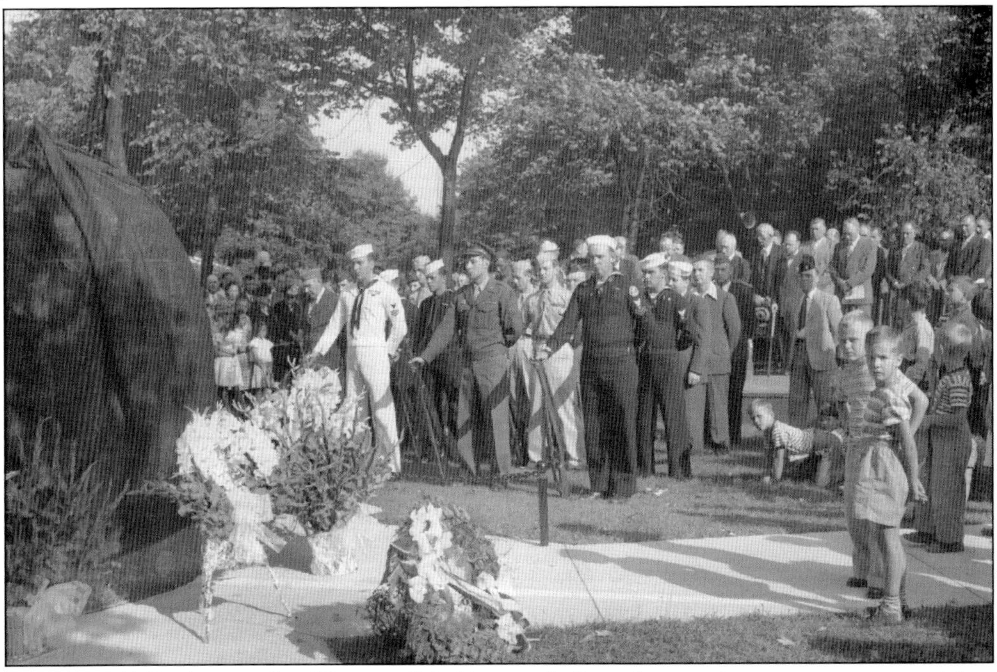

In August 1948, the people of Presque Isle County dedicated a massive stone war memorial to soldiers from the county who died in World War I and World War II. The memorial is on the courthouse lawn in Rogers City. Memorials honoring soldiers lost in Korean and Vietnam have since been added.

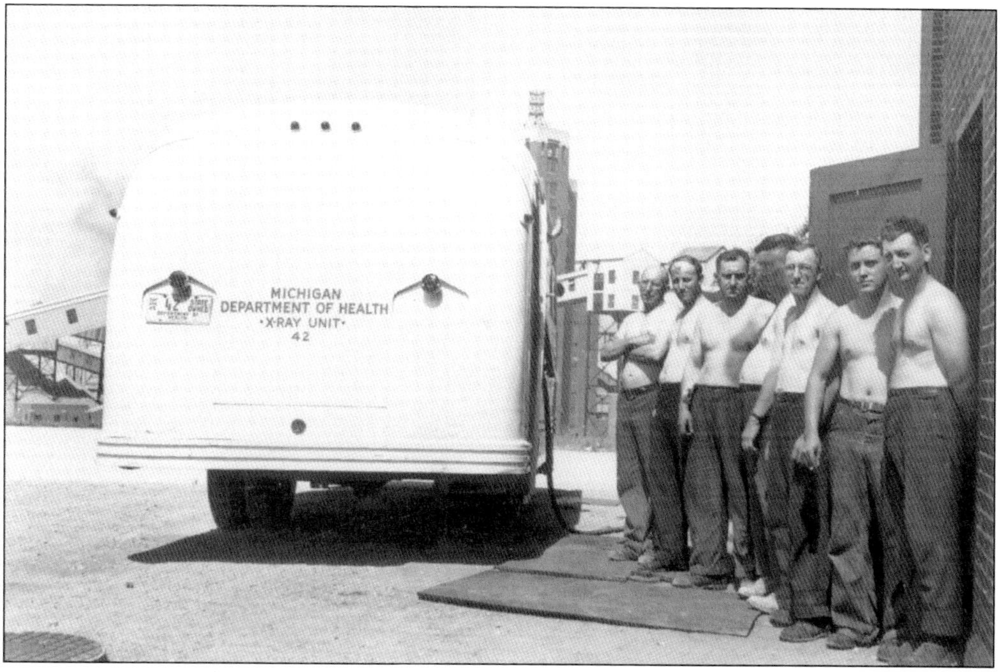

In August 1945, Calcite workers line up for chest x-rays offered at the plant by the Michigan Department of Health.

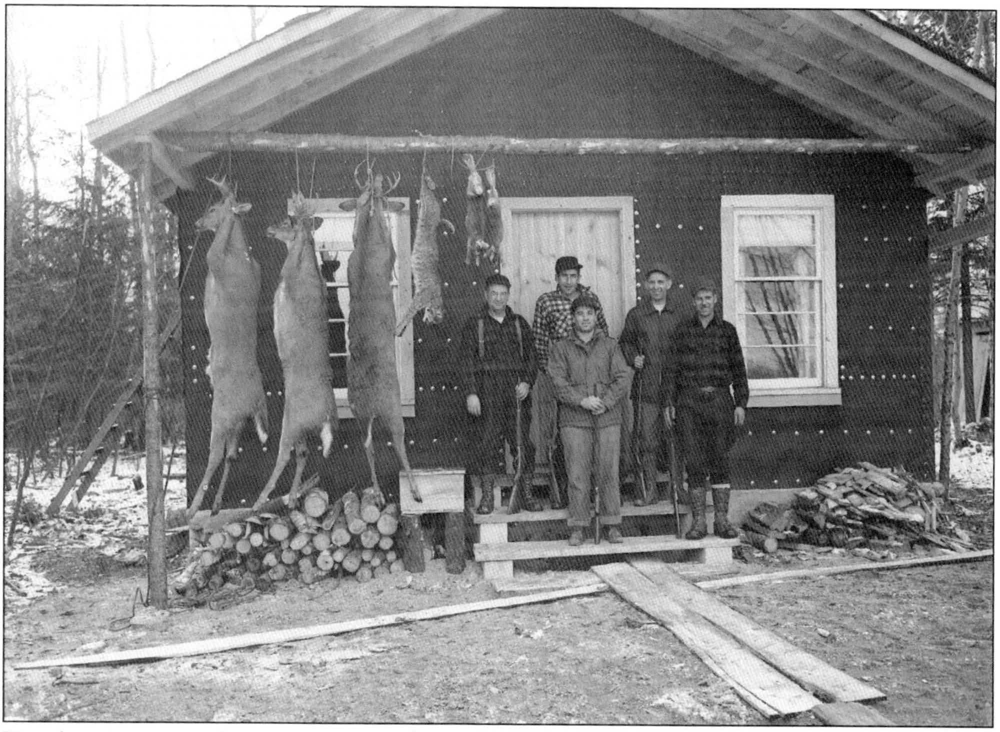
Deer-hunting camps became very popular with many of the veterans who returned from World War II. This photograph shows hunters and the deer, bobcat, and rabbits they bagged at the camp of Charles Kleiber (far left) in November 1949.

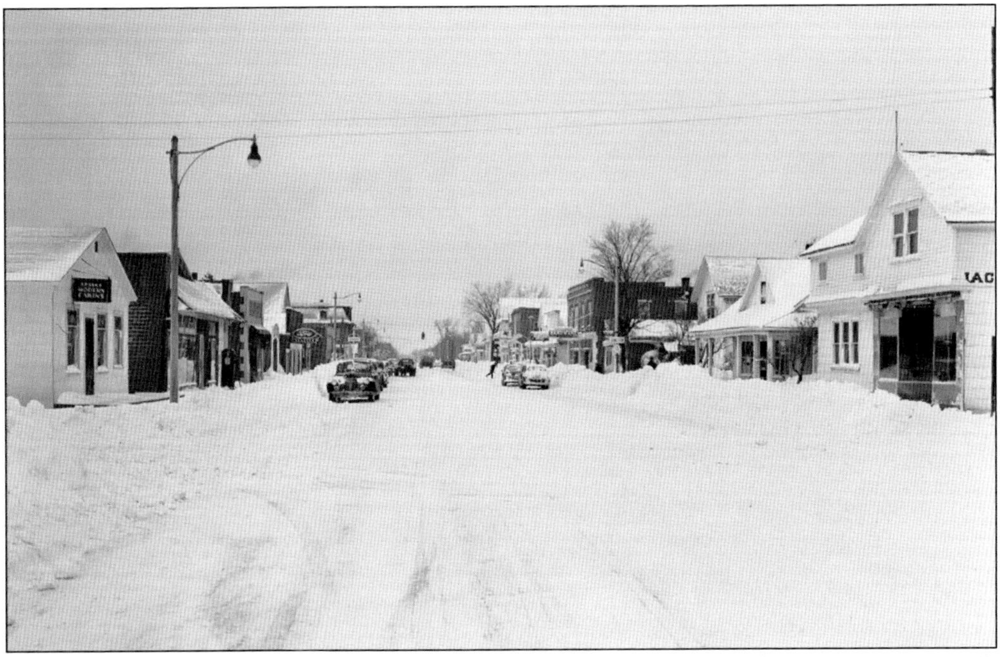

This photograph of Third Street in Rogers City was taken after a typical winter storm in 1949. The street does not look much different today.

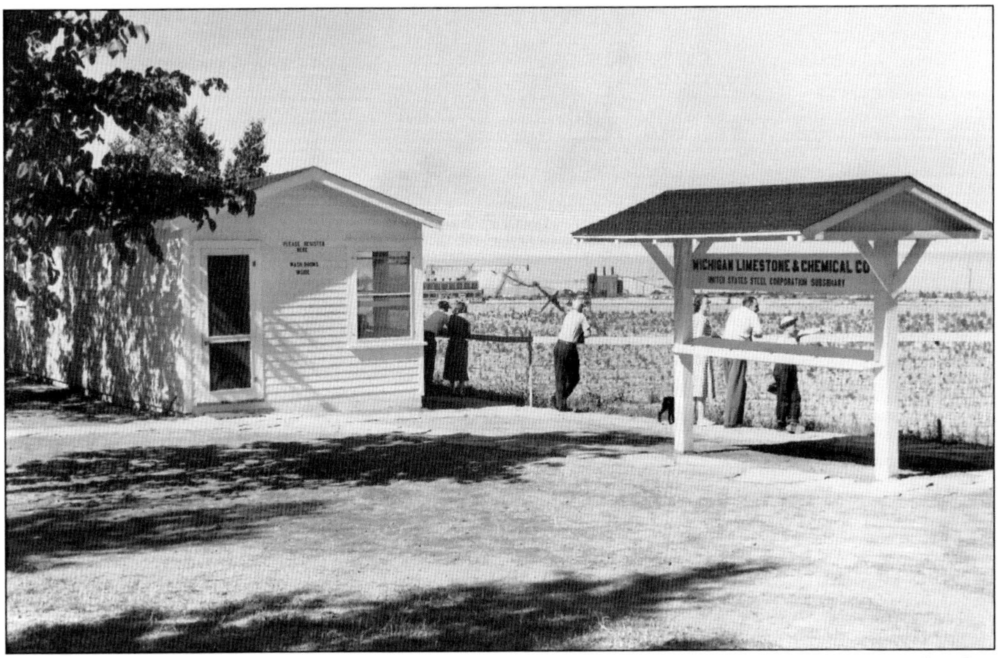

In 1950, Michigan Limestone teamed up with the Rogers City Chamber of Commerce to develop Lookout Point, an observation area on the quarry rim at Calcite that was open to the growing number of tourists visiting the area. The information center at Lookout Point was staffed by employees of the chamber of commerce and contained information about the quarry, the Bradley fleet, and the various uses of limestone. The lookout proved to be extremely popular with tourists, with 50,000 to 70,000 visiting each year.

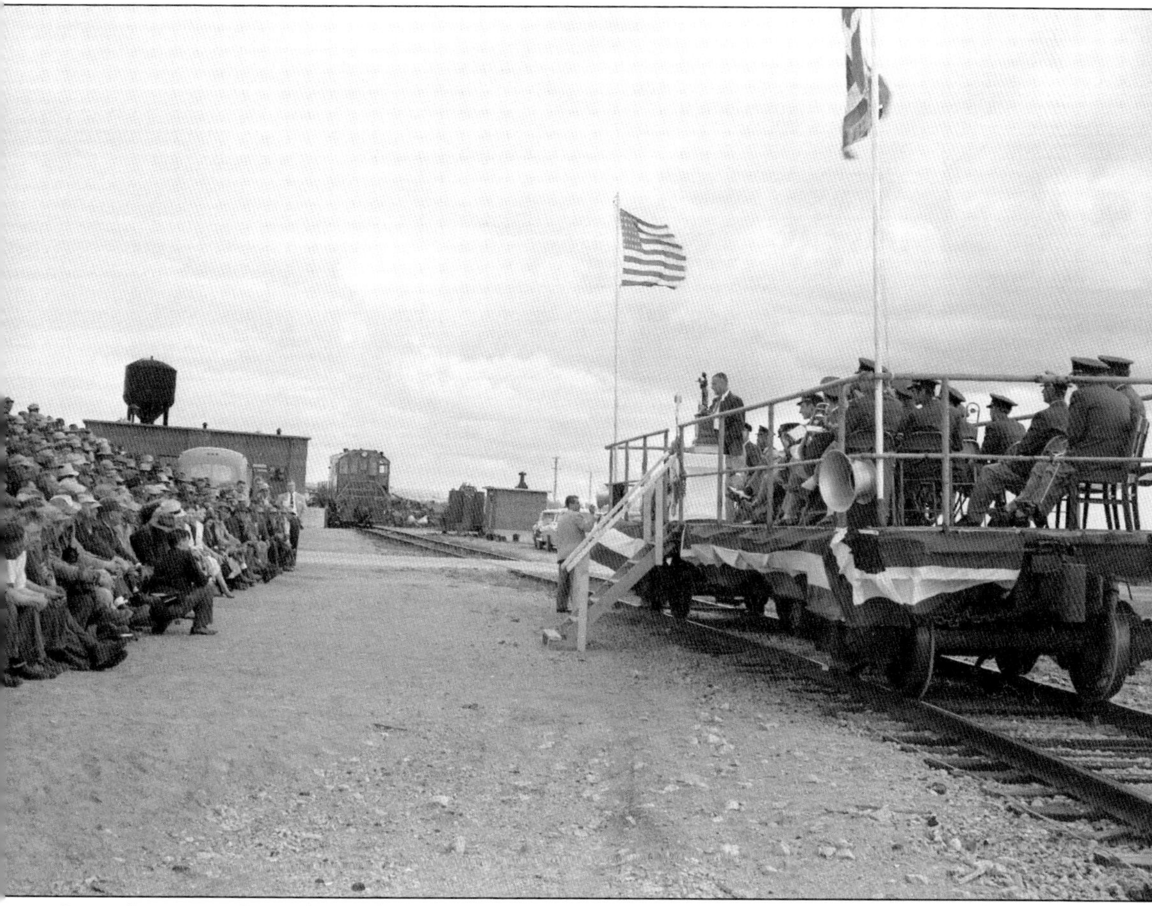

Over the years, the Calcite Plant and the Bradley fleet received many safety awards. Here, employees, company officials, and federal mine safety officials have gathered at Calcite for the presentation of the Sentinels of Safety trophy and flag to the company and its employees in 1951. It is the most prestigious safety award given by the US Bureau of Mines. In 1950, Calcite employees worked 1,273,376 hours with no disabling injuries. It was the fifth time Calcite had received the national safety award.

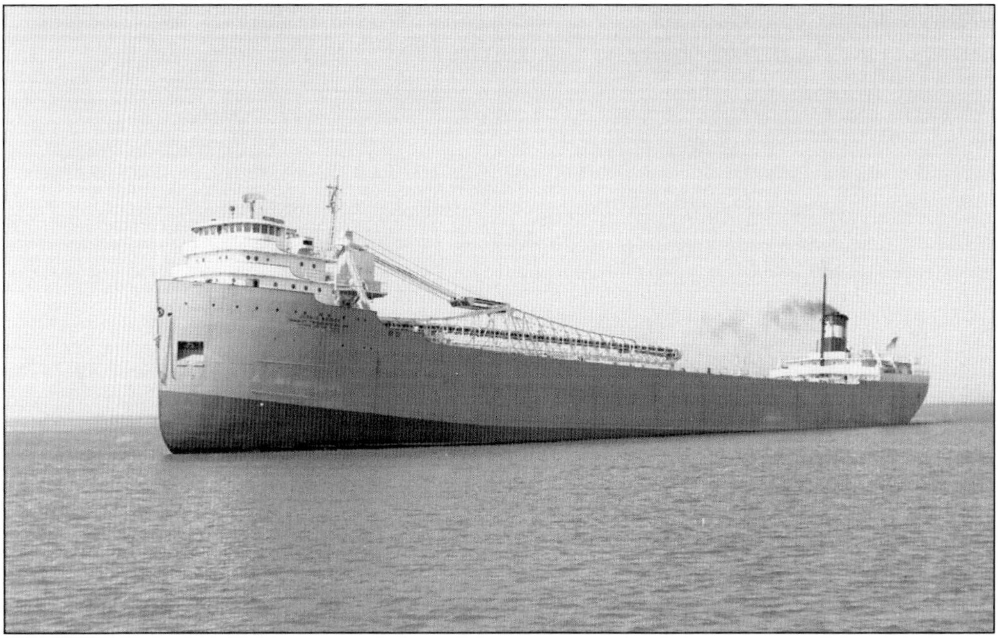

The year 1952 saw the launching of the seventh and last new ship built for Bradley Transportation. The *John G. Munson* was named for the former president of Michigan Limestone and the Bradley fleet, who went on to serve as vice president for raw materials at US Steel. The new ship, built in Manitowoc, Wisconsin, was 666 feet long. It is the only ship built for the Bradley fleet that is still operating today.

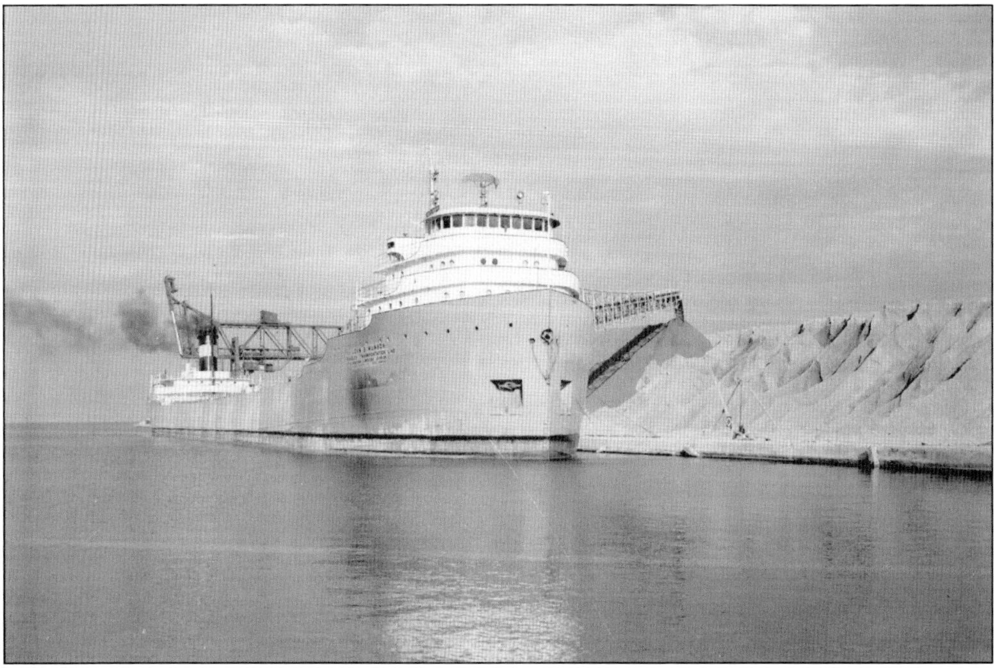

The *John G. Munson* unloads stone at US Steel's Gary Works in Gary, Indiana, on its maiden voyage on the lakes. All of the Bradley ships were self-unloading, meaning they could unload all of their cargo without any assistance from equipment on shore.

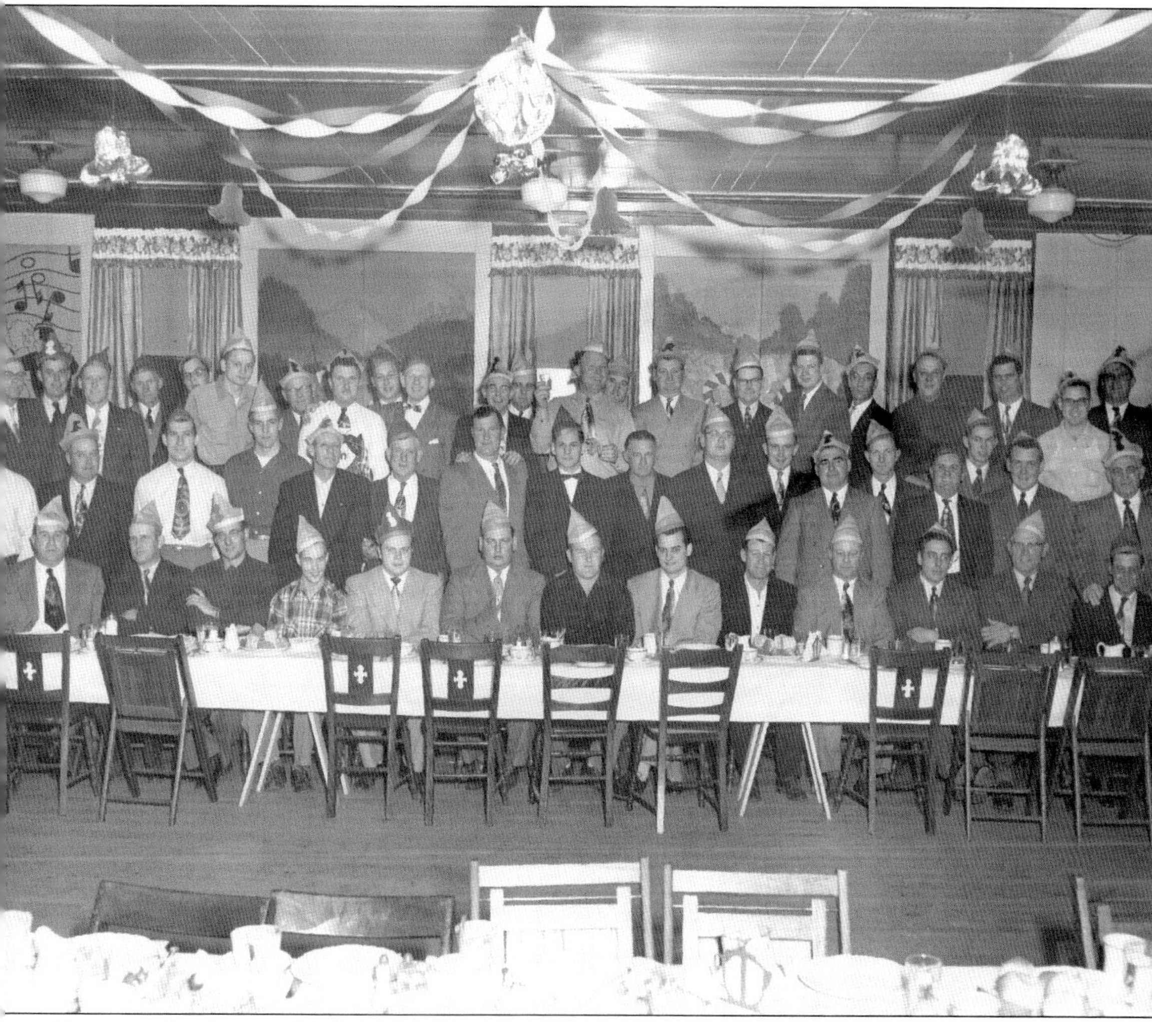

For most of its history, Michigan Limestone was known for the many parties it sponsored for its employees each year. Here, sailors from the Bradley fleet pose at their annual Christmas party in 1952. Crazy hats and exuberant sing-alongs were always required at Calcite and Bradley fleet parties. In addition to the party for sailors, parties were held for the office staff and many other departments at the plant. The largest party of the year, however, honored those employees who had been with the company for 25 years. When employment at Calcite reached 600 workers, that party had to be held at three separate locations in Rogers City simultaneously: St. Ignatius Catholic Church, St. John Lutheran Church, and Westminster Presbyterian Church.

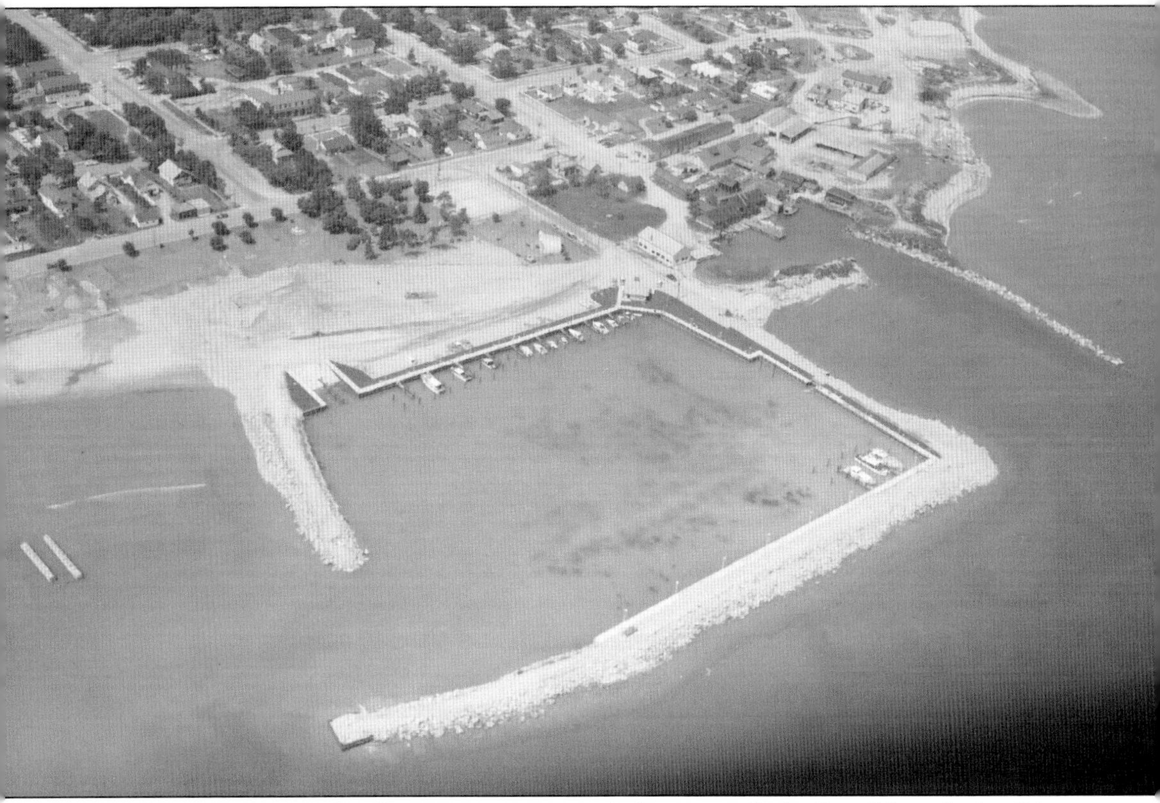

In the 1950s, Rogers City began construction of what was called a "small boat harbor." It was built at the north end of the city's Lakeside Park and featured a sheltered harborage for pleasure boats. To the right of the small boat harbor is the smaller harbor used by fish tugs operating out of Rogers City. The two massive concrete footings on the extreme left once supported Hoeft's lumber dock and boathouse.

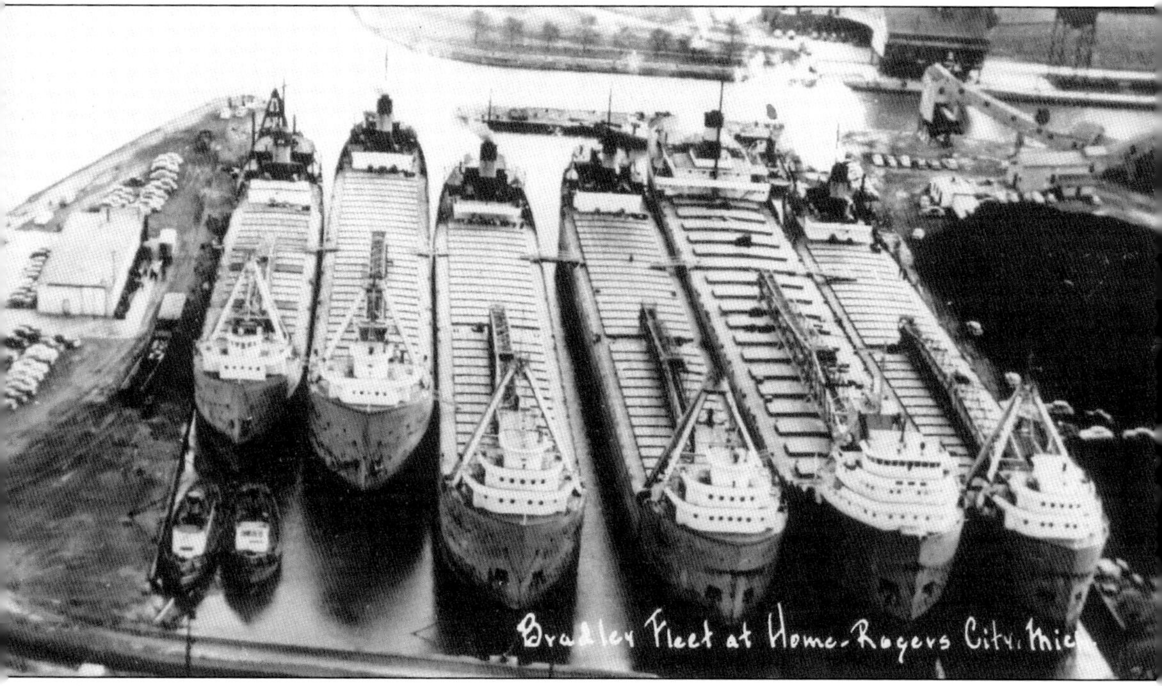

The former tug basin, or frog pond, at Calcite was also expanded over the years in order to accommodate up to six ships from the fleet during the winter months. This photograph shows the laid-up fleet in the winter of 1952–1953.

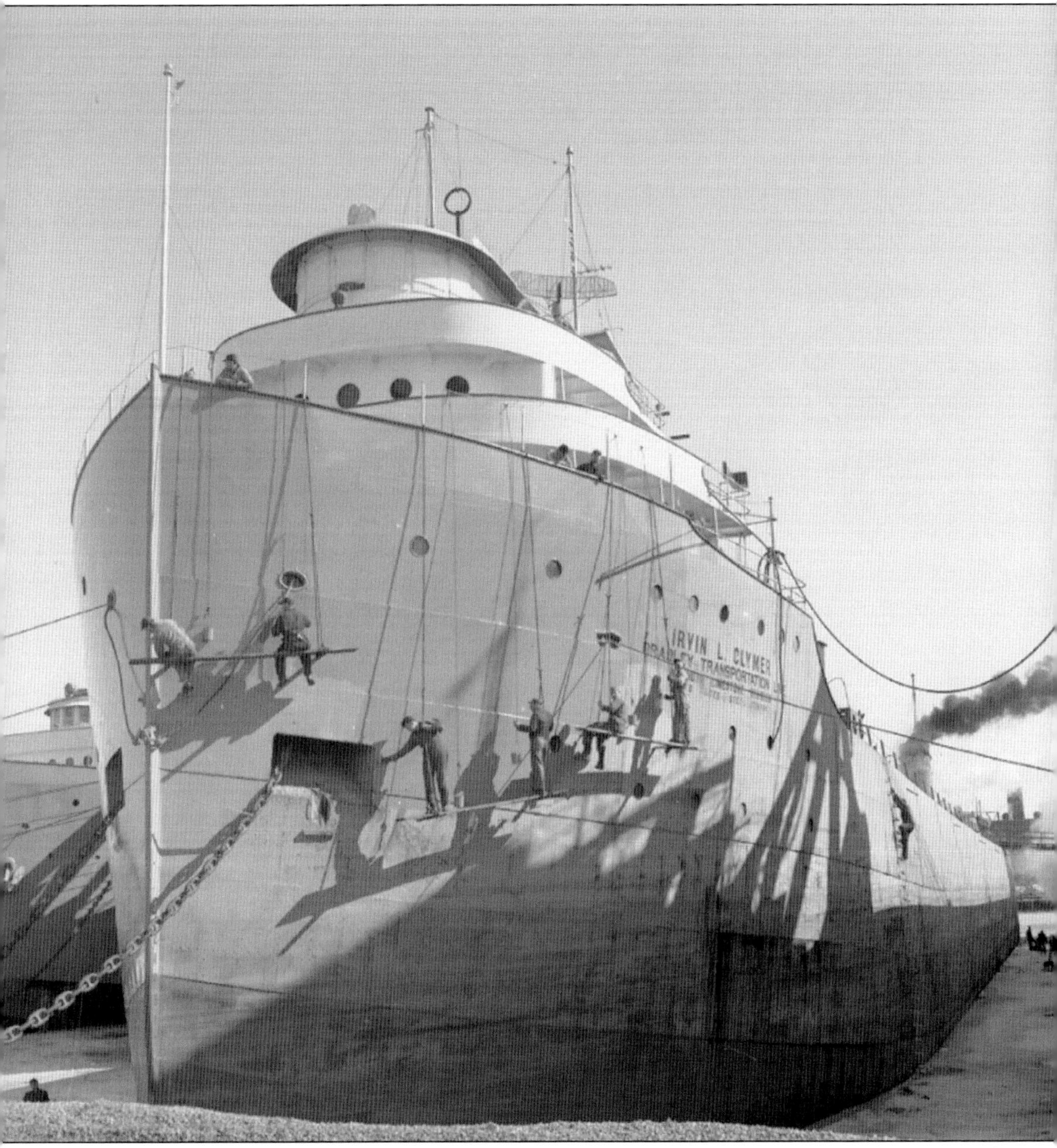

In addition to performing a variety of repair work on the boats during the winter lay-up period, each boat received a fresh coat of paint before setting sail in the spring. This 1953 photograph shows crew members hanging over the side of the steamer *Irvin L. Clymer* putting a fresh coat of paint on the bow.

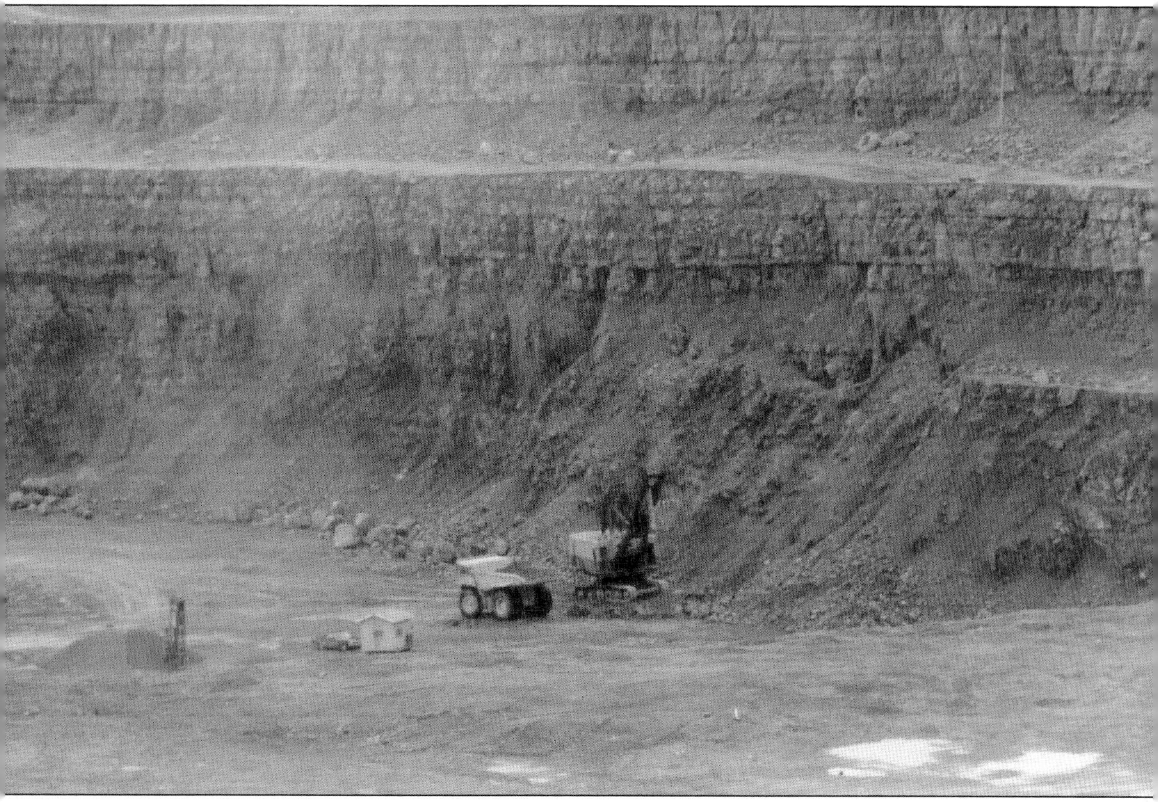

Calcite got some serious competition from a new Presque Isle County limestone quarry in 1954. Five major steel companies joined forces to create the Presque Isle Corporation and build a processing plant and loading dock at a defunct limestone quarry just north of Presque Isle Point, about 18 miles south of Calcite. The partners in the new company included Republic Steel, National Steel, Bethlehem Steel, Jones & Laughlin Steel, and Youngstown Sheet & Tube. Their ownership of the quarry protected their source of limestone in the same way that Calcite secured a guaranteed supply of stone for US Steel. The new quarry, commonly referred to as Stoneport, the official designation of their shipping port, used electric shovels similar to those at Calcite in the mining operation but hauled the stone to the plant's crusher with large haul trucks instead of the trains used at Calcite.

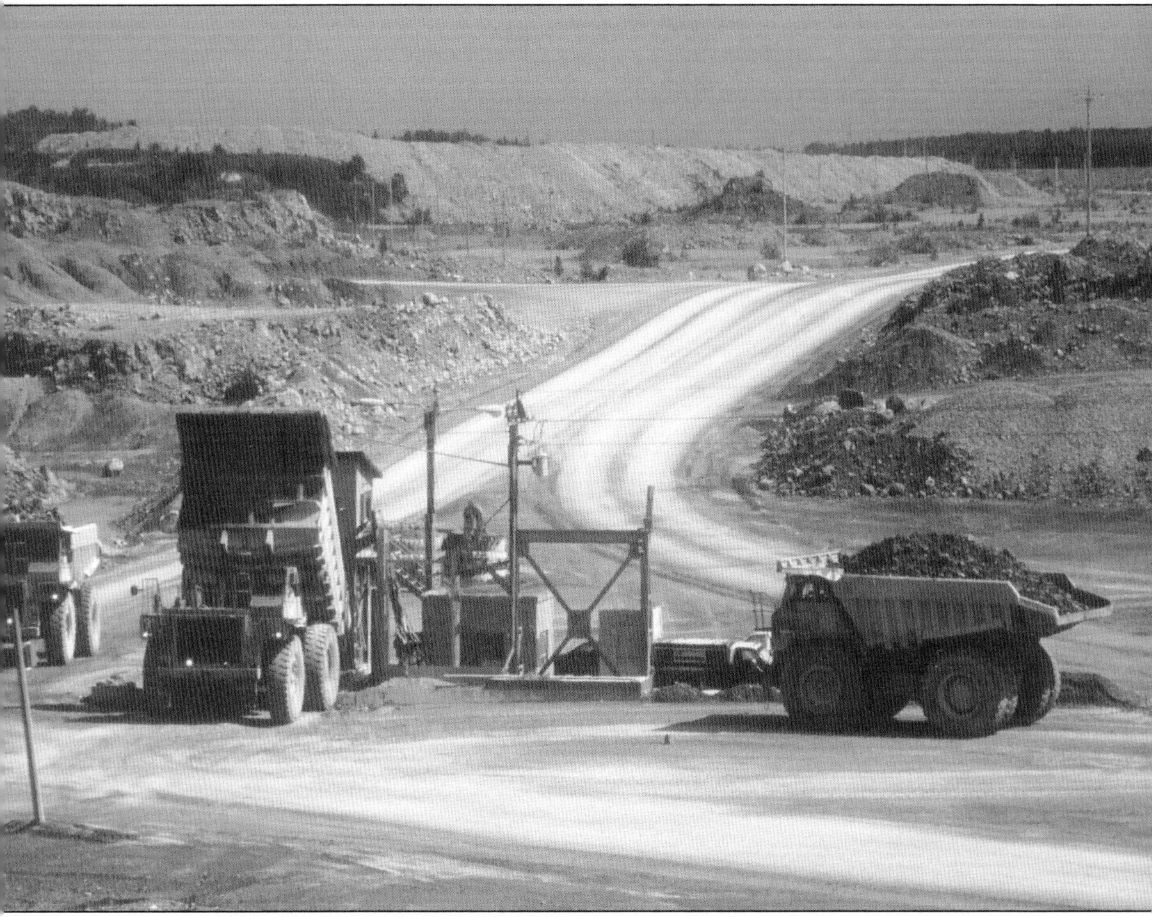

The crusher at Stoneport sits out in the open here in the 1970s, whereas the one at Calcite is housed in a building. This photograph shows Stoneport's huge haul trucks dumping their loads into the crusher. Stone coming out of the crusher is then sent to the mill for further processing via a conveyor system that is partially underground.

In the 1970s, Stoneport abandoned the use of the large, expensive, and labor-intensive electric shovels and began using large Caterpillar 992 loaders to mine stone. The loaders were operated by a single worker, they were less expensive to purchase and maintain than the electric shovels, and they were capable of loading trucks faster.

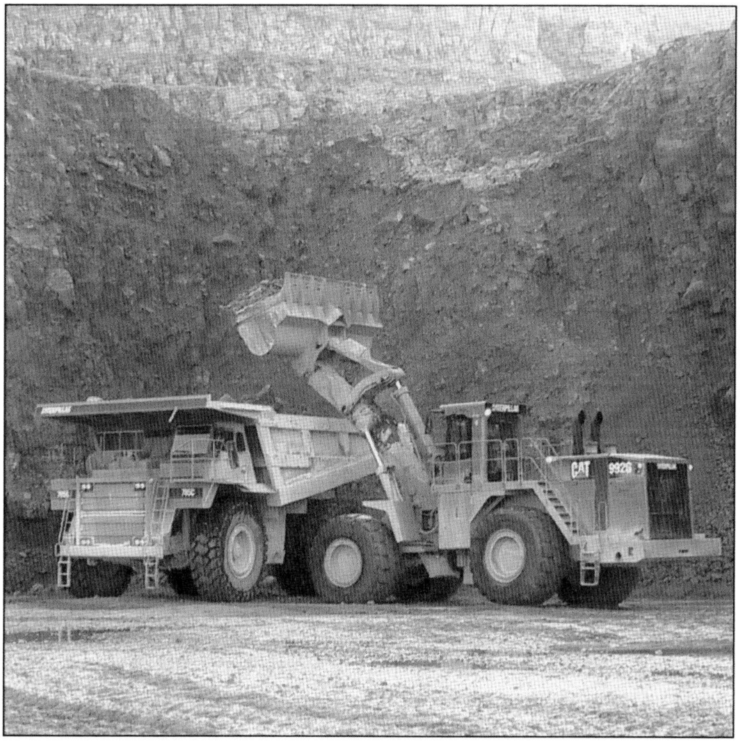

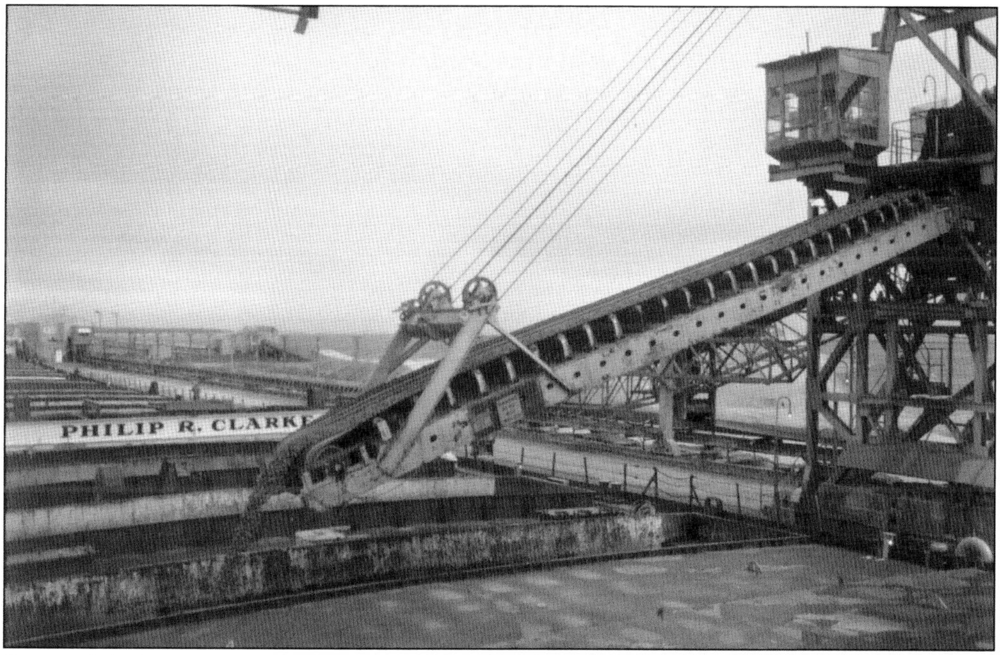

Presque Isle Corporation used a system virtually identical to the one at Calcite to move stone through the processing system and eventually transport it to the ship loader. This 1998 photograph shows the Stoneport ship loader depositing stone in the cargo hold of the Great Lakes fleet's *Philip R. Clarke*. The loader is built on rails so it can move up and down the dock to fill the cargo hold of a ship. The operator sits in a cab above the loader's boom.

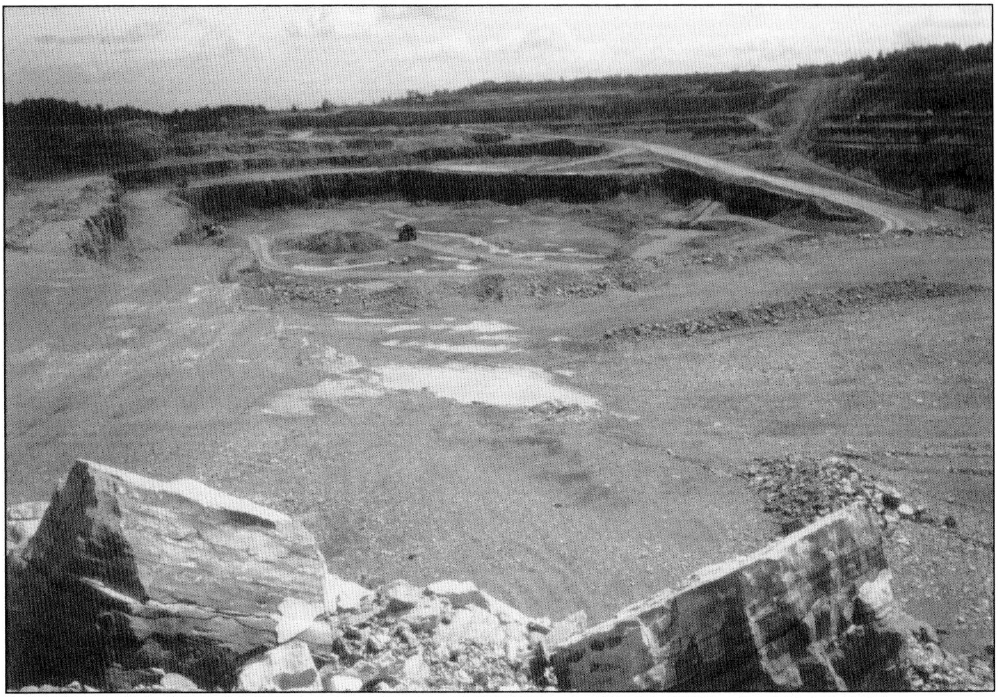

The layers, or cuts, of stone that have been mined at Stoneport are clearly visible in this overview of a part of the quarry. Mining is being done on the far left of the lower level. A rotary drill prepares blast holes on the bank above where stone is being loaded.

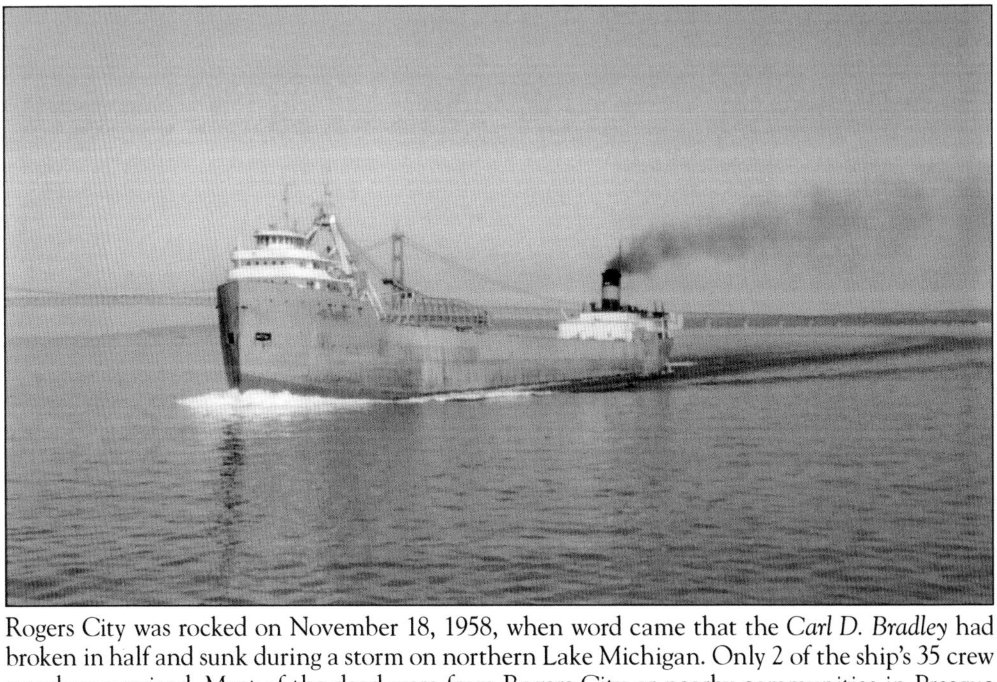

Rogers City was rocked on November 18, 1958, when word came that the *Carl D. Bradley* had broken in half and sunk during a storm on northern Lake Michigan. Only 2 of the ship's 35 crew members survived. Most of the dead were from Rogers City or nearby communities in Presque Isle County. This is one of the last known photographs of the *Bradley*, taken shortly before it was lost.

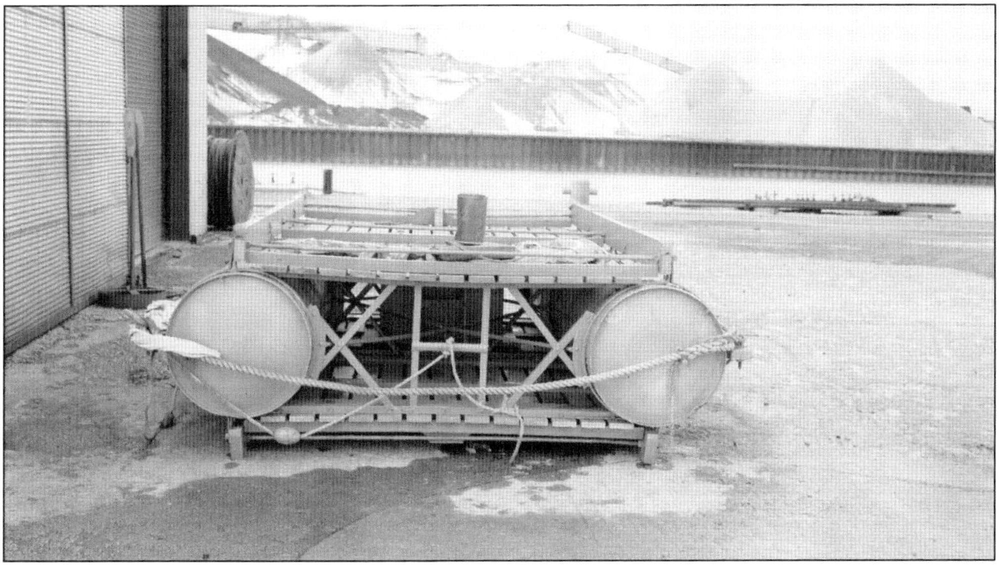

The two *Bradley* crew members who survived the sinking of their ship were found the following morning aboard this raft. After being recovered by the Coast Guard, the raft was returned by truck to Calcite, where this photograph was taken. What happened to it after that is unknown.

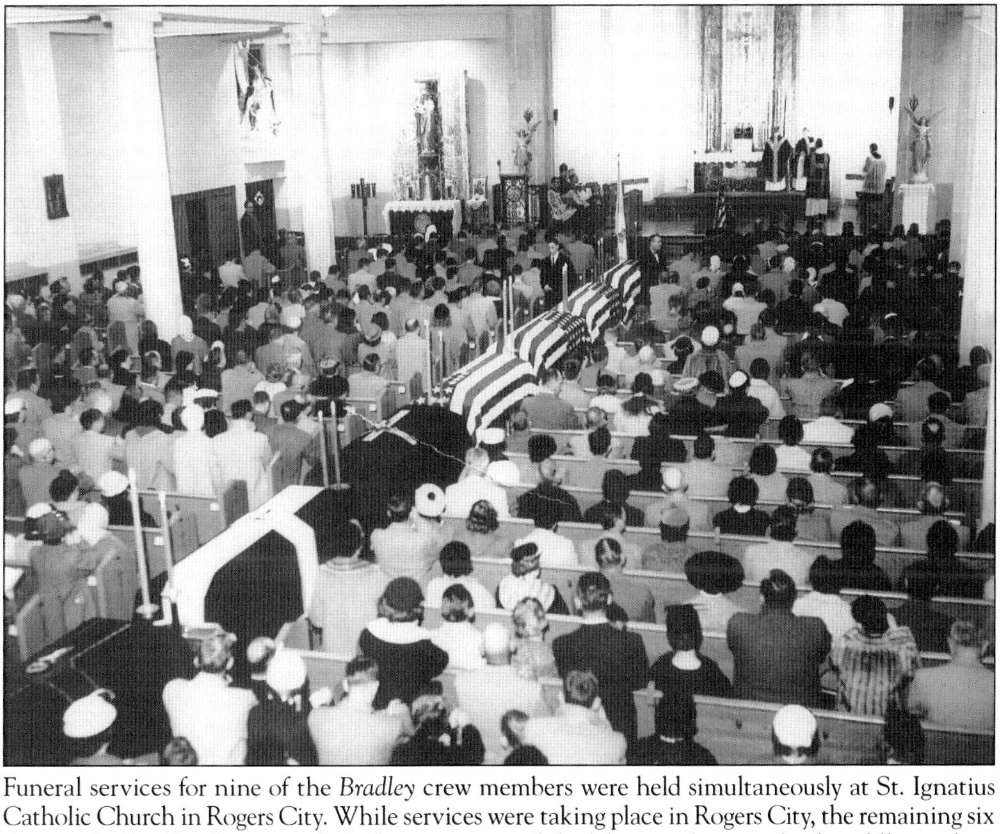

Funeral services for nine of the *Bradley* crew members were held simultaneously at St. Ignatius Catholic Church in Rogers City. While services were taking place in Rogers City, the remaining six ships in the Bradley fleet were docked at ports around the lake out of respect for their fellow sailors. In most cases, pastors from the ports visited the boats and conducted memorial services.

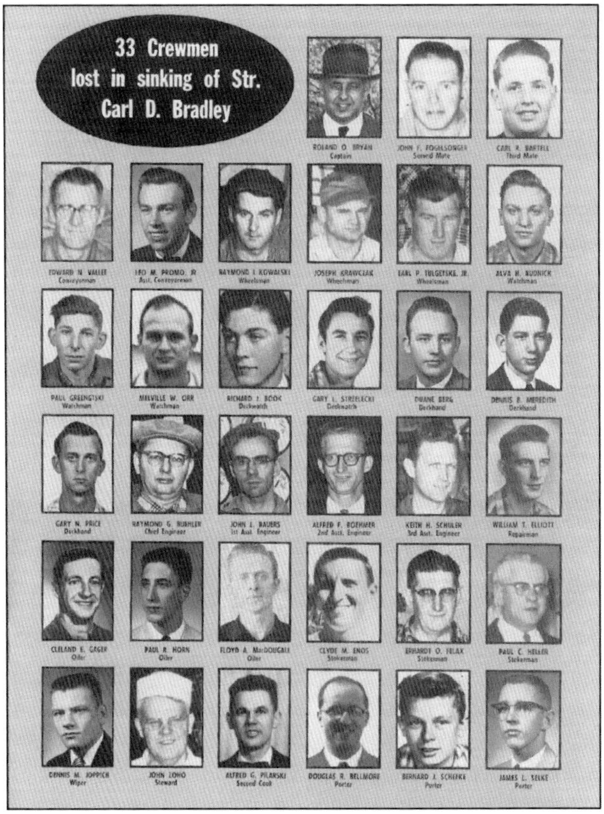
33 Crewmen lost in sinking of Str. Carl D. Bradley

ROLAND O. BRYAN, Captain
JOHN F. FOGELSONGER, Second Mate
CARL R. BARTELS, Third Mate
EDWARD N. VALLEE, Conveyorman
LEO M. PROMO, JR., Asst. Conveyorman
RAYMOND J. KOWALSKI, Wheelsman
JOSEPH KRAWCZAK, Wheelsman
EARL P. TULGETSKE, JR., Wheelsman
ALVA H. BUDNICK, Watchman
PAUL GREENGTSKI, Watchman
MELVILLE W. ORR, Watchman
RICHARD J. BOOK, Deckwatch
GARY L. STRZELECKI, Deckwatch
DUANE BERG, Deckhand
DENNIS R. MEREDITH, Deckhand
GARY N. PRICE, Deckhand
RAYMOND G. BUEHLER, Chief Engineer
JOHN L. BAUERS, 1st Asst. Engineer
ALFRED F. BOEHMER, 2nd Asst. Engineer
KEITH H. SCHULER, 3rd Asst. Engineer
WILLIAM T. ELLIOTT, Repairman
CLELAND E. GAGER, Oiler
PAUL R. HORN, Oiler
FLOYD A. MacDOUGALL, Oiler
CLYDE M. ENOS, Stokerman
ERHARDT O. FELAX, Stokerman
PAUL C. HELLER, Stokerman
DENNIS M. JOPPICH, Wiper
JOHN ZOHO, Steward
ALFRED G. PILARSKI, Second Cook
DOUGLAS R. BELLMORE, Porter
BERNARD J. SCHEFKE, Porter
JAMES L. SELKE, Porter

The 33 crew members lost in the sinking of the *Bradley* are seen here on a page from *Calcite Screenings*, Michigan Limestone's corporate magazine. Virtually everyone in Rogers City lost a relative, friend, or neighbor in the sinking. Mayor Kenneth Vogelheim said the town was too small to hold all the grief. As a result of the sinking, 23 women were widowed, and 53 children lost their fathers.

The people of Rogers City and the surrounding area were again stunned in May 1965 when the steamer *Cedarville* (below) sank in the Straits of Mackinac after colliding with the Norwegian freighter *Topdalsfjord* while operating in heavy fog. When the captain's attempt to beach his mortally wounded ship was unsuccessful, 10 members of the crew were lost.

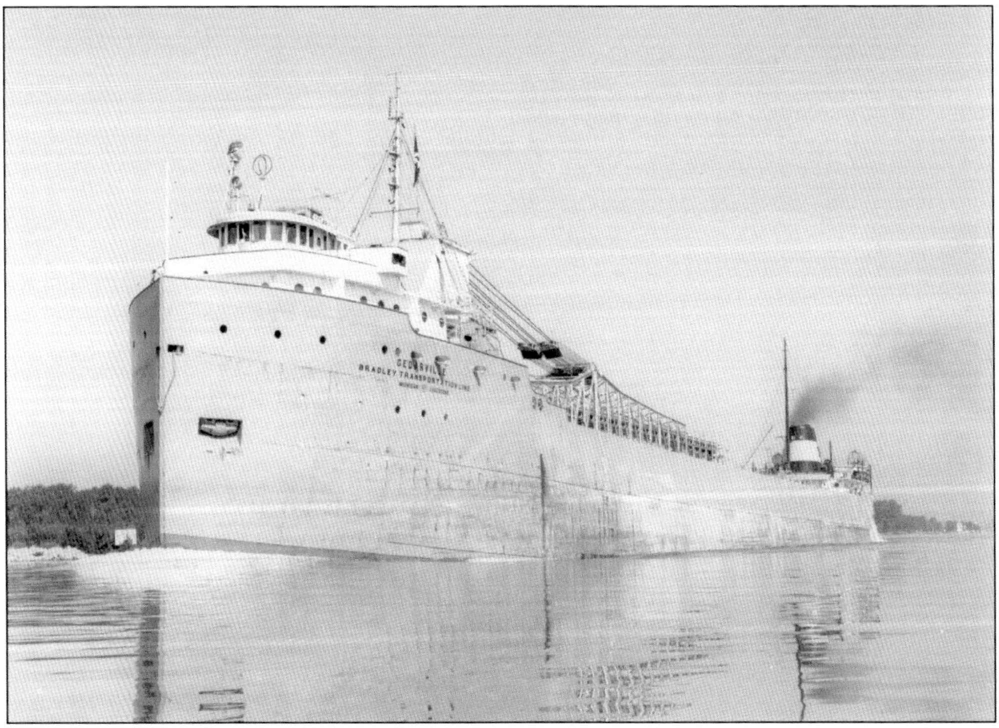

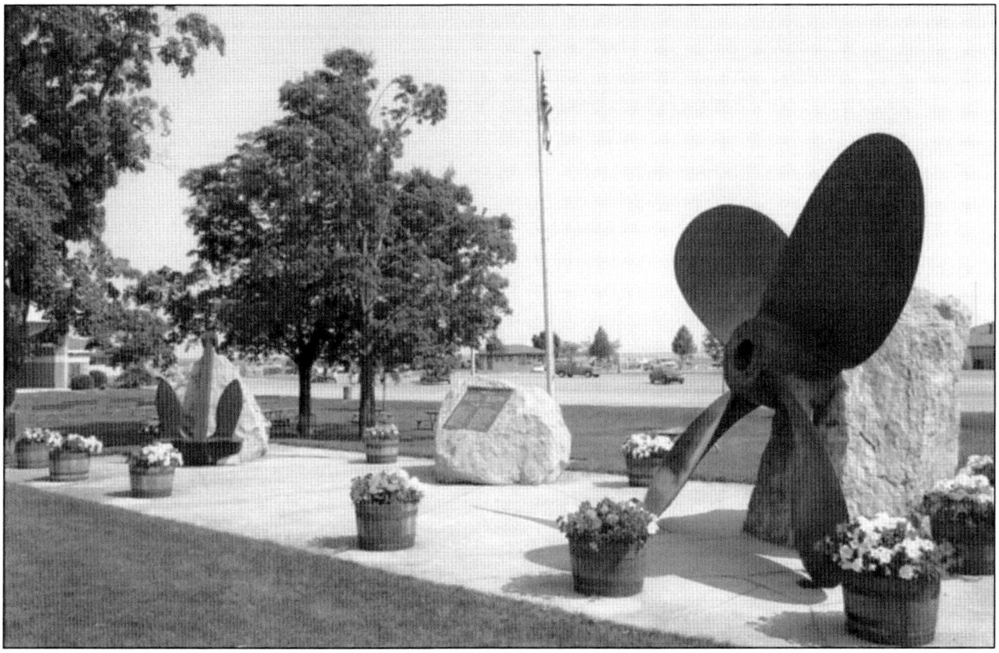

Those lost on the *Carl D. Bradley* and the *Cedarville* are honored at the Sailors' Memorial in Lakeside Park in Rogers City. Each year's Nautical City Festival in Rogers City begins with a remembrance ceremony at the memorial.

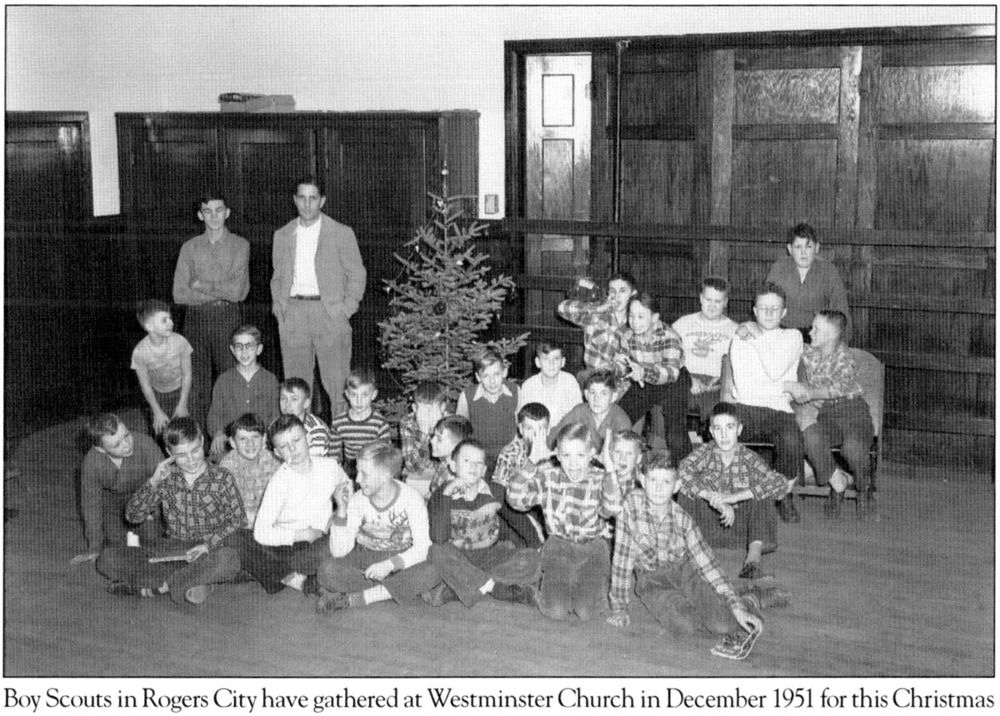

Boy Scouts in Rogers City have gathered at Westminster Church in December 1951 for this Christmas party. The Scout program was very popular in the period after World War II. Most of the Scout leaders were veterans of the war, and many were employed at Calcite. Calcite employees, particularly those in management, were always encouraged to be active in community organizations.

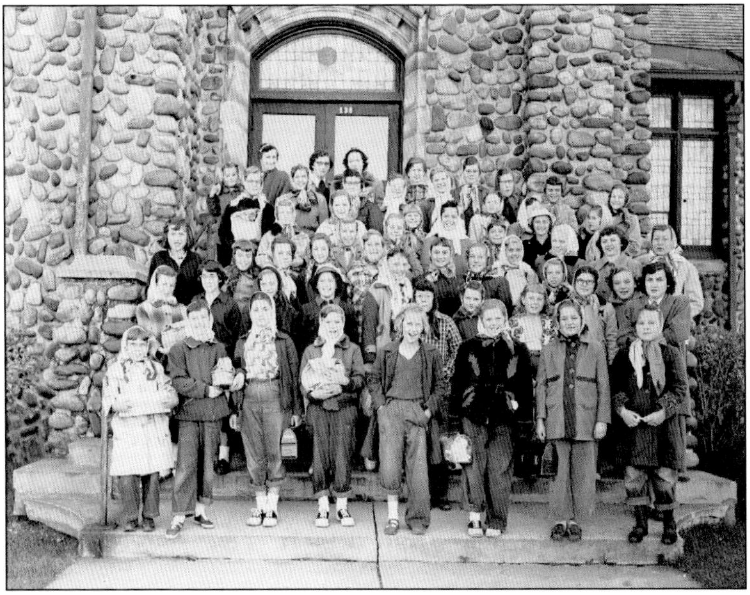

In the fall of 1951, Rogers City's Girl Scouts and their leaders posed for this photograph on the steps of Westminster Church, where they held their meetings. The Girl Scout program in Rogers City is still very dynamic, while the Scout programs for boys have floundered.

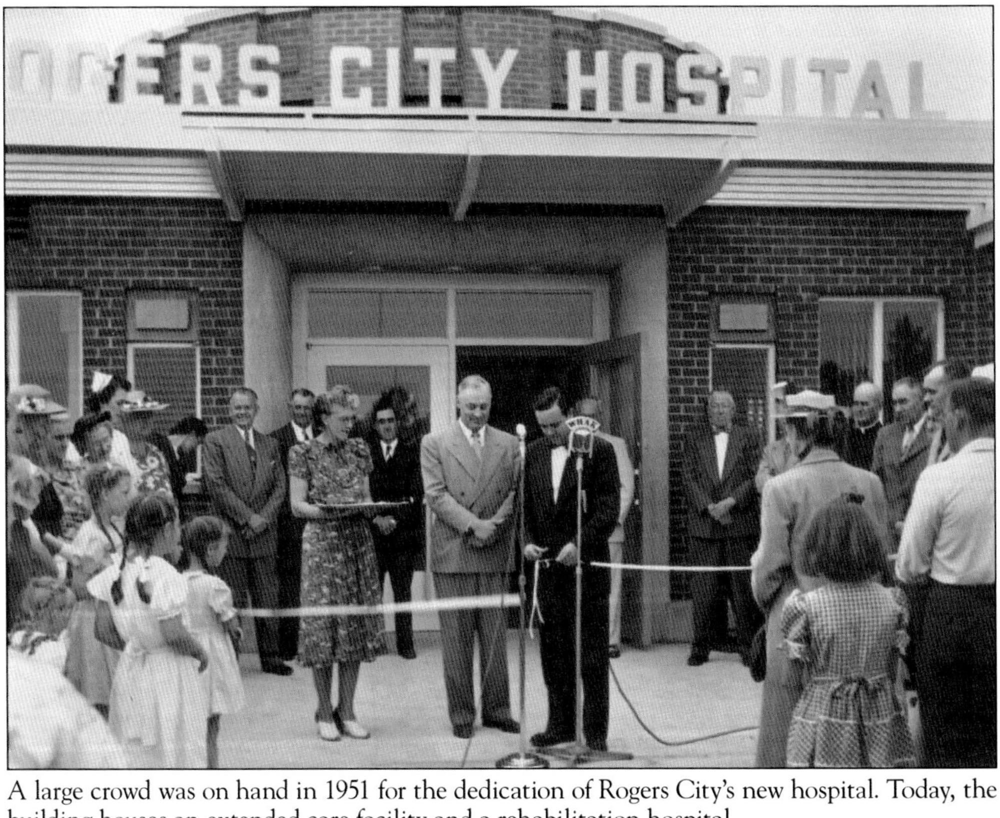

A large crowd was on hand in 1951 for the dedication of Rogers City's new hospital. Today, the building houses an extended care facility and a rehabilitation hospital.

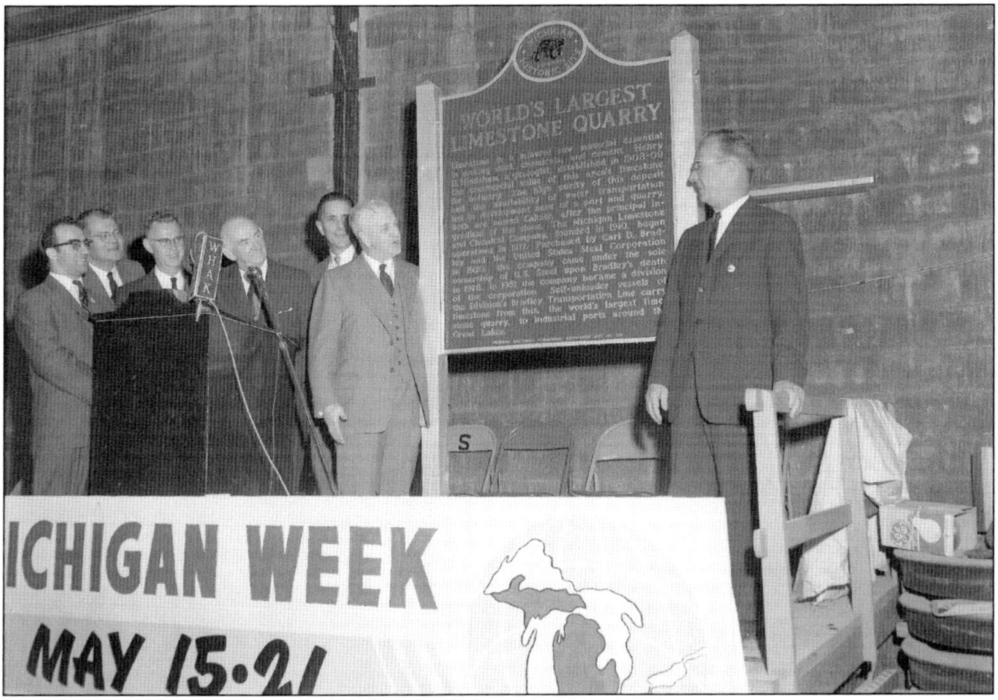

During Michigan Week in May 1960, the Historical Society of Michigan unveiled a marker honoring Calcite as the "World's Largest Limestone Quarry." Michigan Limestone and chamber of commerce officials were on hand to accept the marker, which is now located outside the main gate at Calcite.

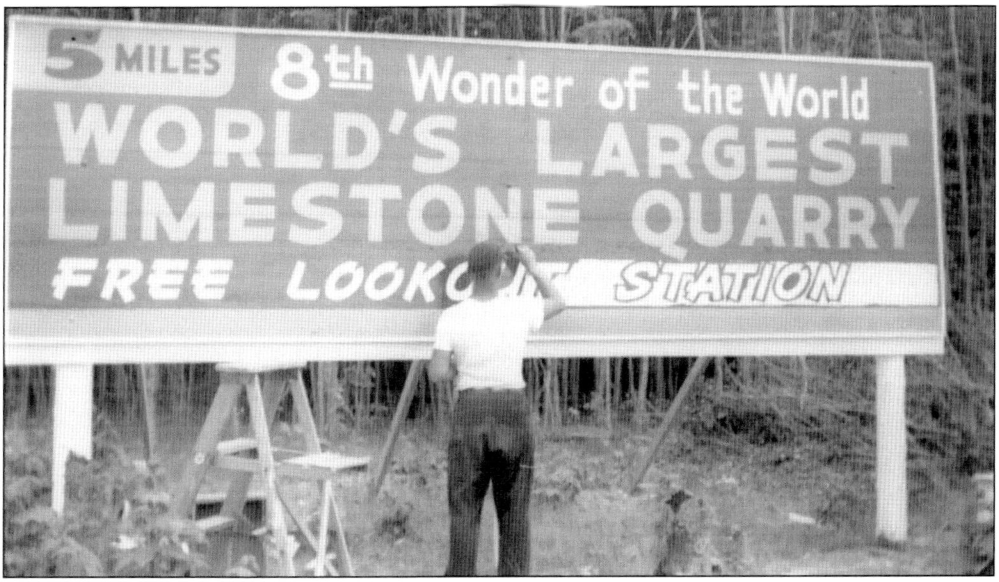

With tourism growing in northeastern Michigan, the chamber of commerce used the Calcite quarry in its marketing program to encourage people to visit Rogers City. Sign painter Roger Parsons is seen here in the 1950s painting one of the billboards that marked the north and south approaches to the community. It not only touted the quarry as the world's largest but also as the "eighth wonder of the world."

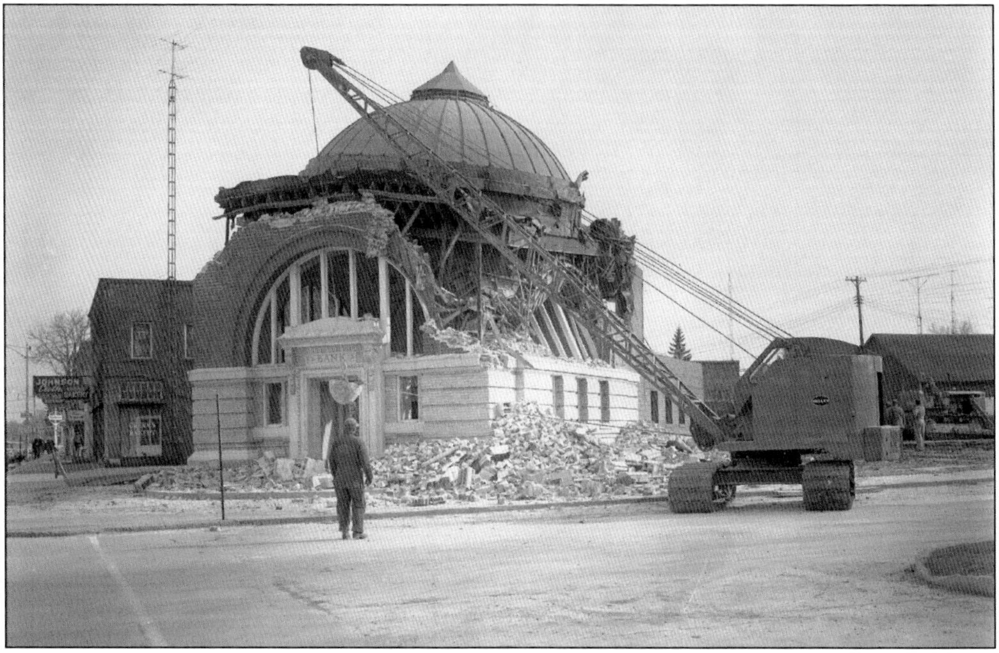

On June 24, 1964, workers began demolishing the domed Presque Isle County Savings Bank to make way for construction of a modern bank building. No structure is missed more by local residents than the stately bank building, which had graced Rogers City's main street for more than 50 years. (Courtesy of John Bunton.)

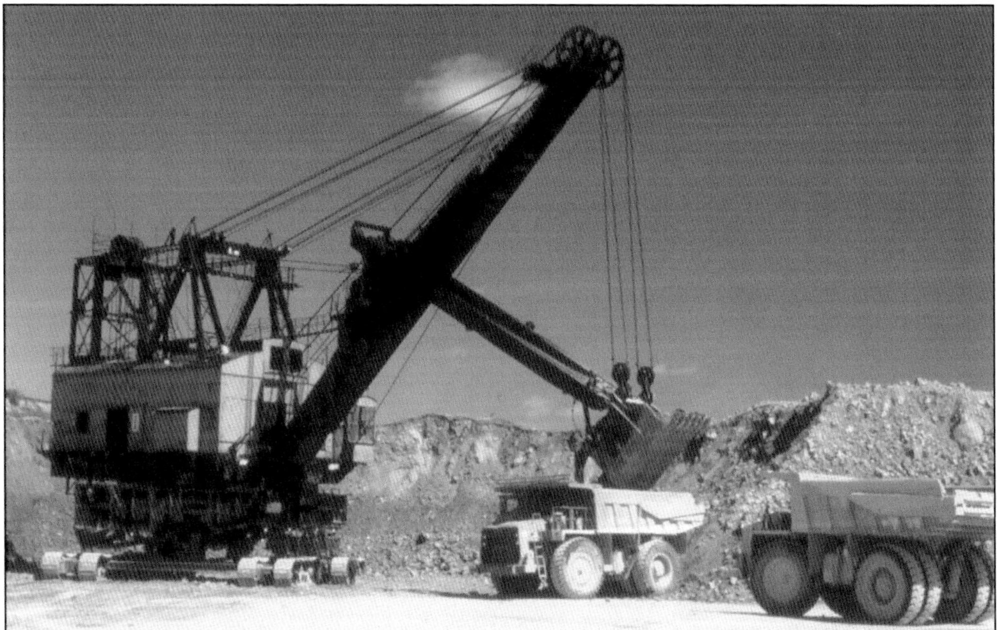

Beginning with the 1984 season, Calcite began using trucks to haul stone from the quarry to the crusher. Also, the railroad system that had been in place since Calcite began operations was shut down and removed. Initially, the trucks were loaded by shovels, as seen here, and were capable of hauling 85 tons per load.

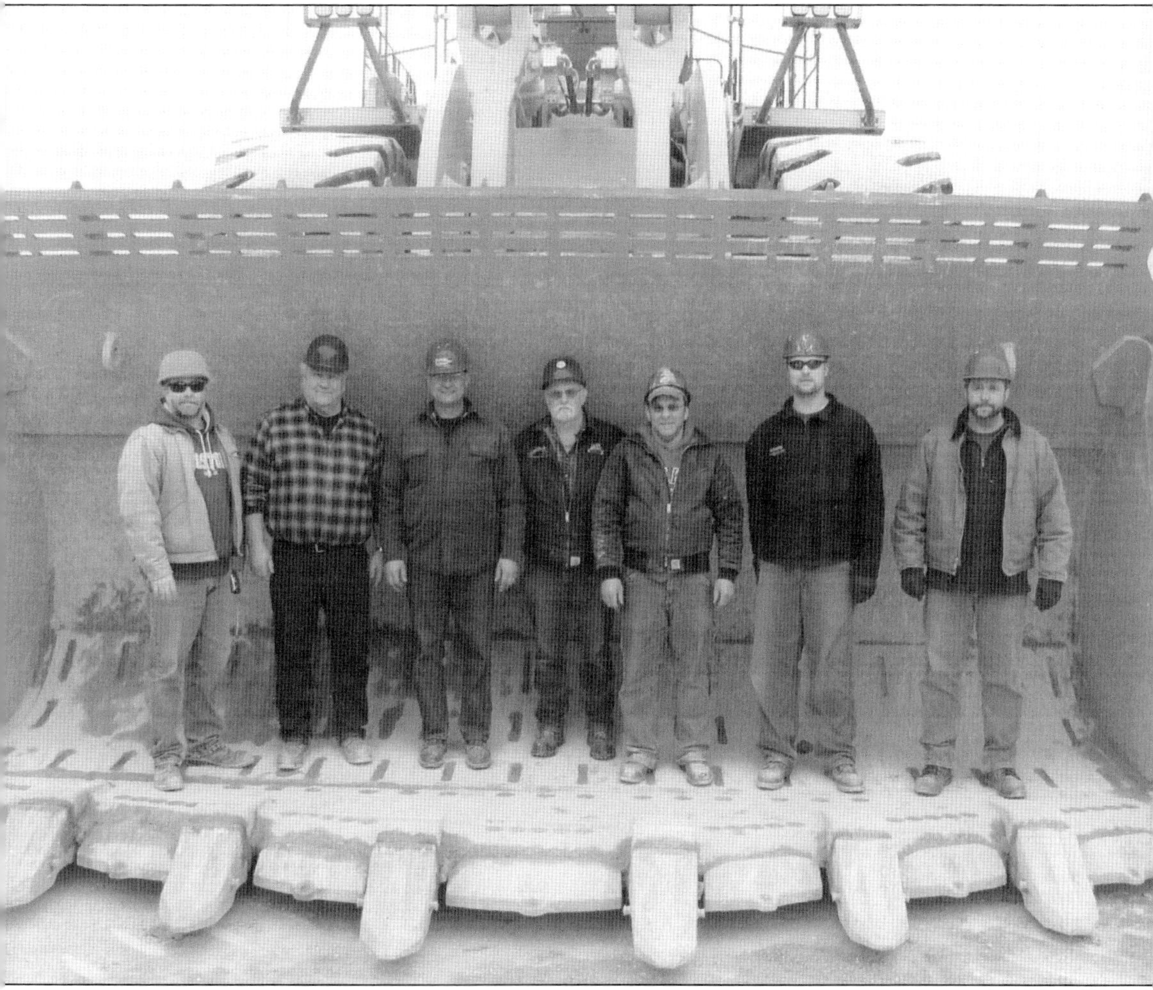

This 2007 photograph shows the operators of the Cat 994 loaders standing in the spacious 25-cubic-yard bucket of one of their machines. Each of the loaders services three of the big haul trucks.

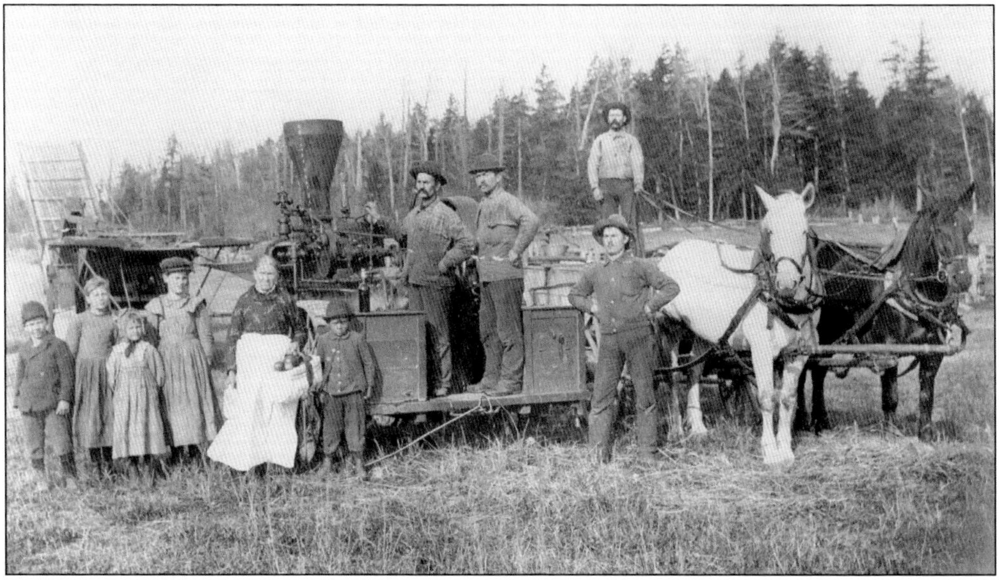

The farming community in Moltke Township lies five miles west of Rogers City, making it essentially an inland suburb. The area was settled in the 1870s, primarily by German immigrants. This photograph shows the crew of the Moltke Threshing Company and some family members in a wheat field during the harvest. They would go from farm to farm with their early steam tractor and threshing machine.

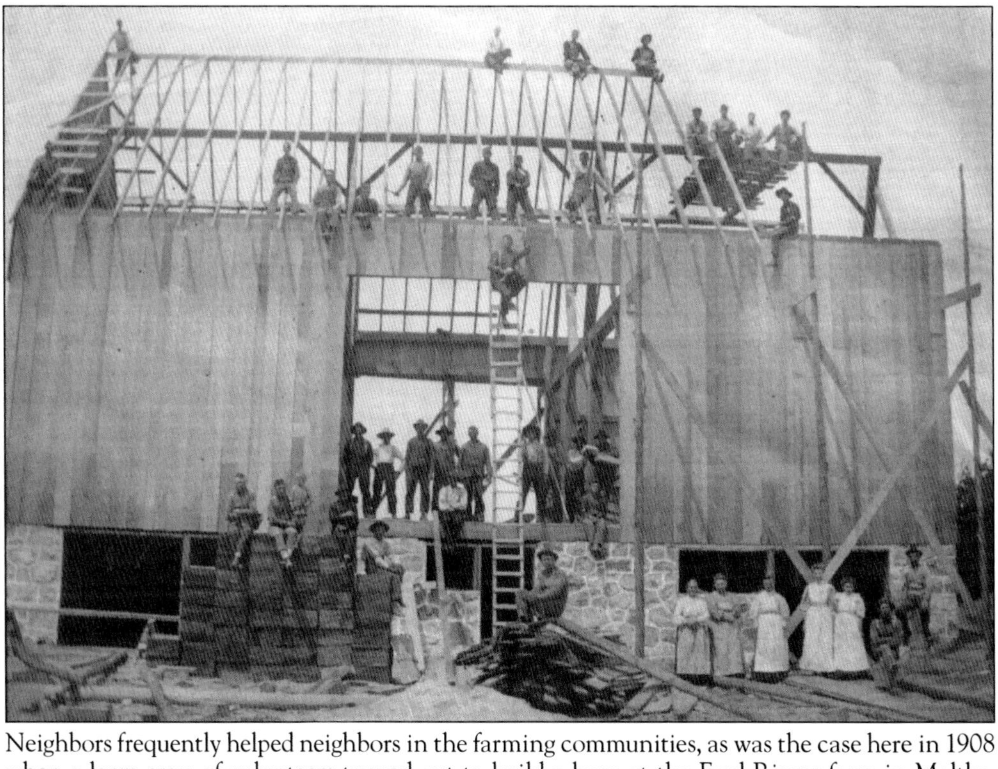

Neighbors frequently helped neighbors in the farming communities, as was the case here in 1908 when a large crew of volunteers turned out to build a barn at the Fred Rieger farm in Moltke. The spacious barn is still in use today.

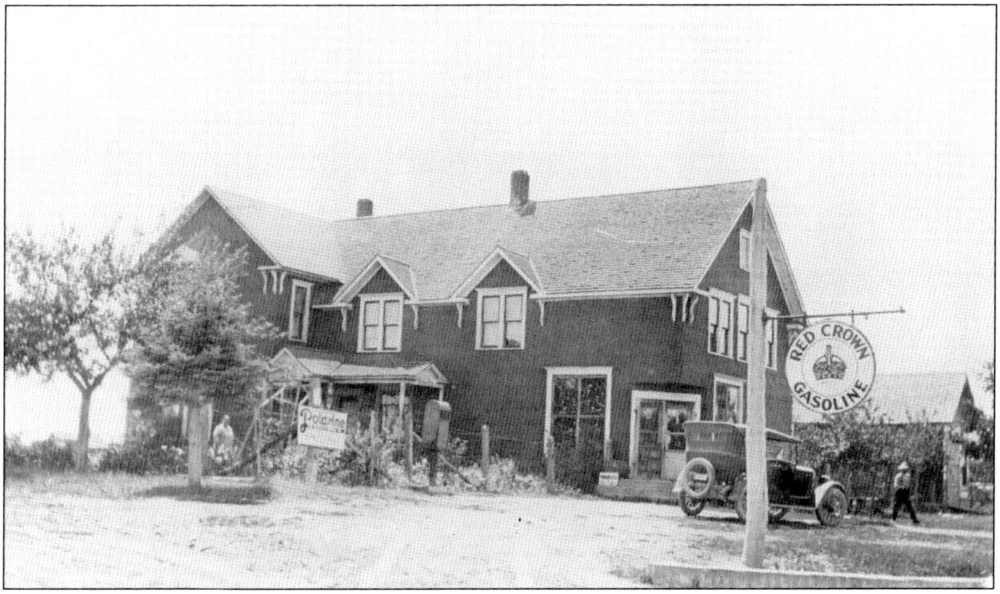

The Tulgetske store, at the main junction in Moltke Township, was one of three small general stores that served the community. All of the stores have since closed, and residents do their shopping in Rogers City or in one of the other neighboring communities. Small general stores are rapidly disappearing from farming communities, as people prefer to shop at bigger stores in the surrounding area. This photograph was taken around 1930.

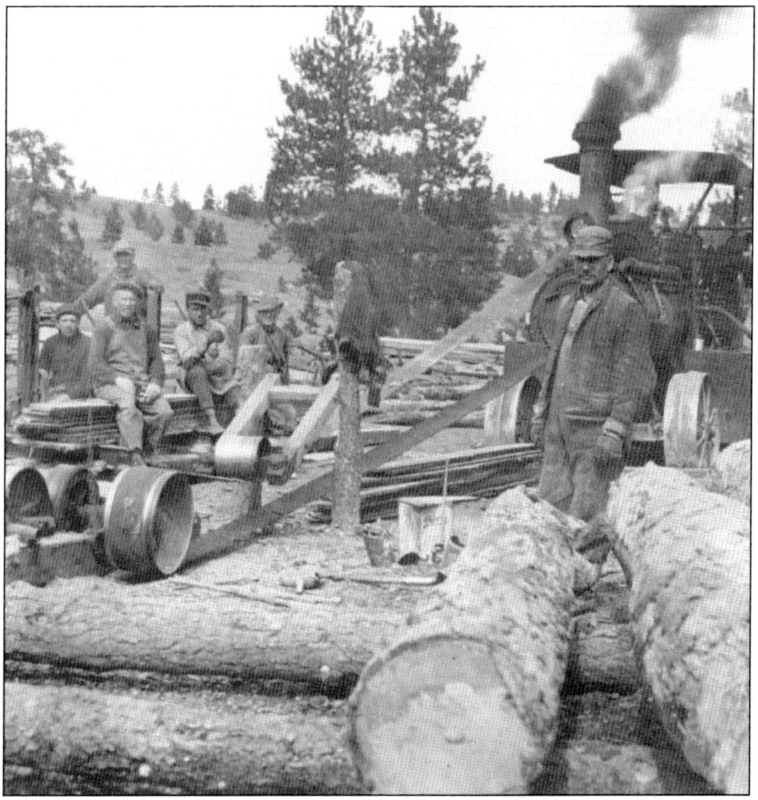

While the lumber boom ended in Presque Isle County in the early 1900s, lumbering continued to be an important business. When the big sawmills closed down, operators of portable mills, like Albert Tulgetske (right foreground), moved from farm to farm to saw logs into lumber.

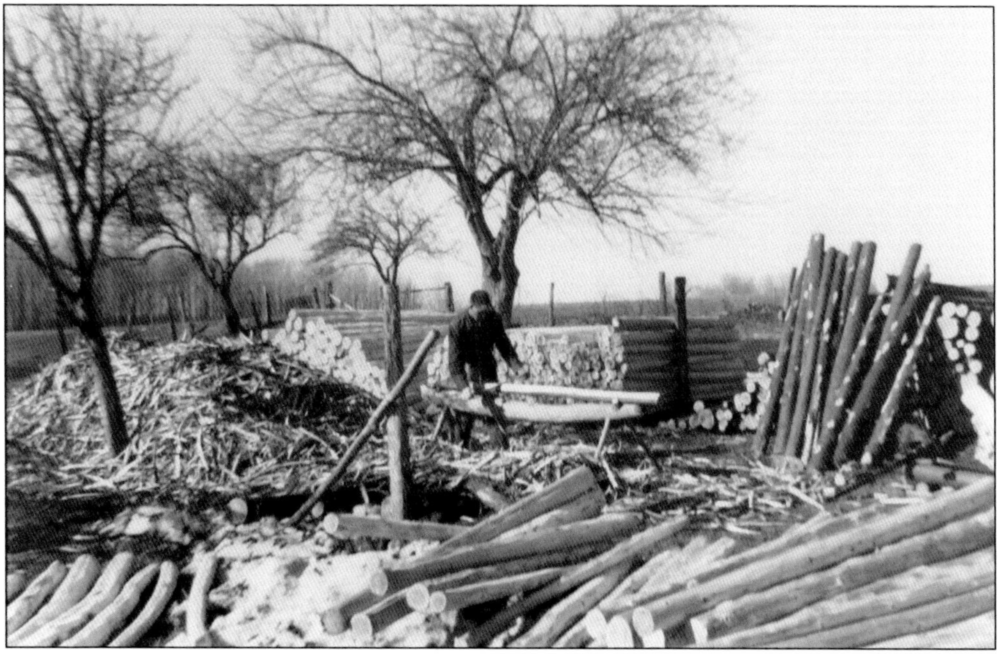

Farmers in the area have traditionally worked in the woods in the wintertime to earn extra money, primarily cutting pulpwood, cedar boughs, or cedar posts. In this 1959 photograph, Moltke farmer Jack Sorgenfrei peels cedar posts to be sold as fence posts.

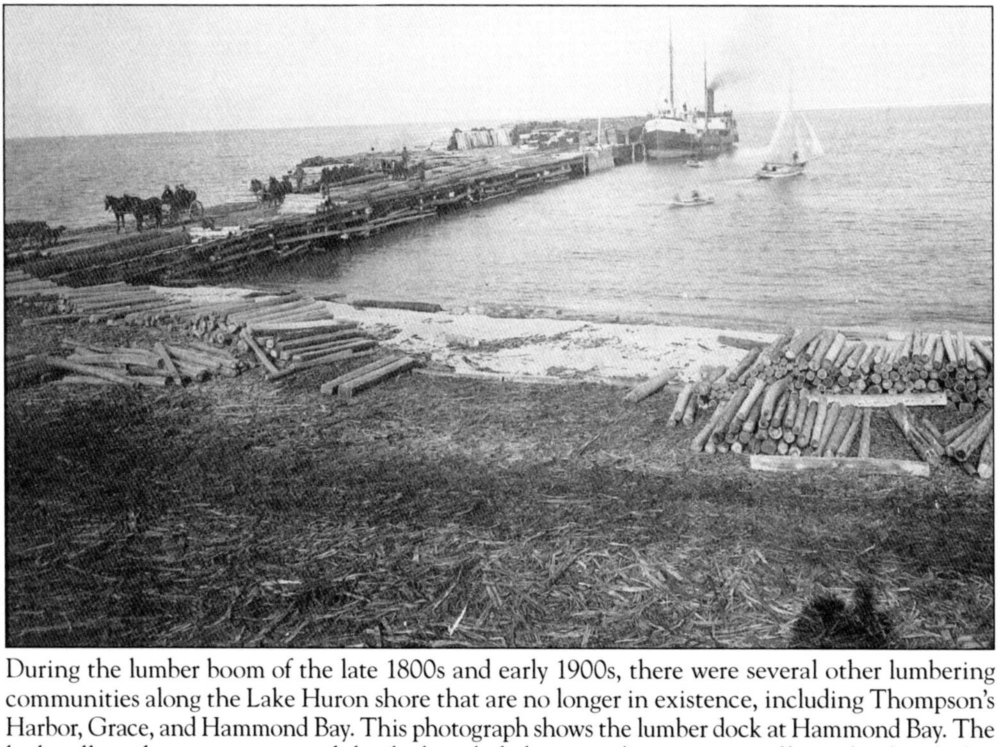

During the lumber boom of the late 1800s and early 1900s, there were several other lumbering communities along the Lake Huron shore that are no longer in existence, including Thompson's Harbor, Grace, and Hammond Bay. This photograph shows the lumber dock at Hammond Bay. The little village that grew up around the dock included a general store, a post office, a lumber dealer, a sawmill, two hotels, an icehouse, a drugstore, a felt factory, a blacksmith, and a shingle mill.

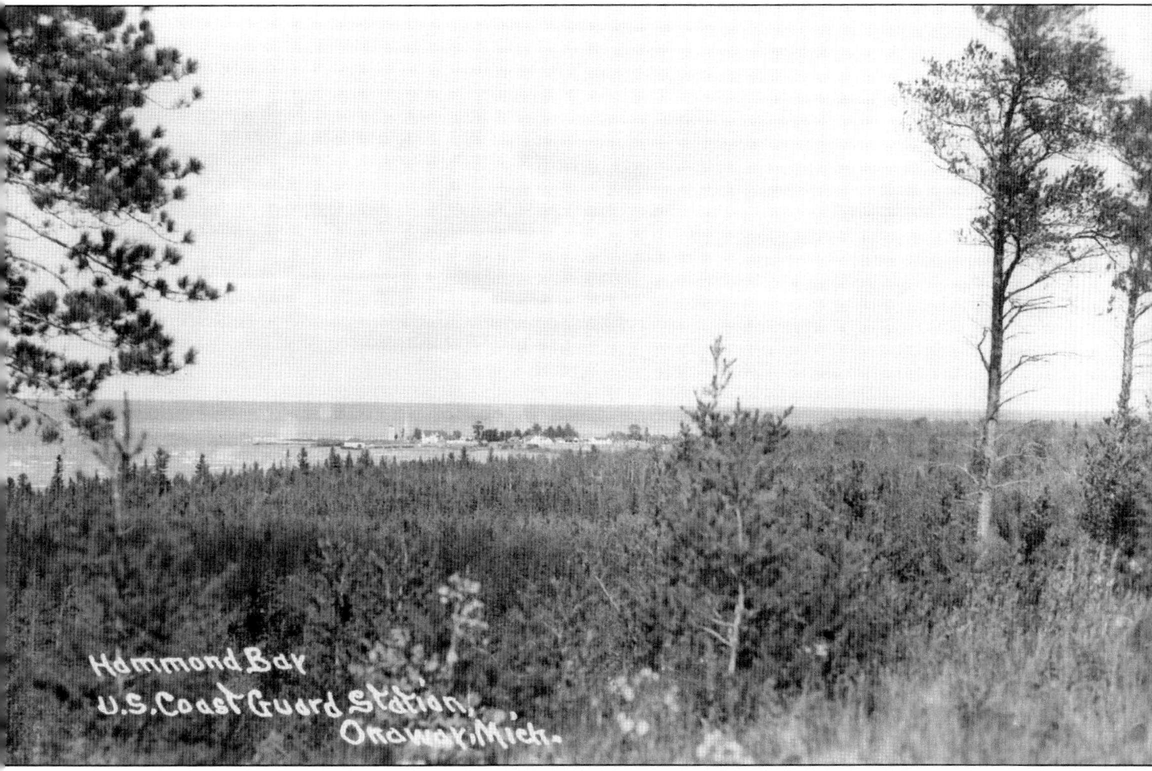

The US Life Saving Service, a predecessor to today's Coast Guard, also operated a station on the south arm of Hammond Bay, assisting vessels in trouble on Lake Huron. This 1950s postcard view of the station was taken from nearby Route 23.

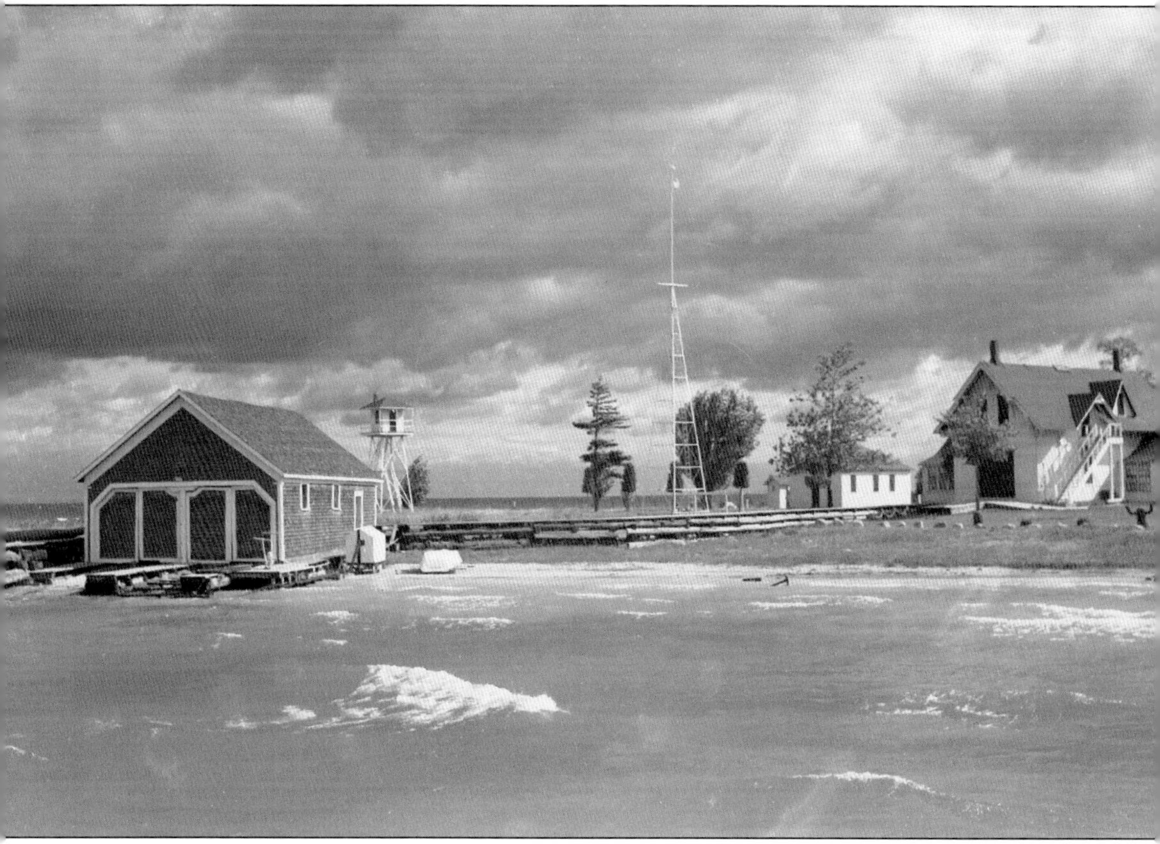

Storm clouds and white-capped waves add to this dramatic close-up view of the lifesaving station at Hammond Bay in the 1940s. On the left is the station's boathouse, where the surfboats personnel used for rescues were stored. Behind the boathouse is a watchtower that was manned by a lookout at night, who searched for signs of ships in trouble on the lake. Crew members assigned to the station spent much of their time practicing with their boats, breeches buoys, and other equipment available to them for use in rescues. Built in 1876 at the peak of the maritime industry on the Great Lakes, the station was decommissioned in 1947. The facility was later taken over by the US Fish and Wildlife Service and used as a research station, with the mission to find a way to combat lamprey eels. The eels, not native to the Great Lakes, were apparently brought to the Great Lakes in the ballast tanks of ships entering from the Atlantic Ocean. By the 1950s, the predatory eels were devastating fish populations in the lakes, which were already suffering from overfishing. Using chemicals developed at the Hammond Bay station, the US Fish and Wildlife Service has been able to control lamprey populations.

Three

WHISTLE STOPS

The settlements along the Lake Huron shore developed there because access to the Great Lakes made it possible to ship things in and out, which was particularly important in the days before the railroad and road systems were developed. While there are reports of a few settlers who arrived in Presque Isle County after hiking north from the Saginaw Valley or Detroit, the vast majority took the easier route: booking passage on one of the steamers that regularly ran up the Michigan shore from Bay City, Saginaw, and Detroit.

The early settlers were almost totally dependent upon passenger and freight steamers to provide them with most of the necessities of life. They brought in most of the groceries and merchandise sold in the local stores, as well as building materials, items people ordered from catalogs, and even livestock and machinery destined for area farms.

At the same time, the economy of the region was initially based almost totally on the timber industry, and the Great Lakes provided the only feasible way to get logs, cut lumber, and other wood products to markets around the region. Even after rail service became available, shipping by water was more economical, giving timber operators in communities along the shore a decided advantage in the marketplace. As the local supplies of merchantable forests were exhausted, mills along the shore were able to survive by importing logs from other areas, particularly from Ontario, Canada, across Lake Huron. Steam-powered tugs and small freighters towed massive rafts of logs across the Great Lakes to meet the needs of the mills, an option that inland communities did not have.

Most of the inland communities have their roots in some individual's family tree, meaning that one person settled in an area of dispersed farms and logging operations and opened a business. It might have been a hotel or an inn, but most often it was a general store. That business then became a magnet that eventually attracted a church, a school, a tavern, a blacksmith shop, and maybe even a post office—the essential components of most early rural communities.

While most of the settlements in the interior regions of Presque Isle County developed along those lines, most did not prosper until they were served by an efficient transportation system. In the case of Presque Isle County and most other counties in northeastern Michigan, that transportation system was the Detroit & Mackinac Railway (D&M).

The railroad lines extended as far north as Alpena in 1886, primarily to serve the lumbering interests of the Thunder Bay region. It was not until 1897 that the rails were extended as far as the village of Posen in southern Presque Isle County. The following year, the line was pushed to Metz and Hawks—named for J.D. Hawks, the vice president and general manager of D&M—and

on to Millersburg, Onaway, and Cheboygan in the western hinterlands of the county. With the coming of the steel rails, these fledgling communities prospered and grew in a way that would have been impossible without an efficient transportation system.

While the extension of the railroad into northeastern Michigan had primarily been based on the needs of the timber industry, it also proved to be invaluable to retailers, hotel owners, and farmers. The D&M also heavily promoted the tourist attractions of northeast Michigan, and people began coming north to experience the rugged frontier and enjoy the beautiful scenery.

Unfortunately, the timber boom in Presque Isle County, like most booms, was short lived, and the presence of the railroad could not significantly moderate the impact of the boom's end. By 1930, most of the little communities along the railroad lines had slipped into a downhill slide that largely continues today.

Some of the lumber towns simply disappeared. The villages of Thompson's Harbor, Providence, Hammond Bay, and Grace are merely designations on old maps, and the rubble of their old foundations are now being crowded out by the second-generation forests and vacation cottages. The demise of Providence, once home to 200 people and three sawmills, might have been forestalled, at least temporarily, if it had not been in the path of a forest fire in 1911. Metz, too, was crippled by the great fire of 1908, which totally destroyed the prosperous little village, as well as the local timber industry that was the backbone of its economy.

It was fire, too, that brought an end to the prosperity of Onaway. When the calendars rolled over to January 1926, it was the largest community in the county, with a population of almost 3,000 residents. The city did not burn, as had been the case with Providence and Metz; instead, a single business burned, and with it the prosperity of the community was destroyed. That business, the Lobdell-Emery mill and its American Wood Rim manufacturing plant—the largest employer in the county—burned to the ground in January 1926. If it had not been for the railroad, the plant might have been rebuilt, but the presence of the railroad made it possible for the wood needed for its manufacturing operations to be shipped to other locations that were more appealing to the company's owners. Within days of the Lobdell-Emery fire, the company left, and businesses on Onaway's busy main street began to board up their windows. In July 1958, another major Onaway business, the Onaway garment factory, also fell victim to fire. After it burned to the ground, the owner opted not to rebuild.

The former lumbering villages of Posen, Metz, Hawks, and Millersburg still exist today—but barely. Their commercial districts are only shadows of what they once were, with many buildings having been demolished or standing empty. None of the towns even has a grocery store anymore. They either already are, or are in the process of becoming, bedroom communities: residents sleep there, but they work and shop elsewhere.

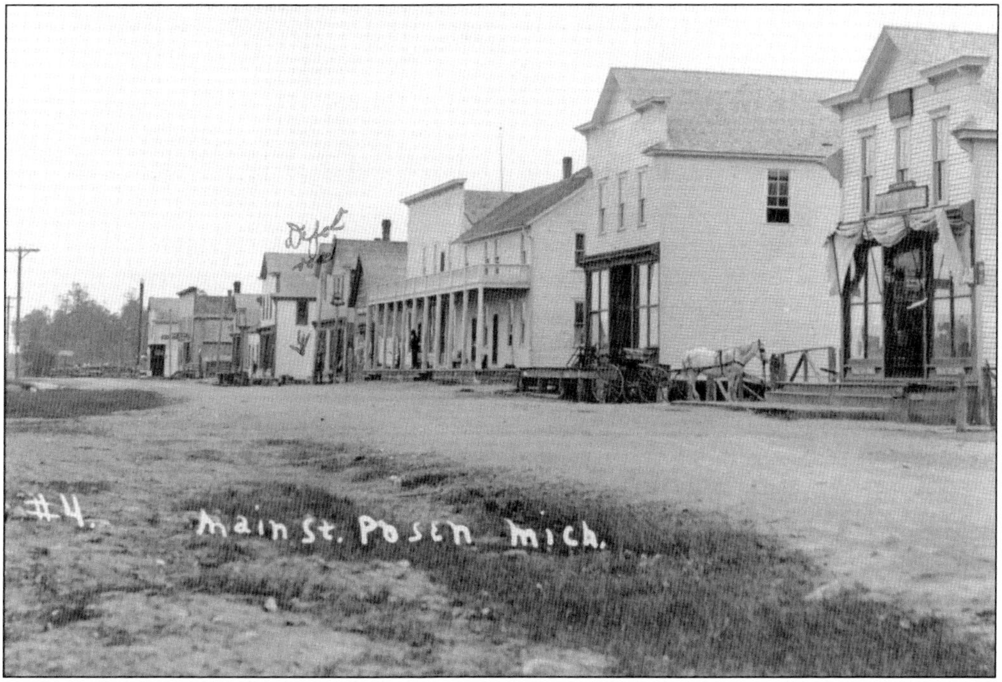

Posen was a busy little farming and lumbering community straddling the D&M tracks when this photograph was taken in 1907. First settled in 1870, the railroad reached it in 1897, but there was no depot until 1907. A post office opened in the village in 1875. Most of the settlers in the Posen area were Polish immigrants, and most of today's residents are still of Polish heritage.

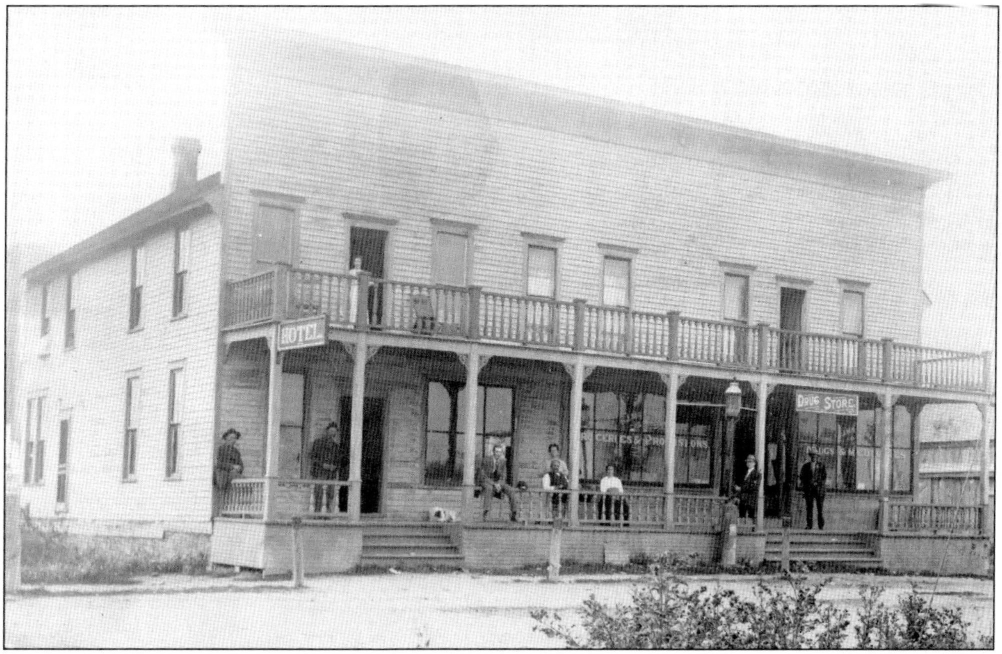

In 1907, one of the busiest businesses in Posen was the hotel that catered to people arriving and departing by train. The lower level of the hotel also included a drugstore and a grocery store.

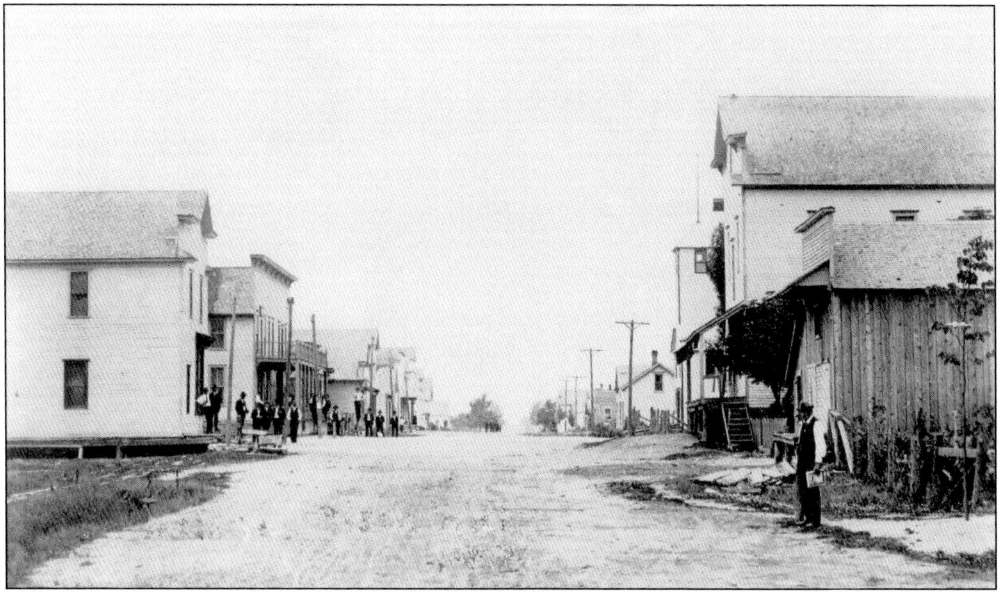

The main street in Posen, now Highway M-65, was even busier in 1914 than it had been in 1907. Based on the dress of the men standing around in the streets, this photograph was probably taken on a Sunday.

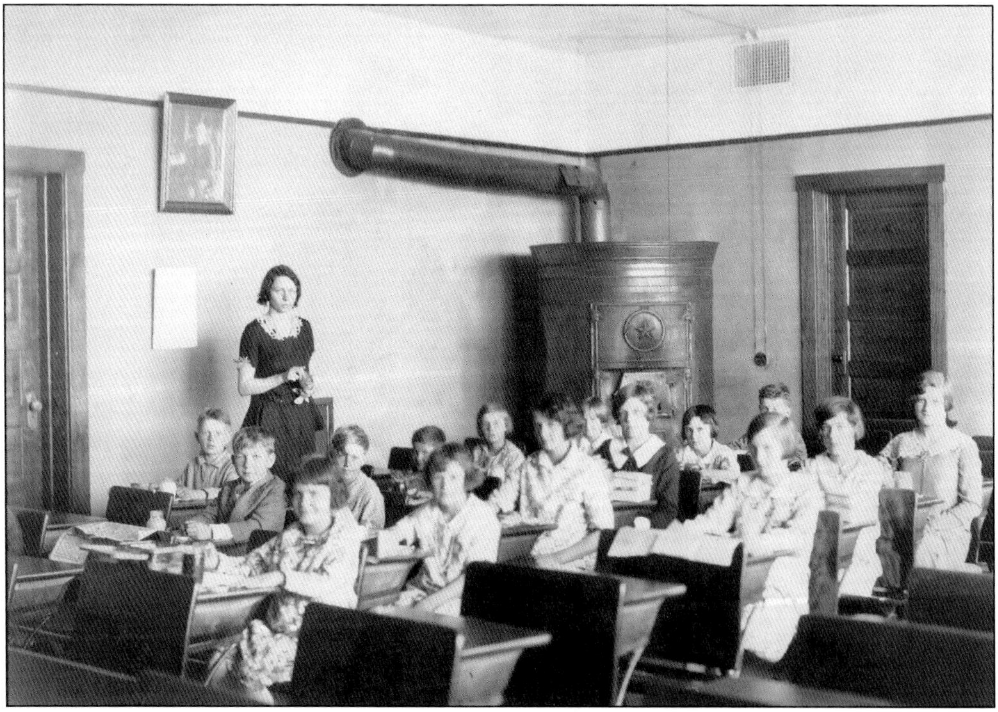

Young Winifred Smilie taught at a one-room schoolhouse in the Posen area in 1930, when this photograph was taken. A high school graduate who attended teacher's training at County Normal, she was responsible for teaching all the students in grades one through eight. She also had to maintain the giant woodstove in the corner that heated the classroom and do much of the cleaning. The photograph on the wall is of Pres. Franklin D. Roosevelt.

Early on, agriculture supplanted lumbering as the mainstay of the economy in the Posen area, which was known primarily as a center for potato production. Each year in the first week of September, the community still celebrates the potato harvest with the Potato Festival, one of the highlights of which is a grand parade. It draws thousands of people to the small community, including many former residents who come back annually for the festival.

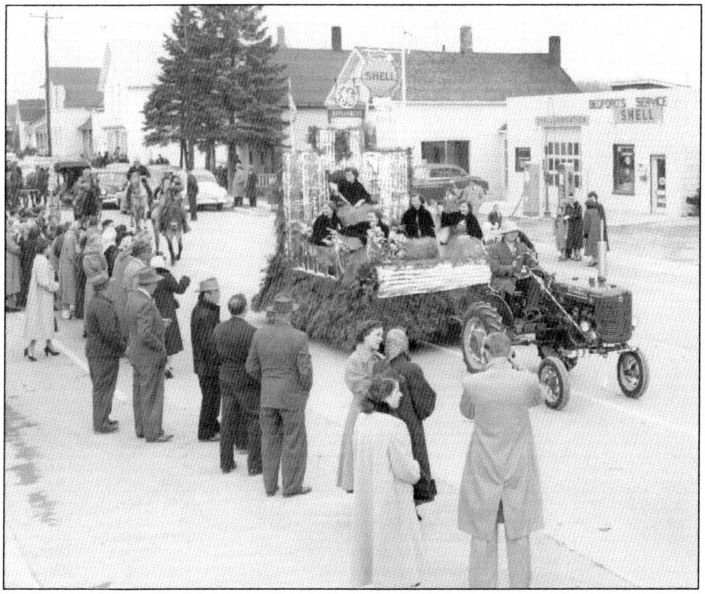

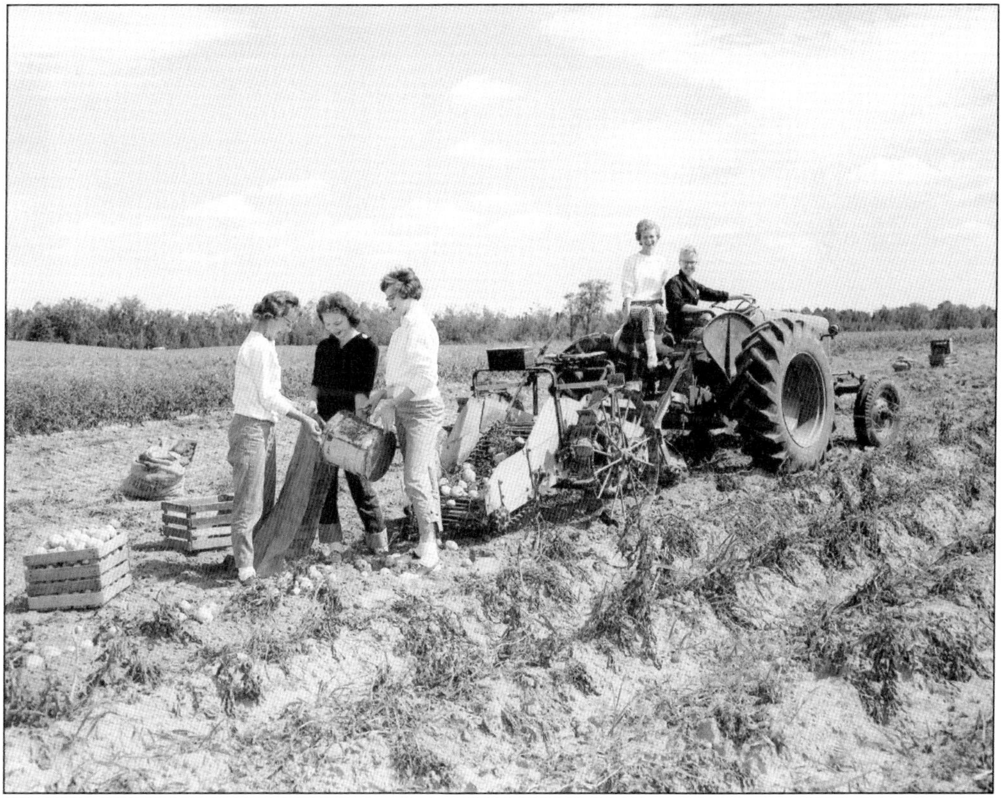

These five candidates for Posen potato queen posed for this promotional photograph in August 1958. From left to right, they are Mayvine Orban, Eileen Molski, Katherine Glomski, Shirley Krajniak, and Elona Kowalski. Back then, potatoes were picked by hand. Today, the process is much more automated. (Courtesy of the Ferris Parsons collection.)

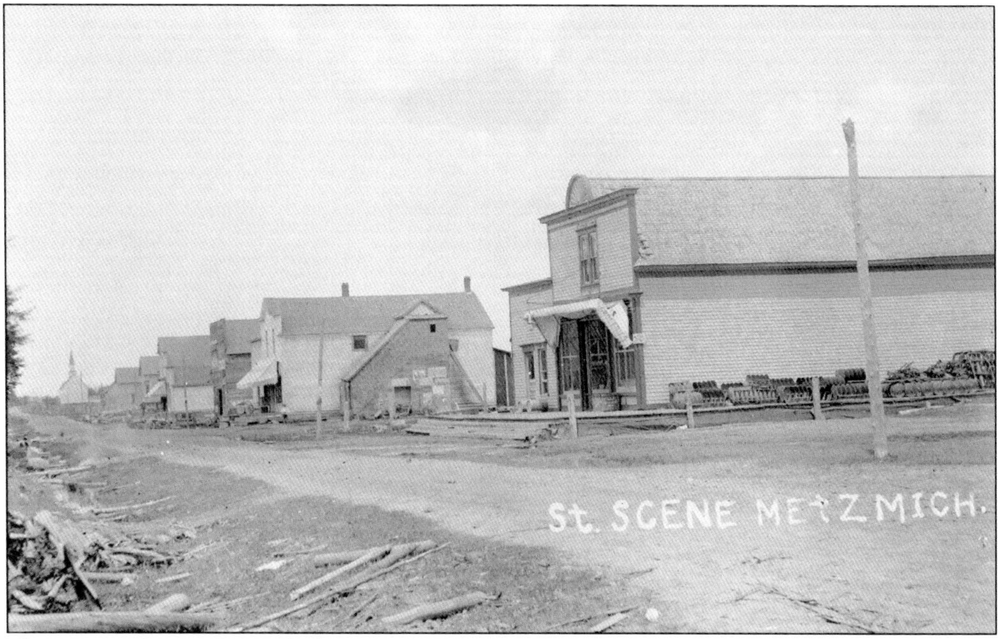

This postcard view shows the business community of Metz shortly before October 15, 1908, the date of the infamous Metz fire, the third-worst forest fire in Michigan's history. The blaze started that morning about 30 miles away in the Millersburg area and, driven by high winds, burned all the way to the Lake Huron shoreline by evening.

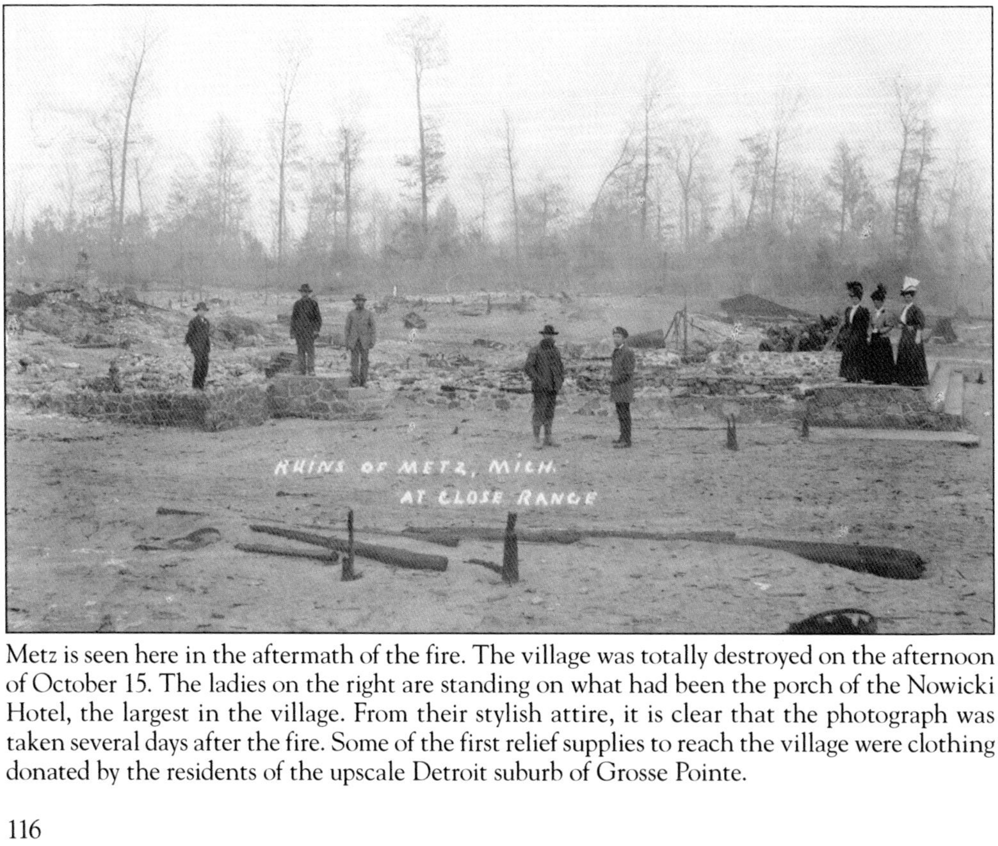

Metz is seen here in the aftermath of the fire. The village was totally destroyed on the afternoon of October 15. The ladies on the right are standing on what had been the porch of the Nowicki Hotel, the largest in the village. From their stylish attire, it is clear that the photograph was taken several days after the fire. Some of the first relief supplies to reach the village were clothing donated by the residents of the upscale Detroit suburb of Grosse Pointe.

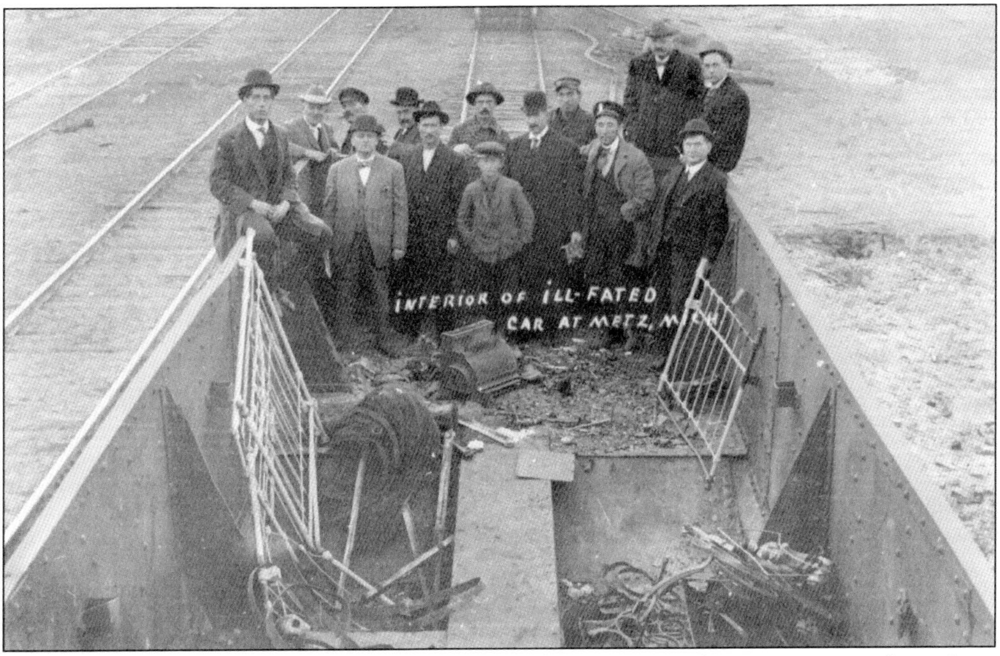

A "relief train" from the Detroit & Mackinac Railway attempted to evacuate residents from Metz, but it derailed amidst a blazing inferno just a short distance east of the village. A total of 16 people died in the fire, including three women, each with three children, who had been in this gondola car.

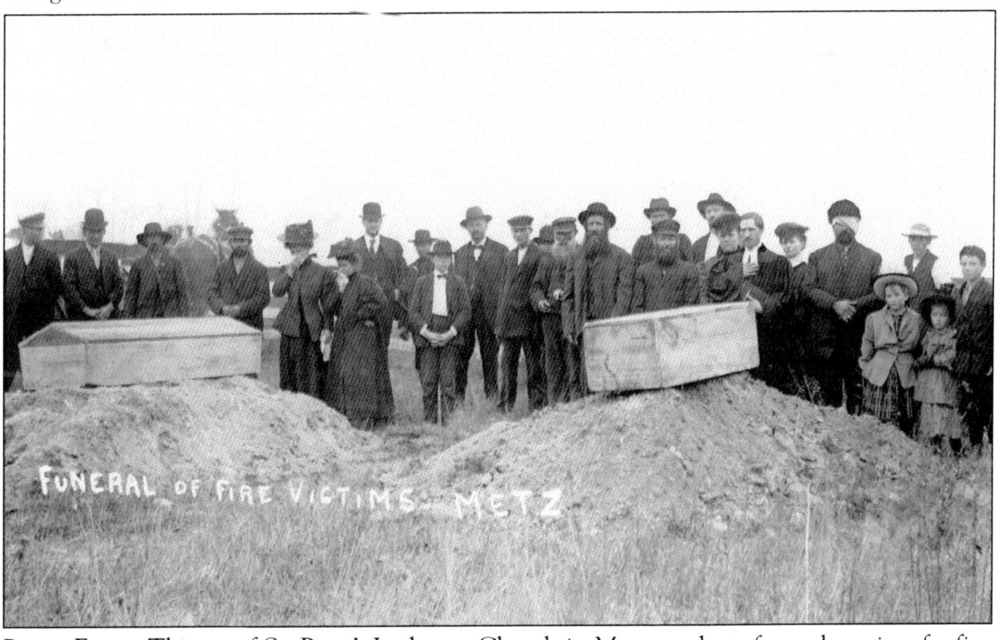

Pastor Ernest Thieme of St. Peter's Lutheran Church in Metz conducts funeral services for five members of his parish who died in the Metz fire. The casket on the left contained the remains of 18-year-old Robert Wagner. On the right is the small casket containing the ashes of Emma Hardies and her three young children, who were incinerated in the gondola car. Her husband and three surviving children are standing to the right of Pastor Thieme.

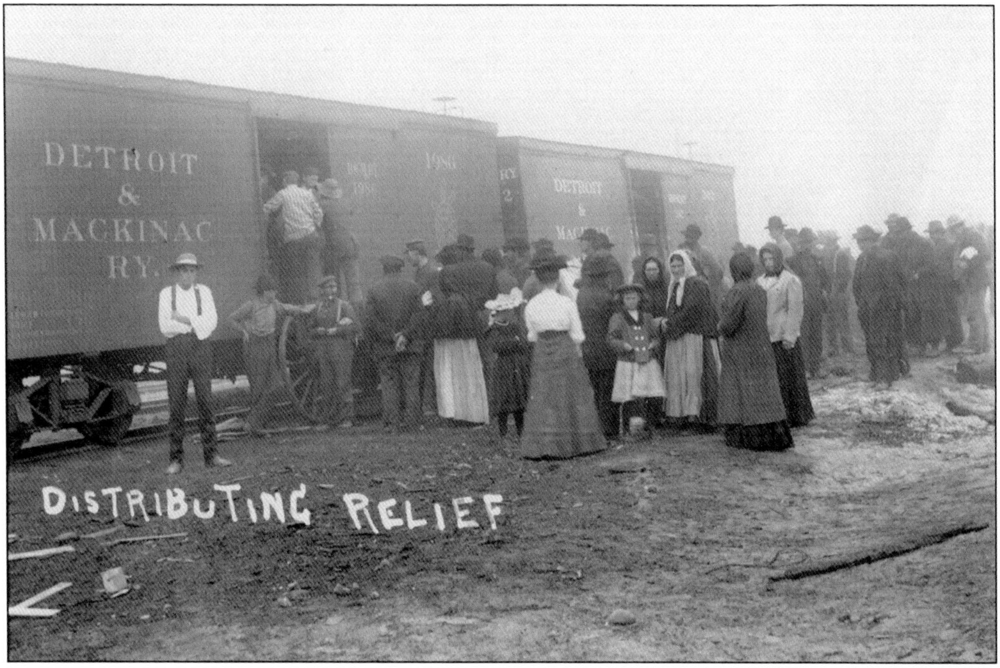

Metz residents, most of them in donated clothing, lined up for a distribution of relief supplies in the aftermath of the fire. In the Metz area, 84 of the 110 families were homeless as a result of the fire. A total of 37 people died in the conflagration, which burned between 200,000 and 300,000 acres.

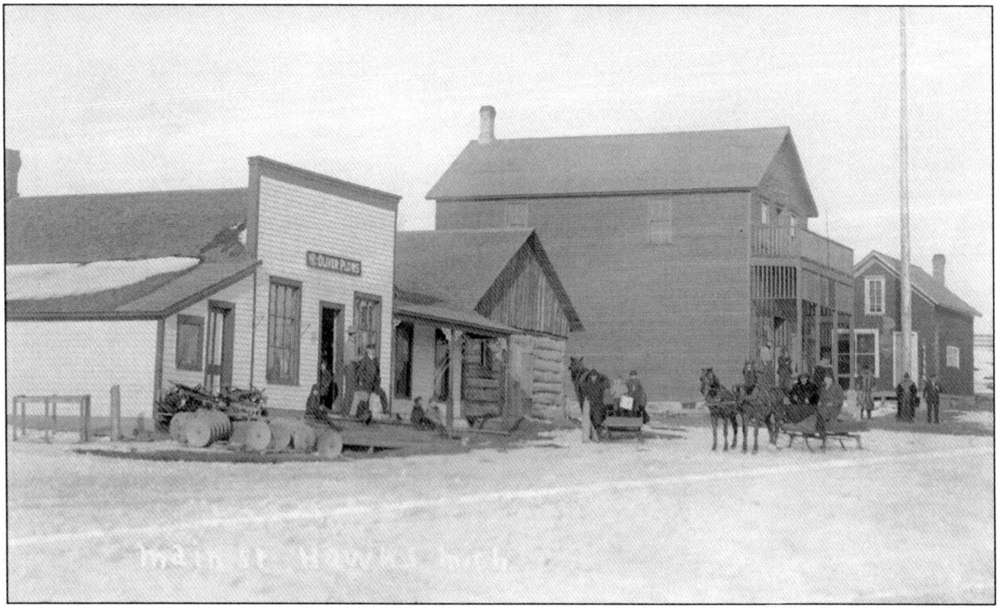

Originally called LaRoque after early resident Donald LaRoque, the name of this village was later changed to Hawks in honor of J.D. Hawks, the vice president and general manager of the Detroit & Mackinac Railway. When this photograph was taken in 1908, the commercial district of the little village included a farm implement dealership, a blacksmith shop, a general store, and a barbershop.

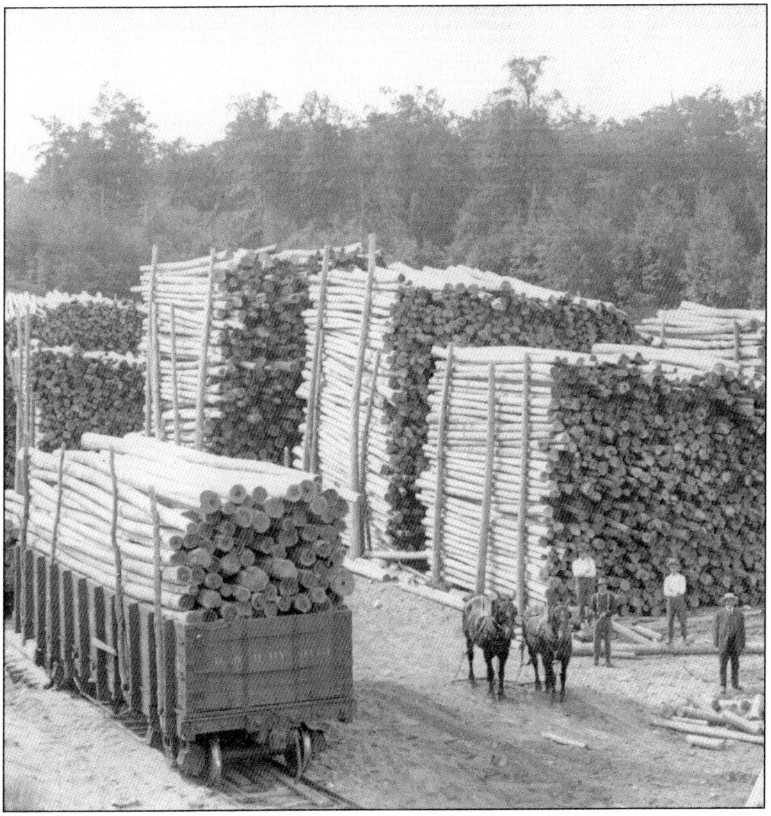

The railroad siding at Hawks seen in this 1908 photograph is full of peeled cedar logs awaiting shipment on D&M trains. Presque Isle County was one of the Midwest's major producers of cedar, which was used extensively for railroad ties, power poles, fence posts, and wooden sidewalks. Cedar is very resistant to decay when exposed to moisture.

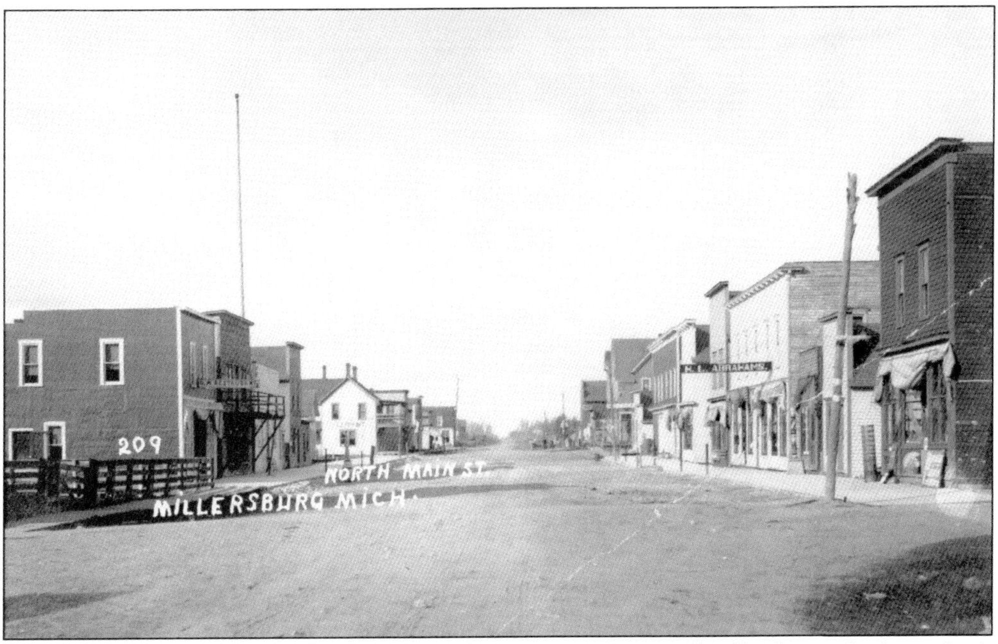

This 1911 photograph shows the two-block-long business district of Millersburg, which was built at the point where the D&M railroad tracks crossed the Ocqueoc River. Like Posen and Metz, the village straddled the railroad tracks. Today, there are only three businesses left in Millersburg.

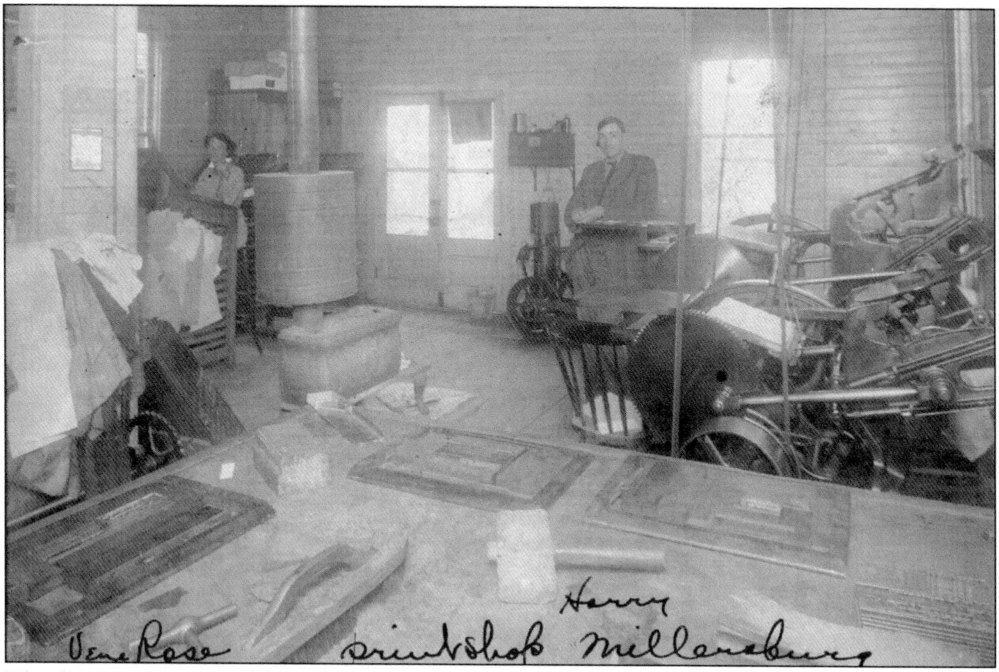

The first newspaper published in Presque Isle County, the *Presque Isle County Advance*, was printed in Millersburg. Publisher Harry Whiteley is seen here in his print shop along with his assistant Vena Rose. The Whiteleys later moved the newspaper to Rogers City, where the weekly continues to be published today.

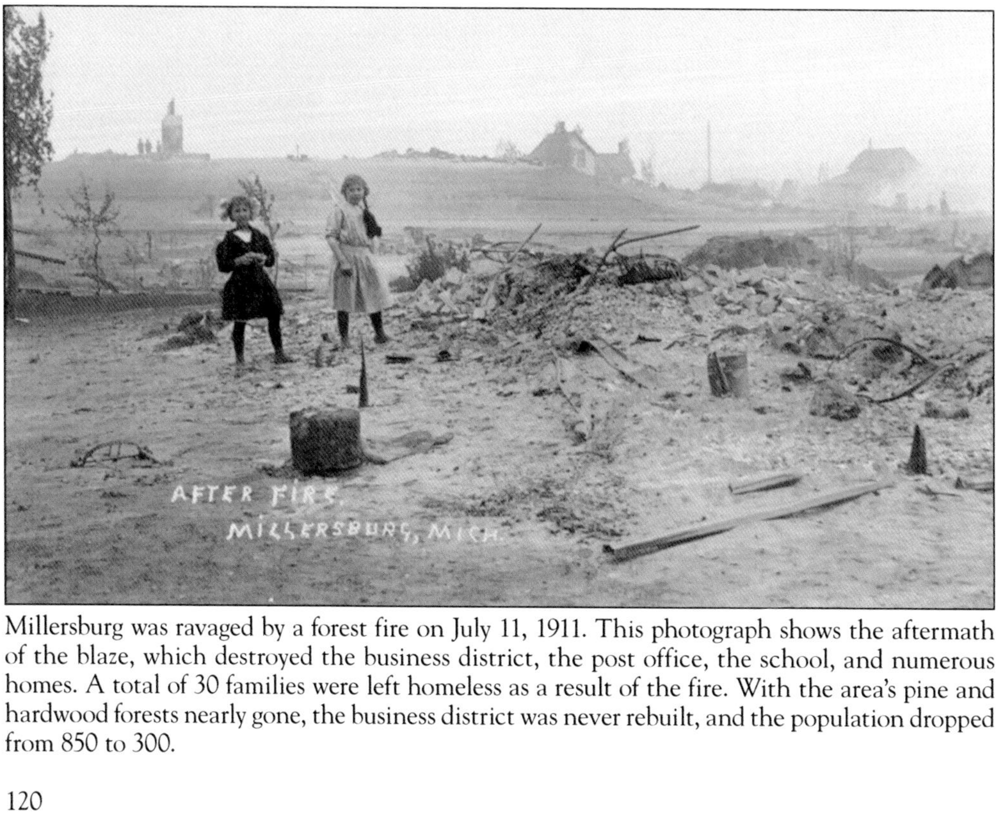

Millersburg was ravaged by a forest fire on July 11, 1911. This photograph shows the aftermath of the blaze, which destroyed the business district, the post office, the school, and numerous homes. A total of 30 families were left homeless as a result of the fire. With the area's pine and hardwood forests nearly gone, the business district was never rebuilt, and the population dropped from 850 to 300.

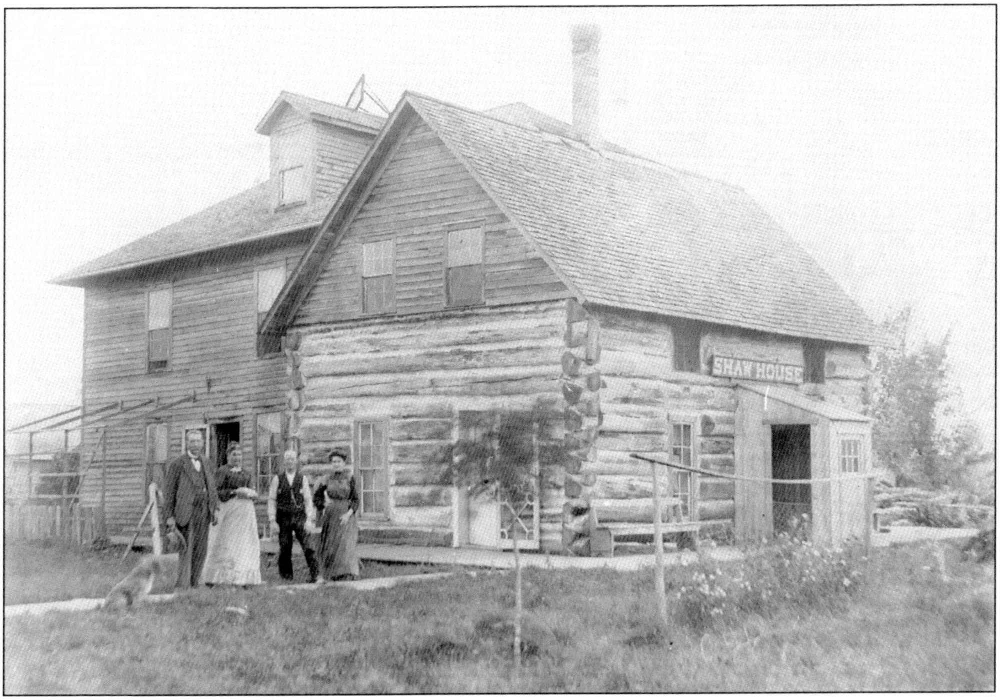

Thomas Shaw and his family stand outside their original log cabin, the first home in the Onaway area, built in 1881. Behind the log cabin is the Shaw House, the area's first hotel. Shaw, a teacher and professor who came north for health reasons, also started the first school in the Onaway area, in 1882, and was the community's first postmaster.

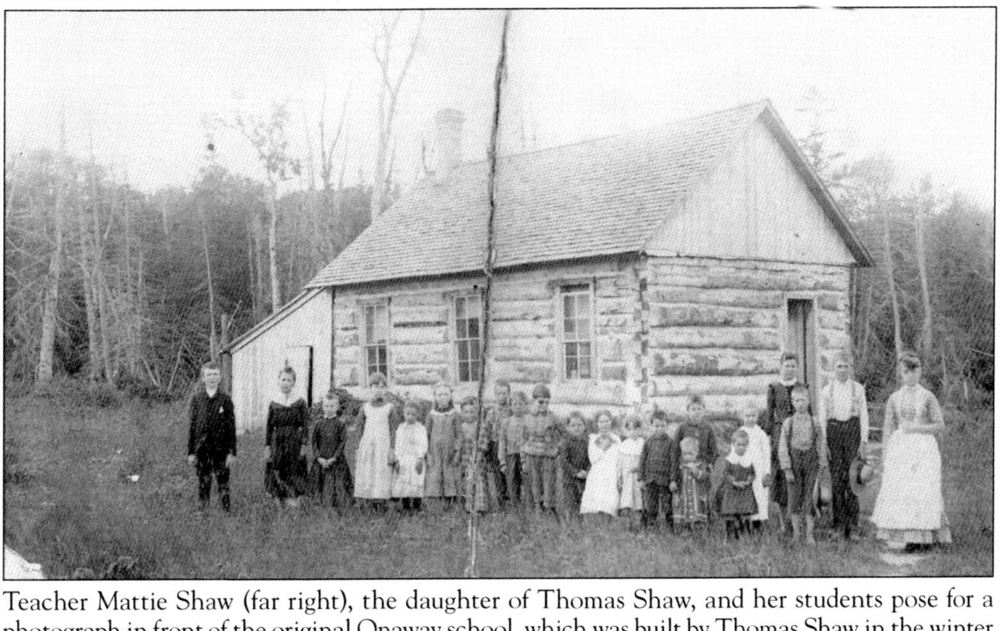

Teacher Mattie Shaw (far right), the daughter of Thomas Shaw, and her students pose for a photograph in front of the original Onaway school, which was built by Thomas Shaw in the winter of 1882. At that time, the little settlement was known as Shaw. The name Onaway was later given to the community by Merritt Chandler, a lumberman and contractor who came to the area in 1886. The word Onaway is from Longfellow's *Hiawatha* and is said to be Ojibwa for "awake."

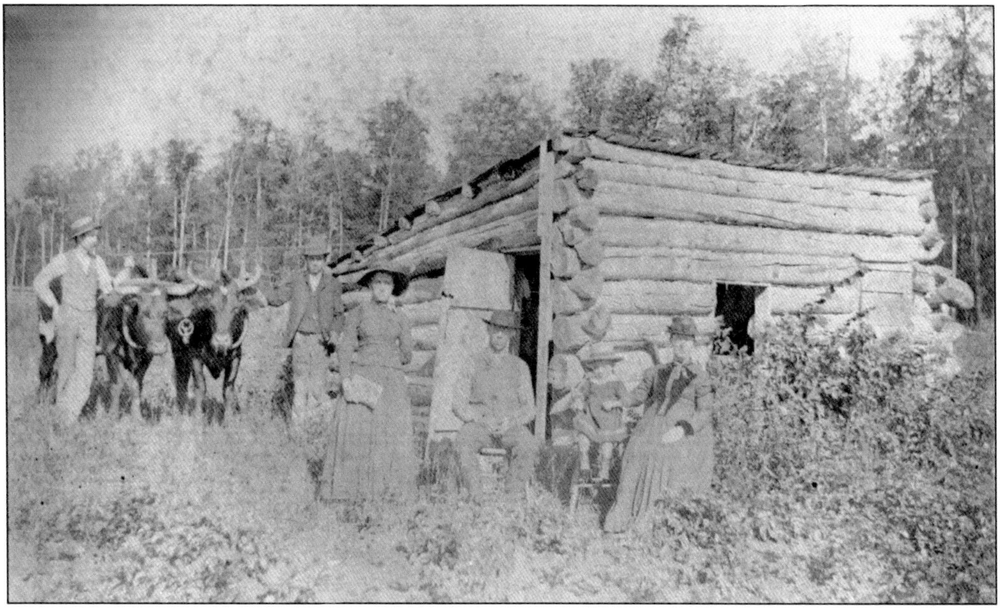

The farm home of A.C. Robinson and his family is seen here. Robinson is seated in the chair, and his wife is standing to the left of him. Robinson built the cabin in 1882 on 80 acres of land that he owned. He and his family lived in this cabin for two years before building a larger frame home on the same site.

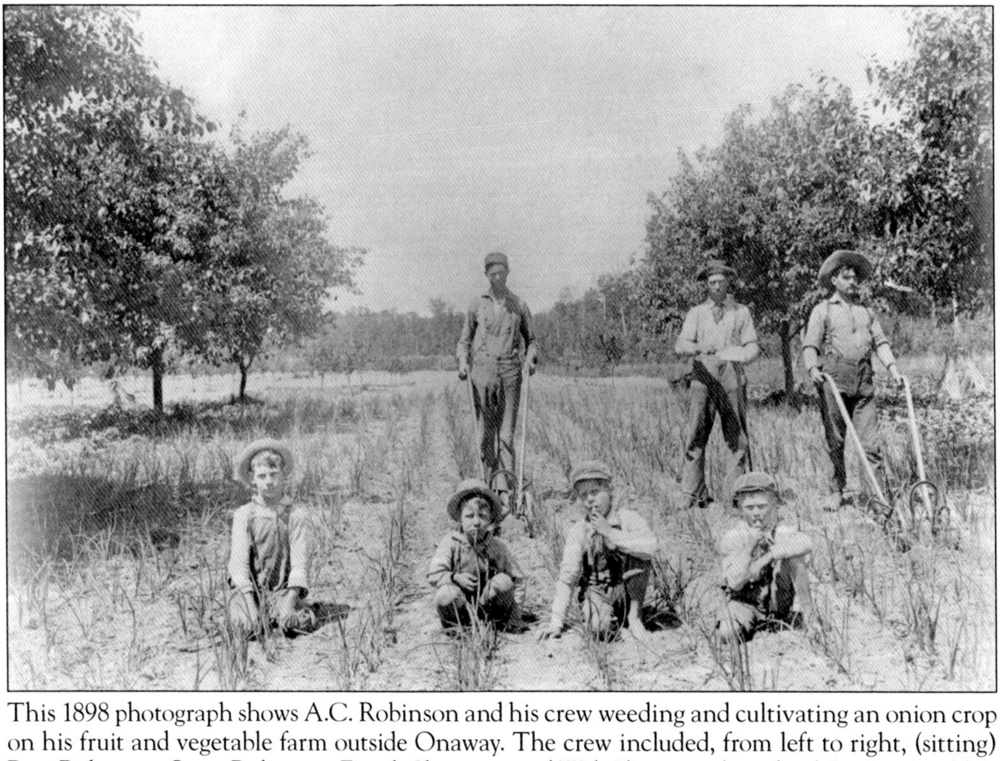

This 1898 photograph shows A.C. Robinson and his crew weeding and cultivating an onion crop on his fruit and vegetable farm outside Onaway. The crew included, from left to right, (sitting) Ross Robinson, Oscar Robinson, Enoch Sherman, and Web Sherman; (standing) Rupert Conklin, A.C., and Dan Burgess.

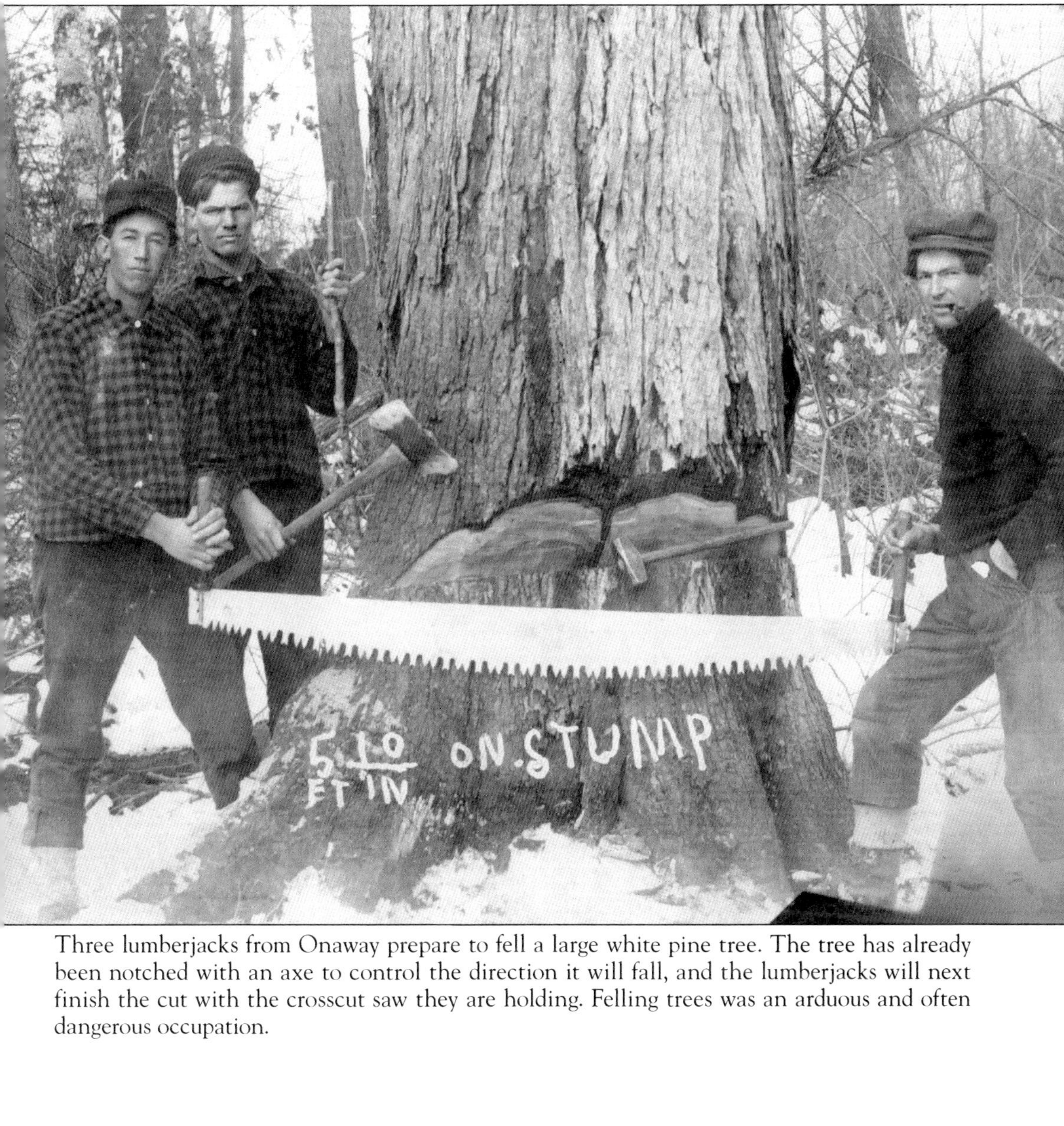

Three lumberjacks from Onaway prepare to fell a large white pine tree. The tree has already been notched with an axe to control the direction it will fall, and the lumberjacks will next finish the cut with the crosscut saw they are holding. Felling trees was an arduous and often dangerous occupation.

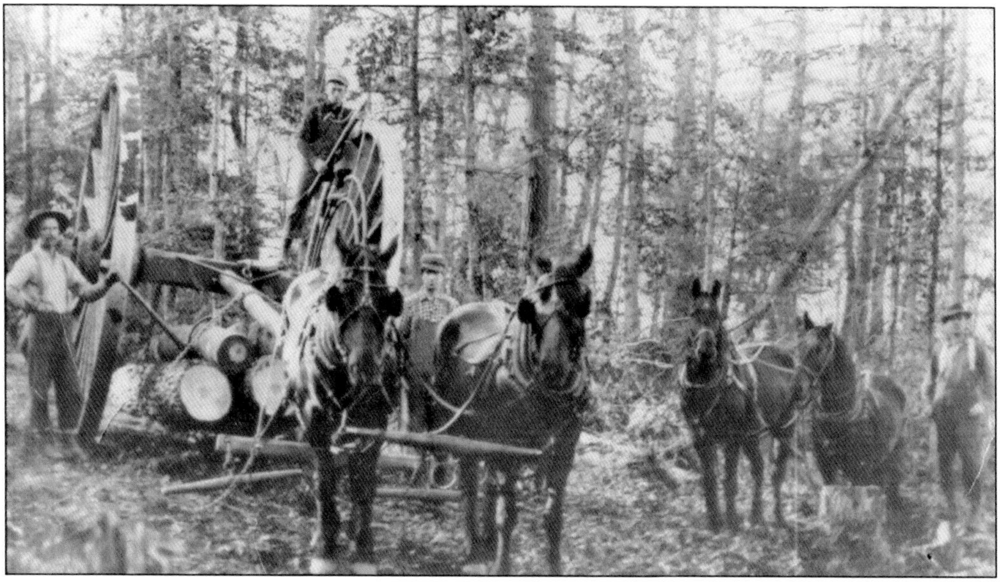

A crew at a lumber camp near Onaway uses "big wheels" to haul logs out of the woods in 1904. Until the big-wheeled haulers were developed, most logging had to be done in the winter, when heavy sleds of logs could be moved over ice-covered roads.

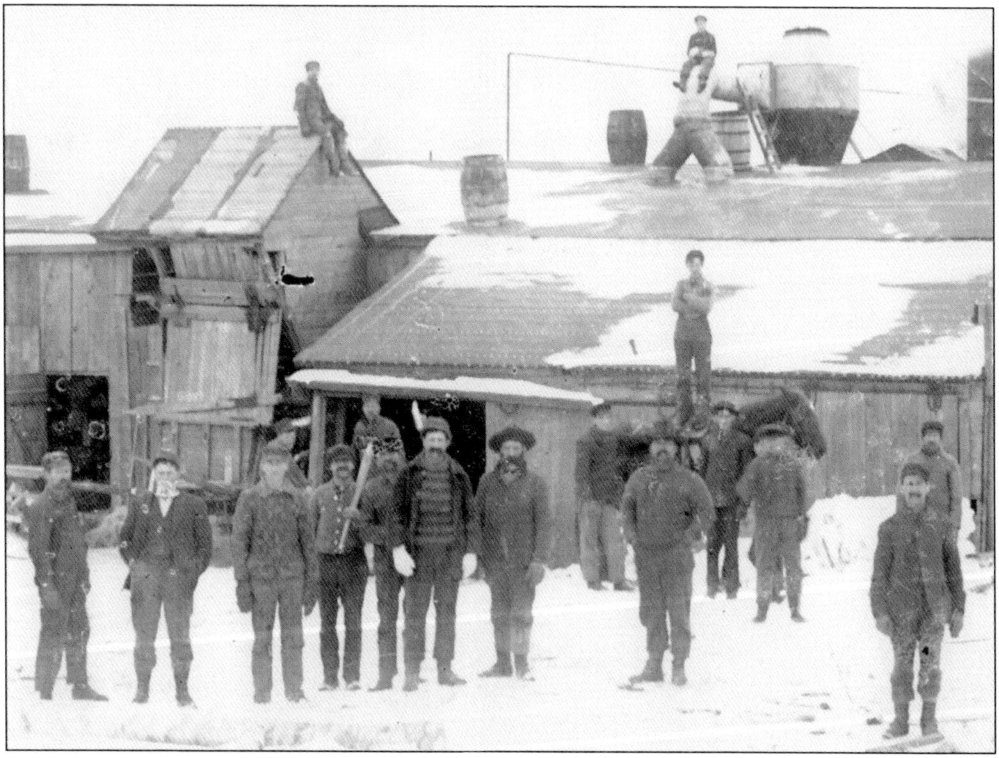

The crew of the Mahoney Brothers sawmill in Onaway poses for a photograph around 1910. The mill sawed timber to make barrel staves and heads, the round ends of the barrels. At that time, most things were shipped in barrels, so demand was high. The barrels on the roof of the mill contain water for use in case of a fire.

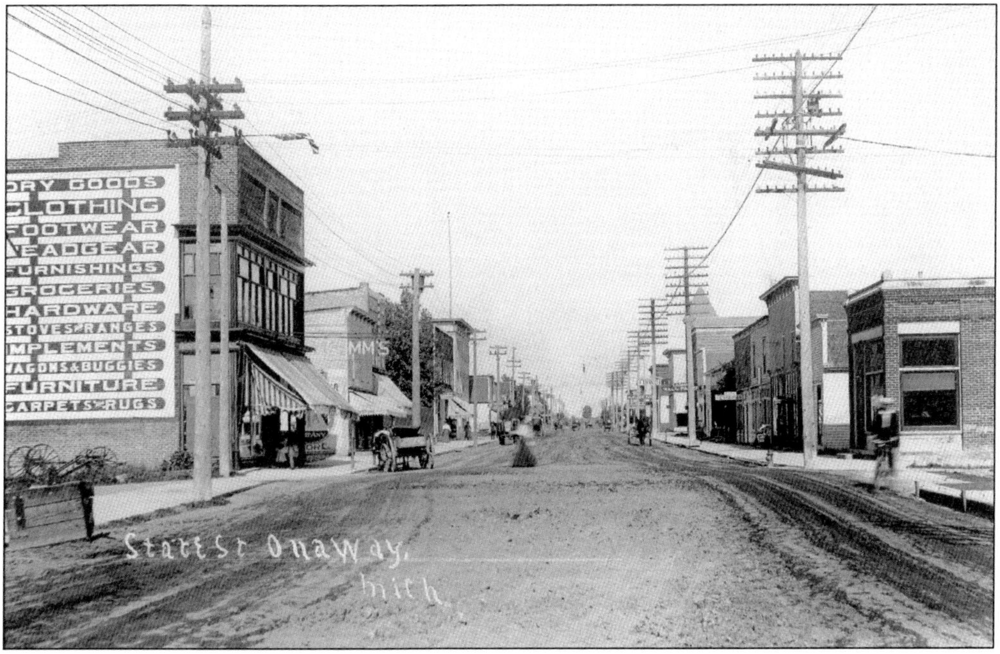

State Street in Onaway was a busy thoroughfare when this photograph was taken in 1908. At that time, the population was about 2,500, while the population of neighboring Rogers City, the county seat, was less than 700. Onaway residents argued for years that their community should rightly have been the county seat.

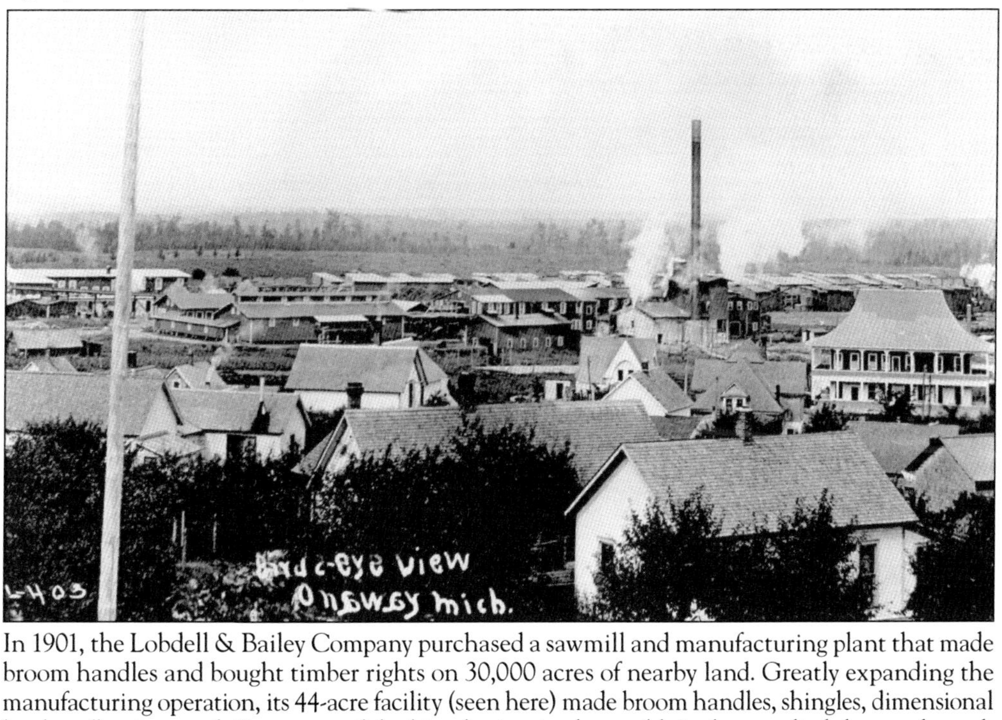

In 1901, the Lobdell & Bailey Company purchased a sawmill and manufacturing plant that made broom handles and bought timber rights on 30,000 acres of nearby land. Greatly expanding the manufacturing operation, its 44-acre facility (seen here) made broom handles, shingles, dimensional lumber, flooring, and 65 percent of the bicycle rims in the world. It also supplied the rough stock for the other 35 percent of bicycles.

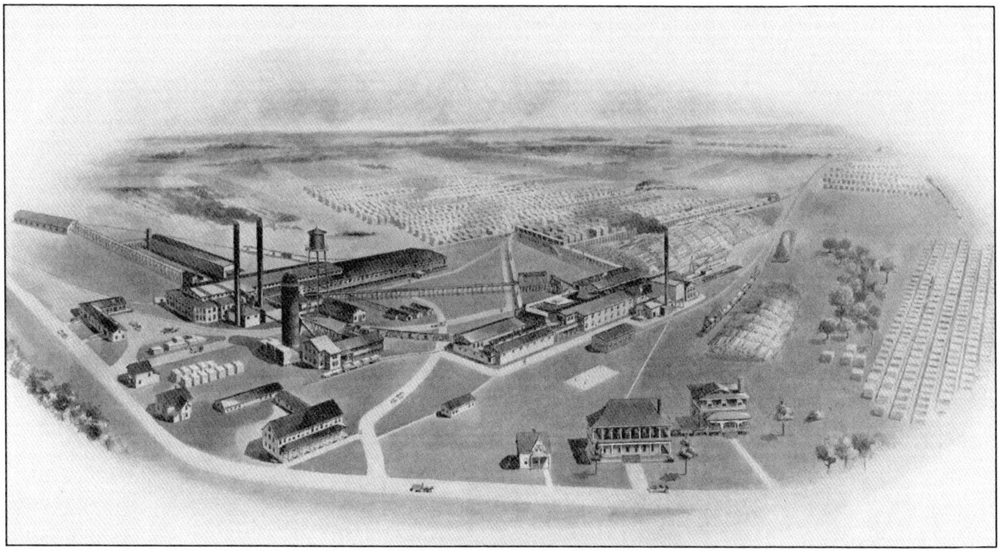

In 1909, Lobdell & Bailey also got into the business of manufacturing steering wheels for automobiles, which were made of an aluminum frame covered with exotic hardwoods, including the rock maple produced by the company's own lumber camps outside Onaway. Before long, the company was the world's largest producer of steering wheels. This etching provides a bird's-eye view of its sprawling plant at the junction of M-68 and M-33 on the south side of Onaway.

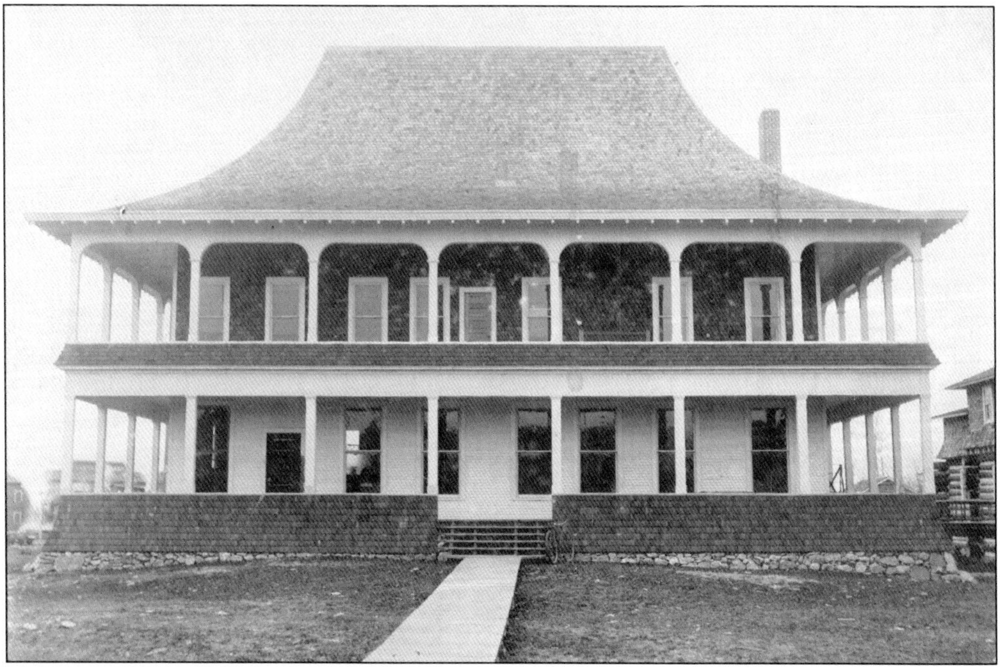

A devastating fire in 1926 destroyed the entire Lobdell-Emery plant with the exception of two buildings, one of which was the company's office building (seen here around 1925). After the fire, Lobdell-Emery decided to move its plant elsewhere. The impact of that decision was more devastating than the fire. The population of the city fell from 2,800 before the fire to about 1,400 after it. The former office building served as the Onaway Masonic hall for many years and was recently acquired by the Onaway Historical Society.

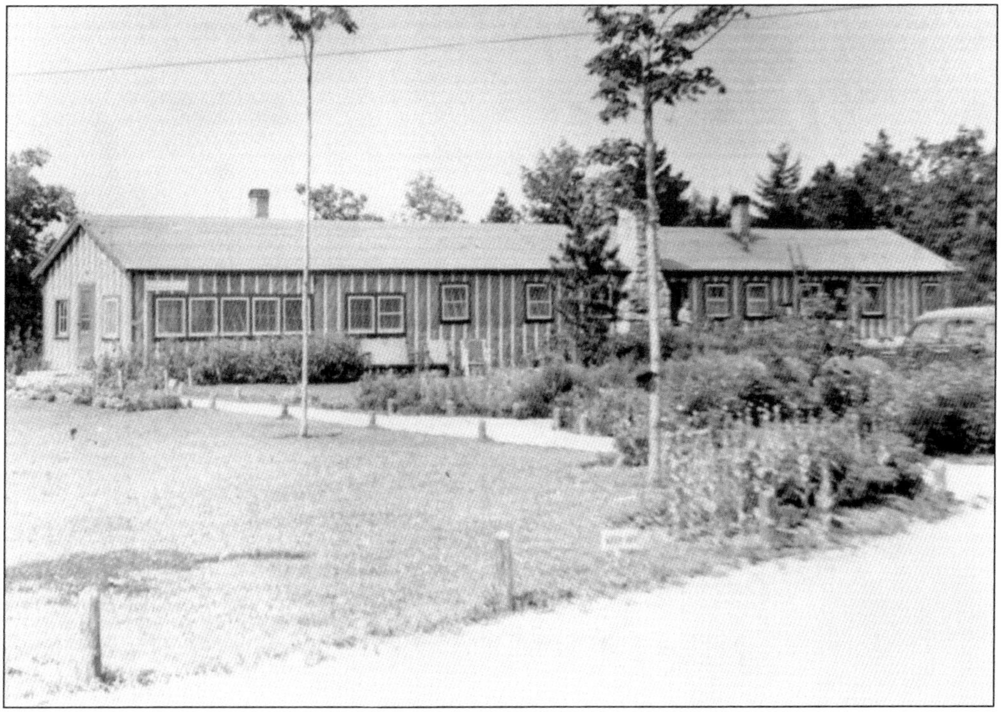

During the Great Depression of the 1930s, the Civilian Conservation Corps established a camp at Black Lake, near Onaway. Most of the camp's buildings have survived, including the one seen here. Maybe one of the most complete surviving CCC camps in the country, it operated from 1933 until 1941. Enrollees in the camp planted trees, improved roads, and built pavilions and other enhancements at Onaway and Hoeft State Parks, working with conservation department personnel on many of the projects.

About the Presque Isle County Historical Museum

The mission of the Presque Isle County Historical Museum is to preserve and interpret the history of the county. Located in Rogers City, the museum has offices and exhibit rooms in the Bradley House and in the adjacent Hoffman Annex. Today, the museum's photographic archives, the source of most of the photographs in this book, include the Calcite, James and Leona Stewart, Ferris Parsons, and Clifford Brege collections, totaling about 75,000 images, as well as another 10,000 historical photographs that have been donated to the museum by past and present residents since it was established in 1973. In each of the past seven years, the museum has drawn on its photographic collections to produce an illustrated local history book. In 2007 and again in 2010, the museum was honored by the Historical Society of Michigan as the state's Outstanding Local Museum. More information about the museum can be found at www.thebradleyhouse.org.